WINGS
OVER
SOMERSET

WINGS OVER SOMERSET

Aircraft Crashes since the End of World War II

PETER FORRESTER

First published 2012

The History Press
The Mill, Brimscombe Port
Stroud, Gloucestershire, GL5 2QG
www.thehistorypress.co.uk

British Library Cataloguing in Publication Data.
A catalogue record for this book is available from the British Library.

ISBN 978 0 7524 6579 1

Typesetting and origination by The History Press
Printed in Great Britain
Manufacturing managed by Jellyfish Print Solutions Ltd

CONTENTS

AUTHOR'S NOTES

Abbreviations

A.E.W.	Airborne Early Warning
A.H.	Army Helicopter
A.O.P.	Air Observation Post
B.	Bomber
F.A., F/A	Fighter Attack
F.A.W.	Fighter All-Weather Attack
F.B.	Fighter Bomber
F.G.A.	Fighter Ground Attack
G.A.	Ground Attack
G.R.	Ground attack, Reconnaissance
H.A.R.	Helicopter Air Rescue
H.A.S.	Helicopter Anti-Submarine
H.U.	Helicopter Utility
N.F.	Night Fighter
T.	Trainer

Aircraft Accidents Categories

Category 1: The damage is repairable within established first-line resources.

Category 2: The damage is repairable within established second-line resources.

Category 3: The damage is repairable on site, but is beyond unit technical resources. Assistance from a repair and salvage unit or civilian contractor is required.

Category 4: The damage is not repairable on site, and the aircraft must be removed to an established repair depot or civilian repair organisation.

Category 5: The aircraft is damaged beyond economic repair or it is missing.

Ranks

The ranks shown of officers and other ranks were the ranks they held at the time. They may also have been either local, acting or substantive ranks. The ranks do not necessarily show the final rank of the officer on completion of his or her service.

PROLOGUE

In 2008, I decided to leave something behind for my two grandchildren to remember me by. My intention was to remind them of their grandfather and maybe generate a fond smile or so in my remembrance. With luck my grandson, Alexander Peter, might at least raise a glass of cider to me when I am at the long bar of heaven; I will be certainly raising my glass to him and his sister, Jessica Lily. After all, by the time they are both old enough to have really got to know me I shall have probably kicked off my mortal coils and raised myself up to a higher level of flight, God willing.

I resolved to write down an account about my youth and leave it as a testament to the golden days that have all too swiftly passed me by. My idea was that in the years to come they may be interested to know how children lived in the 1950s and the 1960s, and perhaps pass it on to their children, and even their children's children. These memories were recorded in *When Grandpa was a Child*.

As time progressed, I jotted down my thoughts each and every night. A strange and sublime thing then occurred. I begrudgingly began to acknowledge the hidden memories that I had successfully locked away in my sub-consciousness; particularly those surrounding the deaths of so many RAF and Royal Naval servicemen. During the 1950s I recall that these gladiators of the sky were flying the exciting and new fast jet aircraft of the era; in particular the Vampire with its strange boom tail and the twin-engine Meteor jet aircraft.

As a young child, I often witnessed these fearless young airmen soaring high in the sky above my home village of Ilton, near Ilminster, in Somerset. These exciting events occurred during every single day and night. On reflection, I can also remember seeing aircraft occasionally tumbling from the sky, some of them streaming a huge plume of flame behind them. I also recall pilots being buried at the cemetery in Ilton. The 303 rifles of the Honour Guard firing a volley, the smell of burning gunpowder, the sounding of the last post and crying women are poignant reminders that remain with me to this very day. One day in 2009, I returned to my home village to check on what I thought I had remembered.

I left a thoroughly disheartened and saddened man at the sight of the graves of these brave young men who had so freely given their lives for their country. They are remembered on no war memorial. I jotted down their names, took some pictures and thought that it would be enough. But of course, it wasn't.

I started delving into the aircraft accidents that had happened in and around Somerset since the end of the Second World War. I was shocked and saddened at what I discovered. What I have learned, I now share with you.

WHY DID THE ACCIDENTS HAPPEN?

Why did so many jet aircraft accidents occur in Somerset in the 1950s and 1960s? To put it in context, the Royal Air Force (RAF) and the Royal Navy (RN) were much larger organisations in those days. The civilian world stayed with the piston-engine aircraft for a much longer period than the military, so there were fewer civil-registered aircraft crashes.

The military flying instructors were also men who had survived the Second World War and who had received their baptism of fire whilst flying piston aircraft. They were just not used to the fast jets and the speed in which sometimes irreversible events could happen.

When acquiring a target from the cockpit of a piston-engine plane the pilot had plenty of time to look around and locate it. The speed of the fast jet did not afford them this luxury, and many pilot error accidents occurred when the pilot simply flew his aircraft into the ground.

Another factor was the Korean War. There was a great urgency to convert piston fighter pilots to the jet fighters and the transition to this mostly outweighed the safety aspects. There was no Health and Safety at Work Act (H&SAW), and the Ministry of Defence (MoD) claimed Crown Exemption at that time and could not be sued for negligence.

Air safety in military aircraft, which included the standard fitting of ejector seats and the engineering out of defects, eventually began to make a marked difference on the high rate of attrition amongst the pilots and crew of the RAF and the Royal Naval Air Service (RNAS). This is not to forget the Army Air Corps, whose transition into the jet age took longer to accomplish. In addition, the introduction of ground trainers during the advent of the computer age also allowed pilots to encounter conditions that hitherto they would only have actually experienced whilst physically flying an aircraft.

As a fall out from these improvements, the safety of civilian aircraft was also considerably improved. On the down side, civil jet aircraft were very much at the cutting edge of new technology and as such many accidents occurred before what caused them could be ascertained.

The most significant military aircraft disasters that caused the most fatalities throughout the UK and in and around Somerset occurred during the early 1950s. These happened in the very first jet training aircraft that were available for pilots to train in: the Meteors and the Vampires.

Again, speed was a major factor. There were also many reported incidents of aircraft colliding with each other, usually with catastrophic results. Air-traffic control, too, had to change its procedures rapidly to reflect the speed at which the modern aircraft approached an airfield or airport. Gone were the luxuries of having ample time to vector and direct an aircraft safely in to an airfield. With modern jets nearing a landing zone at such high speeds, probably travelling at 6 miles a minute or so, it is quite easy to understand the control difficulties experienced in the very early days of jet aircraft.

Jet aeroplanes were still in their infancy and crashes were a commonplace, almost everyday event. Unless an aircraft happened to fall into your back garden or near you it would be most unlikely for you to hear about it. The Royal Navy's Sea Vixen aircraft lost more than fifty air crew, killed in major accidents around the world between 1962 and 1970 – quite a high rate for a specific aircraft type but a lot of these crashes took place at sea and out of sight, and also out of mind, of the general public.

Whichever way you look at it, flying military aircraft comes with an inherent risk. In order to carry out its wartime role, pilots have to practise in peacetime to gain the necessary skills. Sometimes they still have to pay the ultimate price; I have tried to list all those men who have lost their lives since the end of the Second World War where the personnel or an aircraft had a connection with Somerset. In this one shire county alone, the numbers lost are staggering.

There have been civilian aircraft crashes in Somerset or affecting Somerset since the end of the Second World War, but not on the scale of the military aircraft losses. The only major civilian airfield in Bristol and Somerset is the Bristol International Airport, although one crash saw a lot of women from Somerset villages killed in the same accident, but in another country.

Most civilian accidents concerned small private planes that came to grief landing or taking off on private air strips. Modern times have also introduced a new phenomenon – the hot air balloon and microlight aircraft. These, too, have had accidents over the recent years, particularly since 1990. I have also added a couple of 'near misses' as a grim reminder of what might have been. In addition, a large number of pieces of aircraft seemed to have fallen from the sky, but luckily with no deaths or injuries recorded. I have included a few to show how dangerous the skies over Somerset have actually been.

I also acknowledge that I am no 'expert' on aircraft, and my arrival at this point in publishing my book about aircraft crashes has been driven by the fact that so many seem to have occurred with a connection to my home county. I have tried to ensure that the Marks and types of the aircraft shown are the correct ones, although some distinguished and official sources actually do contradict each other. This is not surprising given the number of aircraft that were converted from one Mark to another Mark or type. All in all, a surprising number of aircraft accidents have occurred in Somerset, or have a Somerset connection. Where this has happened, I have tried to show them. Forgive me if I have not.

I also acknowledge the painstaking work that has been done to document the crashes from official sources. Halley, Sturtivant, Burrow, Howard, Cummings, Robertson and Webb, to name but a few, have patiently sifted through the records provided by the Ministry of Defence and left a broad outline of air accidents. By speaking to people who were there in Somerset when the events occurred, and by patiently examining local newspaper archives, I hope to have added to the record – so easily diminished by the rapid passing of time. I have not shown every aircraft crash, but merely recorded those since the end of the Second World War where loss of life has taken place or where, because of the incident, the aircraft never flew again.

1940s

1945

10 September 1945 • Handley Page Halifax B.III • Serial Number RG380 • Coastal Command • Number 517 Squadron RAF • Home Base – RAF Brawdy • Pembrokeshire, South-West Wales

This particular aircraft belonged to the meteorological squadron of the RAF and had been in the air for about nine and a half hours. It had been diverted to Westonzoyland airfield because of bad weather.[1] Due to radio interference, the pilot either did not hear or acknowledge the air-traffic controller, and turning away from Westonzoyland without announcing his intentions, he met with tragedy. During dense fog and at dusk the aircraft flew into the ground at Crowcombe Park on the south side of the Quantock Hills in Somerset. The plane burst into flames on impact and all nine of its crew members perished:

197664 Pilot Officer Keith Gordon Proverbs aged twenty-seven, is buried in the Bath (Haycombe) Cemetery. He can be found in Plot 39, Section H, Row D, Grave 249. He was born in Bridgetown, Barbados, and was one of the few Caribbean pilots of this era.

154868 Flying Officer John Joseph Frederick Hoben aged twenty-one, is buried in the Caterham and Warlingham Burial Ground, Caterham, Surrey, in Section M, Grave 4.

153580P Flying Officer Lindsay George McMillan aged twenty-three, is buried in Stoneham Cemetery in Southampton. He can be found in Section M.3, Grave 102.

191540 Flying Officer Patrick Alfred Bee aged twenty-five, is buried in the church-yard of St Botolph, Barton Seagrave, near Kettering.

1471979 Warrant Officer Roy Donald Cartwright is buried in Watford Cemetery and can be found in Section C, Unconsecrated Row 1, Grave 311.

1608294 Flight Sergeant Robert William Vinton aged twenty-one, is buried in Paignton Cemetery, Consecrated Section, Grave 5,090.

1154488 Flight Sergeant Dennis Norman Everett aged twenty-five, is buried in the Addlestone Burial Ground, Surrey, in Section 23, Grave 28.

1483506 Louis Grimble Groves aged twenty-four, is buried in the churchyard of St Maughold, Kirk Maughold, in the Isle of Man.

1825115 Sergeant John Macilrick Bryce Gordon aged twenty-one, is buried in Kirkton Cemetery at Fraserburgh, Scotland.

10 September 1945 • Hawker Tempest II • Serial Number MW825 • Number 15 Ferry Unit • Home Base – RAF Filton • Bristol

The pilot of this aircraft was undergoing a conversion course to fly another type of aircraft and had been in the air for about thirty minutes when the accident occurred.[2] He was completing a circuit of the airfield and as he went to turn in to make a landing he suddenly stalled the engine and lost control. It was found that the pilot did not have his safety harness set to the locked position and there was some speculation that this is why he was killed in the crash.

56730 Pilot Officer Harry James Marshall Harris was aged twenty-two years when he died. He is buried in the Hinxton (St Mary and St John) churchyard, Cambridgeshire.

8 October 1945   • Gloster G.41 Meteor F.3 • Serial Number EE302 • Number 245 Squadron RAF (Renumbered from Number 504 Squadron RAF late in 1945) • Home Base – RAF Colerne • Colerne, Wiltshire

This aircraft crashed approximately 3 miles west of Frome, Somerset, when the aircraft went out of control with an unintentional spin at about 8,000ft.[3] It recovered briefly at about 6,000ft before spinning to the left and into the ground. The pilot was killed.

182728 Flying Officer Ian Lamont of the RAF Volunteer Reserve is buried at the Kirkapol Burial Ground on the Isle of Tiree, Argyllshire, in Scotland.

16 October 1945   • Brigand T.F.1 • Serial Number RH742 • Bristol Aeroplane Company • Home Base – Filton • Bristol

This aircraft was one of the first of its type and was on a production test flight when it made a very heavy landing in a strong crosswind.[4] The landing wheels were splayed which resulted in the aircraft being declared a Category 4. None of the crew of three sustained any injuries during this incident.

The aircraft was repaired and flew again, but alas on 19 July 1947, when part of the Aeroplane and Armament Experimental Establishment (A&AEE) and flown by Flight Lieutenant L.T. Morren, the aircraft failed to pull out of firing pass during an exercise in Lyme Bay and off the coast of Dorset. It is assumed that there was a dive brake failure and the aircraft went into a slow roll and lost speed while inverted. It then spiralled into the sea. This was the first fatal accident of this aircraft type.

2 November 1945   • Anson I • Serial Number NK876 • Number 10 Radio School • Home Base – RAF Carew Cheriton • Pembrokeshire, South Wales

On landing at Whitchurch airport in Bristol during very poor visibility, the aircraft overran the runway before crossing the road at the extreme end of the airfield's boundary, hitting a hedge.[5] The aircraft ended up in a field but no casualties were reported.

3 November 1945 • Taylorcraft Auster I • Serial Number LB328 • Number 183 Squadron RAF • Home Base – RAF Chilbolton • Near Andover, Wiltshire

This aircraft encountered terrible weather conditions and crashed at Barrow Gurney, Somerset, when it hit a hedge in a forced landing.[6] The aircraft overturned and was damaged beyond repair.

9 November 1945 • Chance Vought Corsair F3A-1 • Serial Number JS852 • Number 1 Naval Fighter School • Number 759 Naval Air Squadron • Home Base – HMS *Heron*/ HMS *Hummingbird* • RNAS Yeovilton/Zeales, Somerset

FX754461 Temporary Acting Petty Officer Pilot Gordon Booth Hughes, aged twenty-one, was killed in a mid-air collision over Devon, near Barnstaple, with another Chance Vought Corsair F3A-1, Serial No JS703. He was born on 31 July 1924. He was the son of Vernon and Helen Ross Hughes, of Powell River, British Columbia, Canada.

This young man lies buried in the Royal Navy Cemetery of St Bartholomew's church in Yeovilton village, Somerset. His final resting place is recorded in Appendix 2.

9 November 1945 • Chance Vought Corsair F3A-1 • Serial Number JS703 • Number 1 Naval Fighter School • Number 759 Naval Air Squadron • Home Base – HMS *Heron*/ HMS *Hummingbird* • RNAS Yeovilton/Zeales, Somerset

Sub Lieutenant D.L. Allen RCN baled out successfully and survived the mid-air collision near Barnstaple, Devon, with Chance Vought Corsair F3A-1, Serial No JS852. The pilot in the other aircraft lost his life.

9 November 1945 • Supermarine Sea Fire III • Serial Number PP997 • Number 761 Naval Air Squadron • Home Base – HMS *Dipper* • Henstridge, Somerset

Temporary Sub Lieutenant (A) Dale Gladstone Carlson, aged twenty, was killed in an air crash. He was on a gun-sighting practice near Sturminster Newton in Dorset when he seemed to lose control and spun into the ground. His aircraft burnt fiercely on impact and he was burned beyond recognition. The aircraft came down in a field at West Orchard, near Shaftsbury. Oddly enough a spanner was found in its burnt out remains that should not have been there and there was some speculation that this item might have been the cause of the accident.

He was the son of Harry and Ida Carlson, of Minneapolis, Minnesota, USA. His nationality is listed in the Commonwealth War Graves Commission as being from the United Kingdom. This officer's final resting place is at Sherborne Cemetery in Dorset and he is listed as being in Section 6, Grave 3.

Source: *Western Gazette*.

22 November 1945 • Consolidated Liberator G.R.8 • Serial Number KH126 •
Number 53 Squadron • RAF Transport Command • Home Base – RAF St David's •
Pembrokeshire, South Wales

On a cold and foggy November morning, a Liberator of RAF Transport Command plunged into the top of the Blackdown Hills at a height of 900ft near Hare Lane, Buckland St Mary, Somerset, shortly after taking off for a routine air-trooping flight to India. The pilot had been briefed that if in cloud when climbing he was not to make a turn until he had passed through the 1,500ft level. All on board were killed.

A memorial stone marks the place where the accident occurred and can be found at Grid Reference ST277155. This memorial can be located by entering the village of Broadway, Somerset, from the A358 and opposite the Ilton turning. Follow the road straight through the village and at the first crossroads go straight across. You are now in Hare Lane. Follow this very narrow road to the top of the hill and on your left-hand side you will see a large field gateway which will easily accommodate a car. There you will find an ash tree, and beneath it there is a large lichen-covered rock with a grey stone plaque placed in front of it. It reads:

Air Crash
22.11.45 Liberator KH126
In memory of the 27 men who perished at this site

Almost opposite this tree and on the other side of the road you will see another field gateway. If you go across to it and look down the hill and slightly to the left of the hedge line, you can, on a clear day, just make out RAF Merryfield lying in the valley below, about 5,000m away.

When you do, you will quickly realise that the really sad thing about the accident is that the plane only needed to have been another 6ft (2m) or so higher and it would have cleared the top of the Blackdown Hills without incident. Such is the difference between life and death.

It is said that the plane had been stripped down to its bare essentials for the long flight and that the men were packed tightly into her, sitting side by side upon the floor of the aircraft.

I acknowledge the help given to me by Hilary Cummings and the Buckland St Mary branch of the Royal British Legion in researching this crash site.

The airmen who lost their lives were:

Pilot Anthony Wize★, buried at Newark.
Flying Officer Gordon Jenkins Myers, buried at Armley Cemetery, Leeds.
Ktp-pil (Flight Lieutenant) Leopold Mieleck aged thirty-four,★ Ilminster Cemetery, Somerset.
Por.-narwig (Pilot Officer) Stanislaw Kleyber aged twenty-five,★ Ilminster Cemetery, Somerset (incorrectly spelt as Kleybor on his tombstone).
Sierz-mech.poki (Flight Sergeant) Jan Brzesinski aged twenty-five,★ Ilminster Cemetery, Somerset.
★ Polish crew

Passengers:

MZ/13494 Major Henry William Gilbert Staunton, Indian Medical Service, aged thirty-seven. He is buried in the Yeovil Cemetery.

1117 Captain Herbert Cecil Buck MC, 1st Punjab Regiment. During the war he had been a member of the Special Air Service and was aged twenty-eight when he died. He was cremated at Reading Crematorium and is remembered on Panel 1.

E/C7914 Lieutenant Peter James Biles, Royal Indian Army Service Corps, aged twenty-two. He is buried in the Yeovil Cemetery.

E/C10780 Lieutenant Arthur George Quick, Indian Signal Corps, aged twenty-six. He is buried in the North Petherton Cemetery.

14621486 Signalman Anthony John Birch, aged twenty. He is buried in the St Lawrence churchyard, West Wycombe, Buckinghamshire.

14902515 Signalman Robert Charles Anderson, aged nineteen. He is buried in the Yeovil Cemetery.

14311367 Signalman Roland Oswin Anderson, aged nineteen. He is buried in the Yeovil Cemetery.

14216739 Signalman James Henry Attwood, aged twenty-two. He is buried in the Marlow Cemetery, Buckinghamshire.

14649020 Signalman John William Alexander Brewis, aged twenty-two. He was cremated at the Warriston Crematorium, Edinburgh, and is remembered on Panel 1.

14366015 Signalman William Armstrong Charlton, aged twenty-one. He is buried in the Mere Knolls Cemetery, Sunderland.

14957177 Signalman Arthur Edwin Clark, aged eighteen. He is buried in the Greenford Park Cemetery.

2368080 Signalman Laurence James Curry, aged twenty-four. He is buried in the Yew Tree Roman Catholic Cemetery, Liverpool.

14646239 Signalman Herbert Donovan, aged twenty. He is buried in the St Patrick's Roman Catholic Cemetery, Leytonstone.

14622999 Signalman Leonard Henry Downes, age unknown. He is buried in the Manor Park Cemetery.

14939236 Signalman Leslie Raymond Dyer, aged nineteen. He was cremated at the Brighton (Woodvale) Crematorium and is remembered on Panel 2.

14916092 Signalman Peter Brown Fairbairn, aged nineteen. He is buried in the Edinburgh Eastern Cemetery.

14945626 Signalman Ronald Douglas Farrance, age unknown. He is buried in the Stone Cemetery, Dartford, Kent.

14394238 Signalman Frederick Walter Gent, age unknown. He is buried in the Kimberworth (St Thomas) churchyard.

14948895 Signalman Roy E.C. Williams, aged eighteen. He was cremated at the Manchester Crematorium and is remembered on Panel 23.

14913071 Signalman Owen Williams, aged eighteen. He is buried in the Yeovil Cemetery.

2392783 Driver Brian Williams Fox, aged nineteen. He is buried in the Atherstone Cemetery, North Warwickshire.

5 December 1945   • Chance Vought Corsair IV • Serial Number Not Known • Number 768 Naval Air Squadron • Home Base – HMS *Dipper* • Henstridge, Somerset

Temporary Sub Lieutenant (Air) James Todd Millar RNVR was detached to RNAS Yeovilton, Somerset, for deck-landing training. During one of these practices his aircraft crashed at sea and astern of HMS *Ravager*. His body was not recovered and he is remembered at Bay 6, Panel 39 of the Lee-on-Solent memorial. He was the son of James and Margaret Millar, of Cowdenbeath, Fife.

6 December 1945   • Chance Vought F3A-1 Corsair III • Serial Number JS769 • Number 768 Naval Air Squadron • Home Base – HMS *Dipper* • Henstridge, Somerset

Temporary Sub Lieutenant (Air) Leonard Rawsthorne RNVR was detached to RNAS Yeovilton, Somerset, for deck-landing training. His aircraft was lost when it carried away the barriers of HMS *Ravager* and went into the sea. He was reported as 'Missing Presumed Killed' and his body was never recovered. He is remembered in Bay 6, on Panel 39 of the Lee-on-Solent memorial.

1946

30 January 1946   • Supermarine Type 358 Seafire F.III • Serial Number NN498 • Number 759 Naval Air Squadron • Home Base – HMS *Heron* • RNAS Yeovilton • Ilchester, Somerset

Temporary Sub Lieutenant (Air) Frank Chappell Eccles of the Royal Naval Volunteer Reserve was killed on a routine training mission in Somerset. His aircraft dived into the ground 2 miles west of Henstridge, Somerset.[7] He was the son of Joseph Maylott Eccles and May Eccles of Ripon. His final resting place can be found at the cemetery in Ripon, Yorkshire, and is located in Section H, Grave 371.

This particular aircraft site was excavated by the Marches Aviation Society in 2007. For a full description of this historical dig log on to www.redkitebooks.co.uk/aa and navigate to Excavations/2007/Seafire Yeovilton.

28 February 1946   • Supermarine Spitfire Mk IX • Serial Number MA579 • Number 58 Officers Training Unit • Home Base – RAF Poulton • Cheshire

The engine of this plane cut out in flight due to a fuel failure and it belly landed in a field 1 mile north of Dunkerton in Somerset.[8] The pilot successfully escaped from the stricken aeroplane.

7 March 1946 • Supermarine Spitfire • Serial Number Not Known • Squadron Not Known • Home Base – RAF Colerne • Wiltshire

Flight Lieutenant S. Lerche crash-landed his Spitfire into a field near Westbury Farm, Tinley near Bath.[9] The plane was badly damaged when it slid along a field leaving a wing behind. The aircraft finished up with a twisted fuselage after going through a hedge and into a field on the other side. The pilot had stayed with his aircraft rather than bale out as he wanted to bring it down safely. He walked away from the incident.

22 July 1946 • Supermarine Seafire F.III • Serial Number NN349 • Squadron Storage • Home Base – HMS *Heron* • RNAS Yeovilton • Ilchester, Somerset

Temporary Sub Lieutenant (A) Edward Graham Mortimer, Royal Naval Volunteer Reserve, was on a test flight in this aircraft when it crashed into the sea 100 yards east of Lulworth Cove after suffering an engine failure.[10] He is listed as 'Missing Presumed Killed' and was aged thirty-nine when he died.

Edward was the son of Samuel Reginald and Annie Beatrice Mortimer and also the husband of Leslie Irene Mortimer of Hook-with-Warsash, Hampshire. His name is recorded on the Lee-on-Solent memorial Panel 41 of Bay 6.

12 November 1946 • D.H.103 Hornet F.1 • Serial Number PX229 • Royal Aircraft Establishment • Home Base – Farnborough Airfield • Hampshire

This aircraft was on a ferry flight to the Torpedo Development Unit at Weston-super-Mare and struck some trees near Warren Farm, Charterhouse in Somerset, during misty conditions. The crashing aircraft then carried on over the valley and into the hill on the other side, leaving a large crater. Its approximate location was at Grid Reference ST498562. It is reported that the pilot had failed to check for the weather conditions before he commenced his flight.[11]

Lieutenant Commander Thomas George Bentley from HMS *Daedalus* was killed in the accident. He is buried in the Haslar Royal Naval Cemetery, Gosport, Hampshire, and can be found in grave G.11.17.

I acknowledge the help of Chris Collins for the grid reference and some of the details of this event.

22 November 1946 • Douglas Boston III • Serial Number AL467 • Air Torpedo Development Unit • Home Base – RAF Gosport • Hampshire

On its approach to RAF Locking, near Weston-super-Mare in Somerset, on a mission to collect stores, this aircraft flew over the road that passed along the perimeter of the airfield.[12] The pilot of this aircraft had recently been in another aircraft accident, although he had been the co-pilot of the plane concerned.

There were the normal signs on the road cautioning drivers about the dangers of low-flying aircraft. These were not obligatory signs but rather a warning to road users so that any drivers would not be startled by a low-flying aircraft. To land at RAF Locking, the Bostons had to come in very low, so any driver would have been unlikely to have seen any approaching aircraft.

It was a Friday and servicemen were eagerly getting away on weekend leave. At that time dusk was also approaching. As three double-decker buses, fully loaded with airmen, drove along the road travelling towards the local railway station, the undercarriage of the descending aircraft hit the middle bus in the line. There were approximately fifty-seven men on the bus at the time. The catastrophe immediately killed seven airmen and another one died later. The strike was so sudden that the aircraft's undercarriage carried away the body of an airman with it. It also seriously injured another fifteen airmen, with others suffering cuts and bruises, mostly sustained from glass from the bus windows. Amazingly, the bus managed to remain in an upright position.

The aircraft landed on grass on its port side as the port undercarriage had been ripped off. Those in the aircraft survived the accident.

The following airmen lost their lives in this tragic incident:

2291223 AC1 (Aircraftman First Class) Sidney Gordon Fairweather, aged nineteen. He was the son of Ernest and Violet Ellen Fairweather and he came from Shepherd's Bush, London. He is buried in the Mortlake Cemetery. He died of his injuries later on during that same day.

2291411 AC1 James Halliday, aged twenty-two. He was the son of Hugh McCallum Halliday and Agnes Halliday, of Dumbarton. He is buried in the Dumbarton Cemetery.

1598231 AC1 Eric Wilfred Bellamy, aged twenty-five. He is buried in the Hull Northern Cemetery.

2260394 AC2 (Aircraftman Second Class) Edward Jackson, aged twenty-six. He was the son of Charles Toynbee Jackson and Martha Jackson, of Nantwich, Cheshire. He is buried in the Manchester (Gorton) Cemetery.

2296456 AC2 Ernest Henry Pearson, aged twenty-three. He is buried in the Ewell (St Mary) churchyard extension.

2285878 AC1 Roy Lawton, aged eighteen. He was the son of John Lawton and Frances Caroline Lawton, of New Ferry, Birkenhead. He is buried in the Bromborough (St Barnabus) churchyard.

2258573 AC2 Frank Wilson, aged twenty-two. He was the son of Reginald Hugh Wilson and Elise Wilson. He was also the husband of Nancy Wilson, of Holmfirth. He is buried in the Upperthong (St John's) churchyard.

3059401 AC2 James Ithel Davis, aged twenty. He was the son of Thomas William Stanley Davis and Margaret Jane Davis, of Llandilo. He is buried in the Llandilo Fawr (St Teilo) churchyard.

1947

3 January 1947 • Douglas C-47A-1-DK • Serial Number G-AGJU • British Overseas Airways Corporation (BOAC) • Heathrow Airport • London

This aircraft first flew in 1943. It had an original American number of 92374 (c/n12169) before going to the RAF as FZ614. It was then sold to BOAC to become G-AGJU.

On landing at Whitchurch, with only a crew of three on board during a positioning flight, it somehow ground looped. The crew escaped unhurt but the damage sustained by the aircraft was so great that it was written off.

23 January 1947 • Supermarine Spitfire L.F.IX • Serial Number MH496 • Fighter Command Communications Squadron • Home Base – An airfield near London

The aircraft was on a flight from its home base and heading for RAF Chivenor. Shortly before midday and near Minehead, the engine caught fire and failed at 4,500ft. The pilot made a forced landing in a field near Larkberrow Farm, 3 miles from Oare (or Oareford – written about in R.D. Blackmore's *Lorna Doone*) and approximately 5 miles west of Minehead. The fire amazingly extinguished itself. The pilot was unhurt and walked to a public telephone to report the incident.

During the war this aircraft was part of the Belgian air force and was in operational use by No 350 (Belgian) Squadron RAF, who were disbanded on 15 October 1946.

Source: *Bristol Evening Post*.

6 July 1947 • Supermarine Spitfire L.F.XVI • Serial Number RW348 • Number 501 (County of Gloucester) Squadron RAF • Home Base – RAF Filton • Bristol

The engine cut out as the rear fuel tank ran dry.[13] The pilot did not change tanks or switch on the fuel-booster pump. He made an approach for an emergency landing but just before touchdown the engine recovered. Because the pilot had left the throttle open after the engine had cut out, there was a sudden and unexpected increase of power that spoiled the pilot's approach. A wheels-up landing was then made when the engine suddenly cut again. The aircraft was written off.

15 October 1947 • Westland Wyvern I Prototype Production • Serial Number TS371 • Westland Aircraft Works • Home Base – Westland's Airfield • Yeovil, Somerset

This particular aircraft crashed near Bailey Ridge Farm, Yetminster in Dorset, killing the pilot, Squadron Leader Peter J. Garner, aged twenty-five years. He had logged some 950 hours' flying experience. The squadron leader was on a test flight, which included air-to-air photographs for *Flight* magazine photographer, John Yoxall, when the engine suffered a failure of the pitch translation bearing whilst returning to Yeovil. The rear unit of the propeller then moved into superfine pitch, which led to a sudden loss of torque. Through superb flying skills the squadron leader made a successful forced landing in a field of stubble.

Unfortunately, he was rendered unconscious by a section of the prop blade which penetrated the cockpit as the aircraft hit the ground. The engine of the aircraft was thrown about 50 yards away from the burning aircraft. The pilot died in the fire that followed the crash. He left behind a wife and two-year-old daughter.

Westland's chief test pilot, Harald Penrose, was flying another Wyvern close by and witnessed the incident. He immediately radioed back to Yeovil for help and a Sikorsky helicopter containing a rescue crew was at the crash site within several minutes, but the blaze was so fierce that there was little they could do.

As a tribute, *Flight* magazine published the final pictures of the pilot flying his ill-fated aircraft on 23 October 1947, on pages 466 and 467.

There has been some confusion as to the exact location of this crash.[14] The AAIB (Air Accidents Investigation Branch) report places it near the small village of Leigh, Dorset, whilst the company records claim that it happened near Cattistock. The location of the crash, Bailey Ridge Farm, is in the Yetminster post code area but physically nearer to the village of Leigh, about a kilometre from the village and north-east from it.

7 December 1947   • Supermarine Spitfire L.F.XVIe • Serial Number TE314 • Number 614, (County of Glamorgan) Squadron RAF • Home Base – RAF Llandow • Glamorgan, South Wales

This aircraft was flying as the No 3, and collided with the lead Spitfire L.F.XVIe Serial No RW355 during a cross-over manoeuvre. The pilot, Sergeant Hodgson, successfully baled out at 3,500ft and he came to earth near Ilchester. His aircraft crashed in a ploughed field belonging to Benedict's Farm at Long Sutton, Somerset.

Source: *Western Gazette.*

7 December 1947   • Supermarine Spitfire L.F.XVIe • Serial Number RW355 • Number 614 (County of Glamorgan) Squadron RAF • Home Base – RAF Llandow • Glamorgan, South Wales

This lead aircraft collided with the number 3 of the flight, Spitfire L.F.XVI, Serial No TE314. A total of three Spitfires had been practising strafing runs and then broke in a cross over. The pilot of TE314 reported that the other Spitfire flew vertically in front of him. The propeller from the sergeant pilot's plane sliced through the tail of RW355 and it broke off. This aircraft came to earth at Othery, Somerset, coming to rest in a ploughed field. On its way down it brought down three power lines and ended up literally just a couple of yards away from a steel pylon. The tail part of the plane landed some 200 yards away.

187267 Pilot Officer David Edward Morgan, Royal Air Force (Auxiliary Air Force) was found lying 10 yards away from his plane with his parachute pack close to him; it had not fully deployed. Unfortunately, the pilot officer broke his neck and fractured his leg on impact, killing him instantly. The aircraft had burst into flames and was burnt out.

He is buried in the Tyncoed Congregational chapelyard, Brecknockshire, and his grave can be located south-west of the chapel.

Source: *Western Gazette.*

1948

7 March 1948   • Supermarine Spitfire L.F.XVI • Serial Number RW391 • Number 501 (County of Gloucester) Squadron RAF • Home Base – RAF Filton • Bristol

During its landing run, the aircraft developed a swing which the pilot failed to correct.[15] It went off the runway and tipped on to its nose, causing the aircraft to be written off. The pilot was uninjured. By this time there was a surplus of Second World War aircraft and some were written off that could have been easily repaired.

17 April 1948   • Supermarine Spitfire L.F.XVI • Serial Number SL675 • Number 614 (County of Glamorgan) Squadron RAF • Home Base – RAF Llandow • Glamorgan, South Wales

The aircraft was seen emerging from cloud in a dive and it appeared to be trying to level off.[16] It struck the water and broke up over Nell's Point in the Bristol Channel, just off the coast of Glamorgan. The pilot was killed. The cause of the accident was never properly discovered.

195753 Pilot Officer Howard Hughes Evans was born on 6 June 1924 and was aged twenty-three years when he died.

4 June 1948   • North American Harvard IIB (AT-16) • Serial Number KF501 • Number 799 Naval Air Squadron • Home Base – HMS *Heron* • Yeovilton, Somerset

Lieutenant (E) William Eric Riseborough lived at Manor Farm, Hardington Mandeville. He was the tutor of this dual-controlled plane and was instructing student Lieutenant Michael Rogers RN in blind flying. The tutor told the student to take control of the plane from the back seat.

Whilst waiting for the signal to take over from the tutor, the student noticed that the nose of the aircraft had dropped. The student thought that the tutor still had control and was not worried until the aircraft started to go into a slow, spinning dive only a couple of hundred feet from the ground.

The coroner recorded that the tutor had thought that the student had taken over control. Only when he realised that the tutor was not in control of the plane did Lieutenant Rogers grab hold of the control stick and pulled it sharply back, thereby preventing the aircraft from crashing nose first. The plane recovered slightly and levelled off, but a wing clipped some trees and crashed on the moor near Long Sutton, Somerset. The student escaped the aircraft and managed to pull the tutor clear of the wreckage. As the aircraft crashed it snapped off both of its wings, and because of this the fuselage ploughed across a field and did not catch fire.

Lieutenant Riseborough was killed in the crash and is buried at the London Road Cemetery in Ilford, Essex. He was born on 22 May 1922 and was aged twenty-six when he died.

Source: *Western Gazette.*

7 July 1948   • D.H.98 Sea Mosquito T.R.33 • Serial Number TW284 • Air Torpedo Development Unit • Home Base – RAF Gosport • Hampshire

The starboard wing of this aircraft suddenly folded up as it became severely overstressed during low-level aerobatics.[17] It crashed at the eastern end of the Weston-super-Mare airport. The pilot and crew were both killed when the aircraft exploded on impact.

39032 Squadron Leader David Alistair Robertson DFC (commanding officer), aged thirty-one, was born on 14 October 1916 and was cremated at the Arnos Vale Crematorium in Bristol.

50646 Flight Lieutenant Anthony George Nichols, aged twenty-eight, was born on 27 April 1920 and is buried at the Weston-super-Mare Cemetery.

14 October 1948   • Bristol 164 Brigand B.I • Serial Number RH824 • Home Base – RAF Filton • Bristol

Squadron Leader Douglas Dennison Weightman DFC was the chief test pilot of the Air Registrations Board (now the Civil Aviation Authority) and aged thirty-six. He was at Bristol specifically to test the Brigand and on loan to cover for staff depletion through sickness and holidays. He was making a second production test flight when the port engine over-sped. All four of the propeller blades on this engine detached, severing part of the nose structure and then collided with the starboard propeller. This overstressed the engine mount and the engine fell away from the wing.[18]

Although Squadron Leader Weightman skilfully managed to make a forced landing at Mill Farm near Northwick in Gloucestershire, he unfortunately hit a tree and crashed into a ditch. Despite being pulled from the cockpit of the burning aircraft by nearby farm workers, he sadly died from his injuries shortly after his rescue. He had 3,500 hours of flight recorded in his log on eighty different types of aircraft and had been demobbed from the RAF in 1946.

1949

23 March 1949   • Hawker Sea Fury F.B.11 • Serial Number VW580 • Number 802 Naval Air Squadron • Home Base – RNAS Yeovilton • Near Ilchester, Somerset

During oxygen-climbing practice over Mounts Bay, Cornwall, the propeller detached itself from the aircraft due to the engine over-speeding and it ditched into the sea.[20] The pilot, Lieutenant Commander R.W. Kearseley, was safely rescued.

6 May 1949   • Bristol 170 Freighter 21 • Serial Number G-AIFF • Bristol Aeroplane Company • Home Base – Filton • Bristol

This prototype Bristol 170 Mk 21 aircraft was performing tests to obtain engine and propeller data under specific climbing conditions. It was possible that the RAF were interested in the aircraft.[19] The aircraft took off from Filton airfield at 10.03 a.m. At 11.10 a.m., the commander of a surfaced submarine, HMS *Truculent* (Lieutenant A.C. Chalmers), saw the aircraft crash into the sea. He reported that he had seen no sign of a fire.

A large object, thought to be part of the wing, was seen fluttering down separately. This aircraft was lost in an extreme-yaw, single-engine climb due to structural failure of the tail fin. The accident occurred approximately 26km from the Portland Lighthouse.

The names of the seven crew members who lost their lives were: Mr J.A.C. Northway, aged forty-one, the company's assistant chief test pilot; Mr John M. Radcliffe, aged forty-seven, head of the Flight Research Department; Mr E.J.N. Archbold, aged twenty-seven; Mr R.M. Pollard, aged thirty-five; Mr R.H. Daniels, aged forty; Mr C.W.E. Flook, aged thirty-six; and Mr J.L. Gundry, aged thirty-seven.

HMS *Truculent* quickly carried out a search of the area and was joined by the frigate HMS *Zephyr* and shortly thereafter by a search-and-rescue (SAR) helicopter from Portsmouth. The submarine located the bodies of Mr E.J. Archbold of Filton, Bristol, and Mr J.L. Gundry of Almondsbury, Bristol. The bodies were transferred to HMS *Zephyr* and taken ashore. The other five crew members were not recovered from the sea.

Another Type 21, G-AHJJ, crashed under very similar circumstances some ten months later, in March 1950, near Cowbridge, Glamorgan. Because of these two accidents a longer and stronger dorsal fin was manufactured, resulting in the production of the Bristol 170 Freighter Type 170 Mk 31.

10 May 1949   • Hawker Sea Fury F.B.11 • Serial Number VW578 • Number 802 Naval Air Squadron • Home Base – RNAS Yeovilton/RNAS Culdrose • Near Ilchester, Somerset and Helston, Cornwall

On return to RNAS Culdrose, the undercarriage of this aircraft failed to lower.[21] The pilot attempted to abandon the aircraft but was unsuccessful in his attempt to get out of the cockpit. The aircraft came down into the sea about 21 miles off Pendennis

Castle, Cornwall. A Sea Otter A.S.R.II (Naval), Serial No RD913 of the Air/Sea Rescue Flight, St Merryn, was sent to rescue the downed flier but damaged its starboard float in the unsuccessful rescue attempt. It sank and the crew were rescued by a motor launch from Falmouth.

Lieutenant Ronald Bernard Francis was born on 27 May 1924 and was aged twenty-four years when he lost his life.

24 June 1949   • Hawker Sea Fury F.B.11 • Serial Number VW235 • Number 50 Training Air Group • Home Base – HMS *Heron* • RNAS Yeovilton, Ilchester, Somerset

This aircraft crashed following a power failure whilst it was performing aerobatics.[22] The aircraft crash-landed in a field of mangol wurzels near to the perimeter fence of the airfield shortly after midday. Naval personnel were quickly on the scene and helped rescue the pilot, Lieutenant H. Umpleby, whose home was in Bradford, Yorkshire. He was taken to the nearby RNAS Yeovilton sickbay where he was treated for minor injuries and shock.

Two farm labourers were working in the field at the time and had to scramble to safety hurriedly as the crashing aircraft plummeted to earth towards them.

Source: *Western Gazette*, 1 July 1949.

27 July 1949   • Avro 652A Anson • Serial Number NK734 • Number 66 Group CF RAF • Home Base – RAF Turnhouse • Scotland

On landing at RAF Locking, near Weston-super-Mare, Somerset, one of the aircraft's tyres burst.[23] The aircraft then careered off the runway and its undercarriage collapsed. The damage was such that the aircraft was written off. This aircraft was being used by cadets at their Air Experience Camp. Luckily there were no casualties amongst them.

24 October 1949   • Hawker Sea Fury F.B.11 • Serial Number VR945 • Number 50 Training Air Group • Home Base – RNAS Yeovilton   • Near Ilchester, Somerset

This aircraft crashed on landing and was burnt out.[24] No other details are known. There were no recorded air-crash deaths that day other than one in HMS *Falcon*, which was located in Hal Fal, Malta. It is therefore assumed that the pilot escaped.

31 October 1949   • Westland Wyvern T.F.2 Pre-Production Aircraft • Serial Number VP113 • Westland Aircraft Works • Home Base – Westland's Airfield • Yeovil, Somerset

A Westland Wyvern airscrew turbine fighter prototype aircraft crashed on two semi-detached council houses near Westland's airfield at Yeovil, Somerset, demolishing one of them.

The aircraft had taken off from the company's base at RAF Merryfield, where it would have normally returned on completion of the flight. While flying over Yeovil the pilot got into difficulties and attempted to land after giving the alarm to those on the ground.

Those killed were the Westland Company's assistant chief test pilot, Squadron Leader Michael Adrian Graves DFC, who lived at Boleyn House, Ash; a child, Ann Wilkins, aged five, the daughter of Mr and Mrs A.A. Wilkins of No 98 Westland Road, who was riding her pedal cycle in the road at the time of the crash; Mrs W. Brown, aged fifty-four and a mother of seven children, of No 30 Westland Road. Her house was severely damaged by the crashing aeroplane.

Another woman, Mrs Hockey, was taken to hospital with serious burns after being trapped in the blazing remains of her house at No 28 Westland Road. Unfortunately she did not recover from her injuries and died in hospital during the early hours of 2 November 1949.

The *Western Gazette* reported at the time:

One eyewitness said that there was a trail of burning fuel 'about 20ft to 30ft long behind the aircraft as it crashed.' The aircraft had been up for about half an hour on a routine test flight and, as it was coming down, in the words of another Observer, 'it plunged' into the council houses, which are close to the airfield. The aircraft experienced engine failure following a high-speed low-level pass across the airfield and climb to 2,500ft. He attempted a crash-landing on the airfield after crossing the boundary at 200 miles per hour but touched down three-quarters of way across the airfield and tragically overshot into a housing estate.

Source: *The Times* and *Western Gazette*.

---

30 November 1949 • Supermarine Seafire XV • Serial Number SR600 • Built by Westland Aircraft Works • Number 767 Naval Air Squadron • Home Base – HMS *Heron* • RNAS Yeovilton, Somerset

Lieutenant (A) Peter Russell Goldsack was born on 2 December 1925 and was the son of Mr and Mrs Maurice Goldsack of No 1 Windsor Road, Boscombe. He was killed, aged twenty-three, when the aircraft he was flying from HMS *Illustrious* crashed at sea.[25]

He was approximately 15 miles south-east of Portland Bill and was completing routine practice deck landings. Lieutenant Goldsack had successfully completed two landings and approached for a third. His arrester hook successfully made contact with the wire but for some inexplicable reason the hook on the undercarriage of his plane snapped off. The plane upended and hit the barrier in a nose-down position. He died within minutes of being removed from the aircraft, suffering from severe shock and fractures of the ribs. He is buried in the Royal Navy Cemetery at St Bartholomew's, Yeovilton village. His final resting place is shown in Appendix 2.

16 December 1949 • Hawker Sea Fury F.B.11 • Serial Number VX650 • Number 767 Naval Air Squadron • Home Base – HMS *Heron* • RNAS Yeovilton, Somerset • Detached to HMS *Illustrious*

This aircraft crashed on board HMS *Illustrious* and broke into two parts,[26] and immediately behind the cockpit. The front end remained upended and entangled itself in the barrier net. The exact date of the accident is not known but it was struck off charge on 16 December 1949. The unknown pilot survived the crash without injuries. This aircraft only served post-war and the last Sea Fury squadron was finally disbanded in 1955.

1950s

1950

16 February 1950 • Supermarine Spitfire F.22 • Serial Number PK545 • Westland Aircraft Works • Home Base – Westland's Airfield • Yeovil, Somerset

This aircraft was flown by a civilian test pilot, Mr Keith Albert Butler of No 58 Limley Road, Cove, Farnborough, Hampshire. It was on its fourth test flight, after reconditioning and modifications,[1] when the aircraft went into an intentional slow roll but lost height whilst inverted and hit the ground at high speed, into a hillside at Yeovil Marsh, a tiny hamlet close to RNAS Yeovilton. A crater several feet deep was formed.

Two farm workers from nearby Marsh Farm had a lucky escape. They were tending a hedge only 200 yards from where the aircraft crashed and witnessed the whole incident. Mr C. Saunders of No 26 Eastlands Road, Yeovil, said he heard the scream of an aircraft coming up behind him – very low and very fast. Working with him was Mr R. White of Marsh Hill Farm, Yeovil Marsh. Sadly, Mr Butler was killed in the accident.

Source: *Western Gazette*, Friday 17 February 1950.

5 March 1950 • D.H.100 Vampire F.1 • Serial Number VF271 • Number 501 (County of Gloucester) Squadron RAF • Home Base – RAF Filton • Bristol

During bad visibility this aircraft overshot on landing and hit a fence; the crash caused extensive damage. It was written off.[2] There were no fatalities.

21 March 1950 • Bristol 170 Freighter 21 • Serial Number G-AHJJ • Bristol Aeroplane Company • Home Base – Filton • Bristol

This aircraft first flew in 1946. It had been recently converted from a type Mk 2A to a type Mk 21 and was on a second test flight in order to achieve its airworthiness certificate. On board were the pilot and three passengers.

About half an hour after the aircraft had departed Filton it went into a spin and, out of control, it crashed, killing all on board. It came down at Cowbridge in the Vale of Glamorgan, Wales. Those killed were Mr J.A. Barraclough, the pilot; Mr F. Pullen, electrician; Mr A. Bolton, radio operator; Mr E.C. Brunt, engineer.

The aircraft crashed into a tree nursery of the Forestry Commission. There were about 100 forestry workers in the area at the time and fifteen of these were in the immediate vicinity of the fatal accident.

The probable cause of the crash was cited as structural failure of the fuselage stern frame. Previously, on 6 May 1949, another Bristol 170 Freighter 21, Serial No G-AIFF, had crashed in very similar circumstances and killed all seven men on board.

13 July 1950 • Supermarine Spitfire F.R.XVIII • Serial Number TP279 • Westland Aircraft Works • Home Base – Westland's Airfield • Yeovil, Somerset

This aircraft had been loaned to Westland's by the RAF when it crashed and was written off.[3] No other details exist except that there were no known casualties.

10 September 1950 • Harvard IIB (AT-16) • Serial Number KF616 • Number 501 (County of Gloucester) Squadron RAF • Home Base – RAF Filton • Bristol

At 3,000ft, the pilot put the aircraft into an intentional spin.[4] Although this was considered to be a safe height for doing this manoeuvre, for some reason the aircraft did not recover from it.

195676 Flight Lieutenant Frank Harvey Hunt was aged twenty-six when he died. He is buried in St John the Baptist Church Cemetery at Chipping Sodbury, Gloucester.

5 October 1950 • Bristol 170 Mk 21 • Serial Number WH575 • Home Base – RAF Filton • Bristol

This aircraft was intended for cold-weather trials in Canada and built for the Ministry of Supply. It was given Serial No WH575 but crashed on take-off from RAF Filton during a simulated engine failure, when both engines actually did fail. The pilot belonged to the Royal Canadian Air Force and as such is unidentified.[5] Happily there were no casualties as a result of this incident. The aircraft was repaired and rebuilt as G-AINK, then as ZK-AYG. Its last known location in 2008 was in Christchurch, New Zealand, where it was privately owned. It is preserved in the Nelson Founders Museum.

3 November 1950 • Westland Wyvern W.38 Wyvern T.3 Prototype • Serial Number VZ739 • Westland Aircraft Works • Home Base – Westland's Airfield • Yeovil, Somerset

On a test flight, this two-seater conversion trainer (and the only one to be built) experienced a turbine fan failure. The aircraft skimmed the roofs of some houses close to the holiday camp at Seaton and forced landed with its wheels up. It careered through some fields next to the railway line for about 400 yards and in the process managed to skip over a water-filled dyke. A wire fence was carried away with it, before it finally came to a rest in the marshes at Seaton, next to the River Axe.

The aircraft was returned to Yeovil via road, where it was found that the centre section spar had been twisted when it had been recovered from the clinging mud of the marshland. It was eventually struck off charge on 30 July 1953 and sold for scrap. The crew for this incident were the pilot, Mr D.A.S. Colvin, and the engineer, Mr R.K. Page.[6]

Source: *Western Gazette*, Friday 10 November 1950.

1951

8 January 1951 • Lockheed Constellation L.049 • Registration G-AHEN • British Overseas Airways Corporation (BOAC) • Home Base – Filton Airfield • Bristol

After having flown some 11,350 hours on BOAC's North Atlantic routes between August 1946 and December 1950, this aircraft overshot the runway when landing after a training flight at Filton and hit the brick-built superstructure of a fuel-storage tank. Fortunately, there was no fire and only minor injuries were sustained by the crew. The aircraft, however, suffered severe damage to the nose, undercarriage and main spar of the wing. This was beyond the company's finances to repair and it was eventually sold for scrap for $244,000.

Later, the salvable parts from this aircraft were combined with those from another L.049 that had been written off by Air France. It flew again as N-74192 for Hawaii Airlines before being finally sold to El Al and ending her days as 4X-AKD.

Source: *Flight* magazine, 1 October 1954.

9 January 1951 • Tempest F.VI • Serial Number NX127 • 1689 Independent Flight • Home Base – RAF Hawarden • North-East Wales, Near Chester

The aircraft was seen to spin into the ground after performing aerobatics very near to the airfield at RAF Filton and the cause of the crash was never discovered.[7] The accident occurred in a field on the boundary of Bristol and close to what is now the M5 near Hallen, South Gloucestershire. The aircraft dived into a marshy area and despite huge efforts to recover the pilot's body by teams from the RAF and local builders, they were unsuccessful. The deepest the teams managed to get was about 12ft before the hole would naturally fill in again. The spot is now marked by a small, muddy pond.

1383280 Flight Sergeant Arthur Leslie Steel was born on 10 January 1920 and was aged thirty when he died. He remains with his aircraft.

8 May 1951 • Bristol 156 Beaufighter T.F. Mk 10 converted to T.T. Mk 10 • Serial Number RD812 • Bristol (Weston) Built • Number 5 Squadron RAF • Home Base – RAF Llandow • South Wales

The aircraft was engaged in a target drop at Watchet Ranges, Somerset.[8] The pilot was flying below the minimum safety height of 250ft and, in an effort to avoid colliding with some high cables, he hit a tree and crashed into a meadow near Williton, Somerset, killing the two crew members. The aircraft broke up and caught fire, setting alight the gorse in the heath land around it.

1892398 Flying Officer Alexander Dean Cordiner DFM (pilot) was aged twenty-five at the time of his death. He is buried in the Heanton Punchardon churchyard near Barnstaple, North Devon.

4006962 Leading Aircraftman James Lawton was aged twenty-five when he died. He is buried in The Hill Cemetery, Ballymacoda, Co. Cork, Ireland.

22 May 1951 • D.H.82A Tiger Moth T.2 • Serial Number N6729 • 12 Reserve Flying School • Home Base – RAF Filton • Bristol

When taking off, this aircraft swung off the runway and hit a hedge.[9] The aeroplane was written off. There were no casualties.

8 June 1951 • D.H.100 Vampire F.B.5 • Serial Number VZ330 • Number 229 Operational Conversion Unit • Home Base – RAF Chivenor • Near Barnstaple, North Devon

The aircraft was taking part in a mock attack on a target. As it approached from a south-easterly direction, the aircraft did not 'peel off' but instead went into a half roll at approximately ST635173 and dived into the ground near the Marston Magna Road, just outside of Sherborne, Dorset, after going through a hedge.[10]

As a pupil at Sherborne School, Patrick Palmer witnessed the crash:

> The aircraft was diving down towards the top of the hill, along with some others. We saw it crash and ran up the hill. It came down into a field just beyond Sheeplands Lane in Sherborne, about 100 yards from the Marston Road. It had almost pulled up in time as it left a furrow about 18 inches deep and about 20 yards long. The engine had broken away from the plane and had carried on up the field.

582233 Pilot Officer Ronald David Jones was aged twenty-three years when he died. He is buried in the Heanton Punchardon churchyard near Barnstaple, North Devon.

29 August 1951 • Hawker Sea Fury F.B.10 • Serial Number TF918 • Number 767 Naval Air Squadron • Home Base – HMS *Heron* • RNAS Yeovilton, Somerset

This aircraft suffered an engine failure and an attempted forced landing was made. It struck the ground by Willow Tree Farm and bounced up into the air near Folke, approximately 3 miles south of Sherborne in Dorset. The aircraft hit the ground again and went through a hedge, snapping in two. The wings and cockpit section were turned around to face the tailend of the aircraft.

Despite immediate assistance from nearby farm workers, including Mr Charles W.H. Barber of Willow Tree Farm, and the releasing of the restraining harness so that they could get him out of his seat, the pilot did not survive the impact.

Lieutenant Michael Edward Stanley was born on 21 July 1923 and was aged twenty-eight when he lost his life. He was a bachelor and lived in Ascot. It is not known where he is buried. Lieutenant Stanley was an experienced pilot with over 850 flying hours, 500 of them in a Sea Fury.

Source: *Western Gazette.*

1952

7 January 1952   • D.H.100 Vampire F.1 • Serial Number TG446 • Number 48 Maintenance Unit • Home Base – RAF Hawarden • Near Chester, North-East Wales

This aircraft crashed whilst approximately 1 mile north-east of Peasdown St John, near Bath.[11] During a ferry flight it simply ran out of fuel and was successfully abandoned in cloud.

Five people, including two children, had a lucky escape when the aircraft came down and hit two cottages at White Oxmead Farm, approximately 5 miles from Bath. The pilot, Flight Lieutenant K.A. Harvey, had successfully baled out about 2 miles away and had landed safely.

8 January 1952   • Westland Wyvern T.F.2 • Serial Number VW867 • Home Base – RAF Merryfield • Ilton, near Ilminster, Somerset

The chief test pilot at Westland's, Mr Harald J. Penrose, was flying this aircraft on handling trials.[12] The aircraft had recently been fitted with a new rear fuselage and a tail parachute. The aircraft made a successful belly landing on the grass next to the runway at RAF Merryfield after it suffered a hydraulic interconnection failure. Mr Penrose was not hurt in the incident. The Wyvern was declared a Category 5. It was eventually sent to RNAY Fleetlands and broken up for spares.

8 February 1952   • D.H.98 Mosquito F.B.VI • Serial Number RF966 • Number 204 Advanced Flying School • Home Base – RAF Swinderby • Lincolnshire

Both engines of this plane unexpectedly cut out and the inexperienced pilot and navigator successfully abandoned the aircraft about half a mile south-east of the village of Sparkford, Somerset.

The tenant of Mill Cottage watched in horror as the still-flying Mosquito steadily sped towards his house. He thought it was going to crash into it but fortunately for him the aircraft narrowly missed. It flew into the ground in a field belonging to Mill Farm, near Weston Bampfylde, Sparkford, and exploded with great violence. The aircraft had disintegrated on crashing and parts of it were scattered over several fields.

The sound of the explosion was so great that people living as far away as Yeovil thought that a huge bomb had been detonated.

The pilot of the aircraft was 4042403 Pilot Officer George Alexander Ironside. His observer was 3058107 Pilot Officer Charles George Wilkinson.

Source: *Western Gazette.*

23 February 1952   • Westland Wyvern S.4 • Serial Number VW880 • Westland Aircraft Works • Home Base – Westland's Airfield • Yeovil, Somersetl

Once again Westland's chief test pilot, Harald Penrose, was involved in a crash test flying an aircraft.[13] This aircraft was undergoing intensive engine trails when the oil pressure was gradually lost. Although Mr Penrose attempted a forced landing at the Weston-super-Mare airfield, the engine finally seized up before he could reach it. He made a wheels-up landing in a field next to the airfield. Although he walked away unscathed, the aircraft was declared a Category 4.

This aircraft never became an active military unit and was retained by Westland Aircraft Works before being written off by them on this crash date. It was sent to RNAS Arbroath in Scotland and used for ground instruction as A2311, where the centre section was used for underwater ejection tests. The remains were finally sent to Abbotsinch, Scotland, in 1957 for scrapping.

4 March 1952   • D.H.100 Vampire F.1 • Serial Number TG352 • Number 208 Advanced Flying School • Home Base – RAF Merryfield • Ilton, near Ilminster, Somerset

The pilot attempted to turn off the runway at RAF Merryfield whilst travelling far too quickly.[14] The starboard undercarriage leg suddenly collapsed and the aircraft slewed on to the grass causing damage that put it beyond economical repair.

16 April 1952   • D.H.100 Vampire F.B.1 • Serial Number TG444 • Number 208 Advanced Flying School • Home Base – RAF Merryfield • Ilton, near Ilminster, Somerset

This aircraft overshot the runway on landing and was so badly damaged that it was written off.[15] It was originally an F.1. that had been converted to an F.B.5 prototype and was the first of its type to fly on 29 June 1948.

22 April 1952   • D.H.100 Vampire F.1 • Serial Number TG377 • Number 208 Advanced Flying School • Home Base – RAF Merryfield • Ilton, near Ilminster, Somerset

While returning to base and after an aerobatics sortie, the aircraft was seen leaving cloud in a high-speed dive.[16] The port mainplane broke away and the aircraft crashed near Babers Farm, Marshwood, in Dorset. It is believed that the pilot entered a well-developed cumolonimbus cloud with a gyro that had toppled as a result of the aerobatics and then he lost control.

2500843 Pilot Officer Douglas John Tart was killed. He was born on 8 July 1932 at Bramley, West Yorkshire, and was aged nineteen when he died. His grave can be found at the Bramley Cemetery in Leeds.

25 April 1952   • D.H.100 Vampire F.1 • Serial Number TG375 • Number 208 Advanced Flying School • Home Base – RAF Merryfield • Ilton, near Ilminster, Somerset

The pilot attempted a wheels-up landing in a field 2 miles west of Chideok in Dorset after engine failure.[17] The aircraft undershot the field it was making for and crashed into a brick wall, ending up in a farmyard. The pilot escaped.

12 May 1952   • D.H.100 Vampire F.1 • Serial Number VF309 • Number 208 Advanced Flying School • Home Base – RAF Merryfield • Ilton, near Ilminster, Somerset

This aircraft crashed in flames close to Yalham Farm, Culmhead, near Taunton.[18] The port mainplane wing had broken off following overstressing of the aircraft and the aircraft went into a spin at 9.00 a.m. The tailplane port half, port mainplane, inner rib port and the elevator starboard half were found in the fields in front of the nearby Holman Clavel Inn, which is to the north-east of where the main wreckage (see plates 3–4) was found. The old RAF station at Culmhead is quite close by and Yalham Farm lies about 900m to the east of the old airfield. The main wreckage of the aircraft came to rest next to a high earth bank.

The *Western Gazette*, dated 16 May 1952, reported:

> Mr A.J. Farley, an agricultural worker, of Higher Yalham, Culmhead, who was working in a field adjoining the one where the plane crashed, said that he heard the plane in the distance and suddenly heard a 'clatter which sounded as if something had gone wrong.' He saw a piece fly from the plane – probably the wing – and the disintegrating machine spiralled to the earth. Mr Farley said, 'I ran for my life. I could do nothing to help the pilot, who was thrown from the plane and killed instantly.' Mr G Westlake, on whose land the crash occurred, was soon on the scene and he telephoned for assistance.

A subsequent RAF Board of Inquiry noted that a test pilot of the de Havilland Company suggested that the fracture of the main wing spar could have been caused by elevator override. To test this theory, one of the de Havilland Company test pilots test flew two Mk 1 Vampires at RAF Merryfield on the afternoon of 15 May 1952. He reported definite signs of elevator oscillation at certain speeds. When HQ 25 Group was made aware of this they ordered the grounding of all Vampires until a modification of the elevators had been made.

4053209 Pilot Officer Peter Nott is buried at Thornbury Cemetery, Gloucestershire. He was born on 25 May 1932 and had just had his nineteenth birthday when he met his untimely end. His gravestone is a family one in the shape of a shield within a curved archway. At its top it has the RAF wings engraved upon it.

26 May 1952 • Hawker Sea Fury F.B.10 • Serial Number TF907 • Number 767 Naval Air Squadron • Home Base – HMS *Heron II* • Henstridge, Somerset

This aircraft was carrying out deck-landing practice on HMS *Triumph*.[19] However, it failed to cut on the signal and carried off the port barrier post, and went over the side. The pilot, Sub Lieutenant John Stanford Brandon, Royal Australian Navy, was rescued unharmed.

28 May 1952 • D.H.100 Vampire F.III • Serial Number VF338 • Number 208 Advanced Flying School • Home Base – RAF Merryfield • Ilton, near Ilminster, Somerset

The aircraft stalled during a roller landing at RAF Merryfield, causing a wing to hit the runway.[20] The aircraft was heavily damaged and, despite the fact that the aircraft was written off, the pilot sustained only minor injuries.

23 June 1952 • D.H.100 Vampire F.1 • Serial Number TG298 • Number 208 Advanced Flying School • Home Base – RAF Merryfield • Ilton, near Ilminster, Somerset

The aircraft broke away from a formation at 28,000ft.[21] Although repeated calls were made to him to rejoin the formation, the pilot failed to acknowledge them. He dived into the ground in a near-vertical dive near Harcombe House, Chudleigh in Devon, despite an appearance of some recovery at 500ft. It is believed that the pilot had suffered from lack of oxygen and had passed out at the controls. An open parachute was found in a field next to the wreckage.

Pilot Officer Allan Durham, aged nineteen, was born on 11 October 1932 at Swallownest in Sheffield. He lies buried in the churchyard of St Peter's in Ilton.

30 June 1952 • Gloster Meteor F.4 • Serial Number RA483 • Number 2 Ferry Unit RAF • Home Base – RAF Whitchurch • Bristol

The aircraft was on a ferry flight and had diverted to St Eval when the pilot had discovered that the ventral tank was not filling with fuel. On arrival he found a low covering of stratus cloud and, despite trying, he could not make radio contact with St Eval, so he diverted towards RAF Merryfield.

The aircraft crashed from 6,000ft and made a large 15ft gap in the bank of the Shepton Beauchamp/South Petherton cross roads when the plane ran out of fuel, throwing lots of earth across the road as it did so. As it crashed, the fuel tanks ignited and the aircraft blew up. The pilot, Sergeant Pilot Berosckiewicz, successfully baled out.

He later told onlookers that he had tried to bale out of the stricken jet three times before he was finally successful. Seconds before the jet fighter hit the bank, a tractor carrying the driver, Mr George Male, and his mate, Tony Welch, had just passed by there. 'That he seemed to be travelling straight towards them but crashed just behind them. Nine times out of ten when one goes past those cross roads something is passing,' Mr Male said. 'It was a bit of luck that we missed it.'

Source: *Western Gazette*, 4 July 1952.

11 July 1952   • D.H.100 Vampire F.1 • Serial Number VF300 • Number 208 Advanced Flying School • Home Base – RAF Merryfield • Ilton, near Ilminster, Somerset

During a tail chase at 8,000ft over Stoke-sub-Hamdon, Somerset, this aircraft entered a slow spin which quickly resulted in a vertical dive and eventually caused the aircraft to break up before hitting the ground, shedding pieces of its tailplane. It crashed in the field opposite Cartgate Junction, on the A358 at approximately Ordnance Survey Map 129, Grid Reference 483188.

Sergeant Lines had commenced flying jet planes on 17 June 1952. Before this flight he had already completed twenty-one hours in Vampires and Meteors.

The flight of three aircraft was led by Flight Officer P.E. Cornell. He had flown over a clearing in the clouds to establish his bearing and then radioed the other two pilots to rejoin the formation. Only Sergeant G.B. Watson appeared. Sergeant Lines had acknowledged the radio instructions to rejoin but then there was no further radio contact with him.

Sergeant Watson had last seen Sergeant Lines on top of a roll in an inverted position at about 8,000ft. Lines then dived into a cloud.

3508089 Sergeant Pilot Richard Butler Lines was born at Hinckley in Leicestershire on 15 February 1929. He was aged twenty-three when he was killed in this aircraft accident. He is buried in Hinckley Cemetery in Leicestershire.

Brian Pittard recalls that he later dug this area with other members of the Aviation Archaeologists Society and removed at least three trailer loads of artefacts from the aircraft's impact site (plate 5). He arrived there soon after the crash to view the remains of the aircraft and recalls that by the time of his arrival the RAF recovery crew had been and gone. The impact area is marked by a slight indentation in the ground about 20–30 yards out from the corner of the hedge next to the main A358 road.

Source: *Western Gazette*, 25 July 1952.

14 July 1952 • D.H.100 Vampire F.1 • Serial Number VF265 • Number 208 Advanced Flying School • Home Base – RAF Merryfield • Ilton, near Ilminster, Somerset

This aircraft collided with a Vampire TG297 at 30,000ft over Cardiff. Large pieces of the aircraft crashed into a Cardiff hotel, killing a civilian on the ground, Mrs Georgina Ethel Evans, aged fifty-three – a chambermaid.

She was working in a third-storey bedroom of the hotel when the debris from the collision crashed into the building before finally ending up in the basement of the hotel. The residents of the hotel were having their lunch when the crash occurred, which filled the dining room with smoke and debris. Many a person experienced a lucky escape that day.

The pilot, Pilot Officer G.H. Patterson, of Houghton-le-Spring, County Durham, parachuted to safety and landed at Cardiff airport.

Source: *The Times.*

14 July 1952 • D.H.100 Vampire F.1 • Serial Number TG297 • Number 208 Advanced Flying School • Home Base – RAF Merryfield • Ilton, near Ilminster, Somerset

This aircraft collided with Vampire VF265 at 30,000ft over Cardiff.[22] The pilot, Pilot Officer B.F. Shaw, successfully parachuted to safety and landed in the Bristol Channel, whereupon he was rescued by a Swedish vessel and taken to Barry. The aircraft crashed at Pont Camma Farm, Llandaff, Glamorgan, Wales.

Source: *The Times.*

6 August 1952 • D.H.100 Vampire F.1 • Serial Number TG305 • Number 208 Advanced Flying School • Home Base – RAF Merryfield • Ilton, near Ilminster, Somerset

The aircraft was engaged in a tail-end chase but the pilot lost sight of the aircraft he was meant to pursue.[23] He was so intent on looking for his leader that he did not notice that he had allowed the aircraft to descend. Due to a calm sea and hazy visibility, the pilot did not realise how low he was until it was far too late. The aircraft hit the sea in a slightly nose-down attitude and broke up near Barry Dock.

2506570 Pilot Officer Derek John Atkins was born on 15 October 1932 at Winchmore Hill, Southgate. He was aged nineteen when he lost his life. He is buried in Bradstone Cemetery, Dorset, and his grave can be found in Section B, Grave 645.

28 August 1952
• D.H.100 Vampire F.1 • Serial Number VF313 • Number 208 Advanced Flying School • Home Base – RAF Merryfield • Ilton, near Ilminster, Somerset

The aircraft dived into the ground out of cloud near Bagbear Farm and struck some trees 2½ miles south-south-west of Great Torrington, Devon.[24] Unfortunately, the pilot was killed.

This aircraft was being flown by Pilot Officer Alan Harvey, aged nineteen. He was born on 1 January 1933 at Abertillery, Monmouthshire. He is buried in Ilton Cemetery in Section U, Grave 1.

25 September 1952
• D.H.100 Vampire F.3 • Serial Number VF279 • Number 9 Flying Training School • Home Base – RAF Merryfield • Ilton, near Ilminster, Somerset

The pilot was briefed to conduct his assigned sortie clear of cloud at all times. On returning to base he requested advice as there was a large cumolonimbus cloud ahead. Almost immediately the aircraft 'was seen by Mr Henry Robert Pope of Moortown, Curry Rivel. He said he was in a field when he saw a Vampire come out of the cloud at about 1,000ft. The plane was diving at an angle of about 450 with the engine going.'

It made a crater 18ft square by 10–12ft deep. The pilot, Gillard, had enlisted in the RAF in March 1951 and started flying in October 1951. He qualified as a pilot in June 1952. He had approximately 230 flying hours and was on a course at Ilton for jet-propelled aircraft that lasted three months. This was his fourth aerobatic sortie in a Vampire.

It is believed that the aircraft entered the cloud and the pilot opened the hood in an attempt to clear ice off the windscreen. The air stream removed his helmet and probably knocked him unconscious. His helmet was located over a mile away from the impact site. The aircraft crashed close to Burton Woods, Curry Rivel.

Pilot Officer John William Gillard, aged nineteen, was born on 6 March 1933 at East Greenwich, London. At the time of his death he lived at No 28 Ballard House, Thames Street, London, SE10. Pilot Officer Gillard is buried in the churchyard of St Peter's church, Ilton. His grave lies close to the main entrance gate.

Source: *Western Gazette*, 3 October 1952.

11 October 1952
• D.H.100 Vampire F.B.5 • Serial Number VV698 • Number 229 Operational Conversion Unit • Home Base – RAF Chivenor • Near Barnstaple, North Devon

This aircraft's engine blew up and it was forced to crash-land upon the beach north of Burnham-on-Sea, Somerset.[25] The pilot escaped from the aircraft. The aircraft was recovered from the beach and taken to No 49 Maintenance Unit at RAF Colerne, where it was finally struck off charge as a Category 5 (S) on 3 November 1952.

7 November 1952   • Gloster Meteor T.7 • Serial Number WL433 • Number 209
Advanced Flying School • Home Base – RAF Westonzoyland • Bridgwater, Somerset

The aircraft was on an asymmetric training sortie when it entered a spin at 1,000ft. This was corrected but the aircraft then stalled, dived towards the ground and exploded on impact, 2 miles east-south-east of Baltonsbury, Somerset, and near Westwood Farm, West Lydford.

> The Control Tower was in wireless communications with the aircraft and at 11.14 a.m. at his request, F.O. Evans was given a course to fly back to the station. When the aircraft had been airborne for 30 minutes it had been called on all frequencies, but there was no reply.

John Parham, farm worker, of White Hart Hotel, Castle Cary, said that he was working in the yard at Grange Farm, West Lydford, when he heard the sound of a jet plane overhead and looked up. At first glance it was flying quite normally. One wing, he thought the left-hand one, was beginning to drop as if the aircraft was starting to turn. He imagined it was at about 1,000ft up, heading roughly in a northerly direction, and the turn became steeper and steeper.

It appeared to go over on its back and start to fall in a wide spiral, revolving at the same time. It did this very slowly and he watched it disappear behind one of the farm buildings. About five seconds later he heard a crash and saw a column of thick, black smoke go up into the air. When he got to the scene he and some other people tried to put out the flames by throwing dirt on them, and using an extinguisher from a cattle lorry that had arrived.

4074458 Pilot Officer Samuel Bruce Frankel was born on 25 May 1933 in Hydrabad, India, and was aged nineteen when he was killed. His grave can be found at Westonzoyland Cemetery, Section 1, Grave 52.

His crew mate, 607097 Flying Officer Tony Roland Valland Evans, was born on 8 December 1929 at Harrow, Middlesex, and was aged twenty-two when he was killed in the same air crash. He is buried at Dovercourt Cemetery, Essex.

Source: *Western Gazette*, 14 November 1952; www.gatwick-aviation-museum.co.uk.

20 November 1952   • Hawker Sea Fury • Serial Number Not Known • Number 804
Squadron Naval Air Service • Home Base – RNAS Brawdy • Wales

> Farm workers searched snow and mist this morning for the pilot after a Naval Sea Fury plane had dived in flames to crash and burn out in a field 300 yards from the centre of Hinton Charterhouse, six miles from Bath.
>
> Ignoring the danger of an explosion, one man peered into the blazing cockpit before the heat drove him back. He saw an empty seat.
>
> Later police flashed a message to the searchers: 'Pilot safe; baled out at Faulkland', three miles away.

The pilot was later named as Commissioned Officer W.A. Newton, of Monmouthshire.

A Faulkland farmer said that Newton knocked at the farm and asked if he could use the telephone. Newton had parachuted safely into a soft field.

His plane was one of a flight of eight Sea Furies that were on their way from the Naval Air Station at Brawdy, Haverfordwest, to Lee-on-Solent. They were making a fly past before the Queen tomorrow [21 November 1952].

The aircraft had lost oil pressure in flight and the engine caught fire, cutting out. At this point the pilot abandoned his craft which continued to circle, but on fire. Eventually it crashed.

Source: *Bath & Wilts Chronicle and Herald*, 20 November 1952.

1953

25 January 1953   • Gloster Meteor T.7 • Serial Number WL432 • Number 209 Advanced Flying School • Home Base – RAF Westonzoyland • Bridgwater, Somerset

Whilst in the process of landing this aircraft, coded 49, undershot the runway and was so badly damaged that it had to be written off.[26]

2 February 1953   • Gloster Meteor F.4 • Serial Number VT265 • Number 209 Advanced Flying School • Home Base – RAF Westonzoyland • Bridgwater, Somerset

The aircraft dived into the ground 2 miles north-east of RAF Oakington during a sleet storm.[27] The pilot was on his fifth solo flight and it is believed that he lost control in the obscured visibility.

Flying Officer John Arthur Stephens was killed. He was born on 26 August 1932 and is buried in the Congregational churchyard at Long Buckby, Staffordshire.

9 February 1953   • Gloster Meteor T.7 • Serial Number WL455 • Number 209 Advanced Flying School • Home Base – RAF Westonzoyland • Bridgwater, Somerset

Pilot Officer Woods was about halfway through his flying course. On the day in question he had been instructed to carry out instrument-flying practice; Sergeant Stockley was his instructor. The weather over Exmoor was not very good that day but the decision had been taken to fly there.

The aircraft was seen to climb steeply towards the clouds and then it was heard circling. Shortly afterwards, it emerged from the clouds and dived into the ground about 3¾ miles north-west of Dulverton, Somerset. The aircraft was presumed to have iced up.

The aircraft crashed in the valley between Liscombe Farm and Tarr Steps. The body of Pilot Officer Woods was located close to Knaplock Farm, about half a mile away from the crash site. His watch had stopped at 10.53 a.m. and his parachute was unopened in his pack, which was still attached to his body.

Sergeant Stockley's body was found in Westwater Wood, about 1 mile from the crash site. His parachute cords were attached to his harness but the parachute itself was missing. It is presumed that after baling out his parachute snagged on the doomed jet and tore itself away.

3134036 Pilot Officer Raymond Kenneth Woods, aged twenty, was born at Guildford in Surrey on 28 December 1932. He is buried in Westonzoyland Cemetery in Section 1, Grave 53.

4029506 Sergeant Frederick James Samuel Stockley, aged twenty-three, was born at Swanage in Dorset on 8 January 1930. Sergeant Stockley is buried next to Pilot Officer Woods in Westonzoyland Cemetery, in Section 1, Grave 54.

Source: *Western Gazette.*

9 February 1953   • Gloster Meteor F.4 • Serial Number VT229 • Civil Registration of N229VT • Number 12 Flying Training School • Home Base – RAF Westonzoyland • Bridgwater, Somerset

This aircraft collided on take-off with a Gloster Meteor T.7, Serial No WA608.[28] It received sufficient damage to downgrade it to instructional airframe status. The last known location of this aircraft was in July 2009. By this time it had found its way to the Fantasy of Flight Museum, Tamiami, Florida.

9 February 1953   • Gloster Meteor T.7 • Serial Number WA608 • Number 208 Advanced Flying School • Home Base – RAF Merryfield • Ilton, near Ilminster, Somerset

This aircraft collided with Gloster Meteor T.7, Serial No VT229, on a pairs take-off.[29] It yawed and crash-landed. The damage sustained was such that it was written off.

11 March 1953   • Gloster Meteor F.4 • Serial Number VT304 • Number 209 Advanced Flying School • Home Base – RAF Westonzoyland • Bridgwater, Somerset

The aircraft he was piloting dived into the Bristol Channel on a night training flight just off of Minehead, Somerset. It was reported it was heard at Weston-super-Mare at approximately 2300 hours in the evening but many of the reports said that the engine sound was not like the familiar high pitched noise. It was presumed that the pilot suffered anoxia (This means a total decrease in the level of oxygen, an extreme form of hypoxia or low oxygen). Unfortunately, the pilot was killed and his body was never recovered.

2531284 Pilot Officer John Nuttall Shaw, aged nineteen, was born on 22 May 1933 in Leeds, Yorkshire.

Source: *Western Gazette.*

17 April 1953   • Gloster Meteor T.7 • Serial Number WG998 • Number 209 Advanced Flying School • Home Base – RAF Westonzoyland • Bridgwater, Somerset

This two-seater training aircraft lost power on take-off.[30] Despite the instructor taking over control, the aircraft overshot the runway, went over a ditch and crashed into a field. It was repaired and finally transferred to the Dutch navy as I-304 on 14 March 1959, finally being scrapped on 17 December 1959.

11 June 1953   • Gloster G.A.5 Javelin Prototype • Serial Number WD808 • Test Pilot • Home Base – Moreton Valance • Gloucestershire

This aircraft was the second prototype of its kind, after the loss of the original prototype WD804. WD808 went into what was termed 'a super stall' near Flax Bourton in Somerset whilst on a test flight. It crashed into a field of tall grass at Ashton Court Park. It was discovered afterwards that at high angles of attack the elevators became masked from the airflow by the wings and therefore they became totally ineffective. Recovery from this 'super stall' was impossible.

The crash occurred on a playing field near Bristol and, in the words of a statement issued by the Gloster Aircraft Co. Ltd, Lawrence died 'in heroic circumstances'. Pending the disclosure of further information at the inquest, or subsequently, these circumstances are related in the statement, which said that the pilot 'had been flying for half an hour when he radioed to his home base, Moreton Valence, that he was in trouble'. At this point he was at over 20,000ft. If he had baled out then he would have been safe, but he elected to crash-land with minimum damage to the aircraft and homes and people on the ground. He came down in a glide, seeking to avoid built-up areas with houses, and just before landing found himself over playing fields where teams of boys were playing cricket. He stayed with the aircraft all the way down to 250ft, put it into a straight slow run in, and baled out using his ejector seat. However, he had waited too long, and he was killed on impact with the ground. The aircraft swept over the heads of the boys and landed in a field, flat. The wings and tail were undamaged 'on landing'.[31]

Lieutenant Peter G. Lawrence MBE (a former Royal Naval officer) landed about 300m from the crash site but still in his ejection seat because the parachute had failed to properly deploy in time. He received fatal injuries and did not survive. He was buried at Hessle, near Hull, on 17 June 1953. Canon A.E. Smallwood, who conducted the funeral service, said, 'He could have saved himself by leaving the machine earlier; by remaining in it and guiding it over homes and playing-fields, he saved others.'[32]

To prevent this type of accident happening again, a stall warning system was developed for the aircraft. This was a sensor placed on top of the wing that activated a buzzer in the pilot's headphones which alerted him if the pressure at the wing's leading edge began to drop.

18 June 1953   • Gloster G.41G Meteor F.4 • Serial Number VT266 • Number
209 Advanced Flying School • Home Base – RAF Westonzoyland • Bridgwater, Somerset

Take-off of this aircraft was abandoned when both engines suddenly lost power at
the same time. The aircraft overran the runway and went on over a ditch and into a
field.[33] It was declared a write-off.

10 July 1953   • Gloster G.43 Meteor T.7 • Serial Number VW445 • Number 209
Advanced Flying School • Home Base – RAF Westonzoyland • Bridgwater, Somerset

This aircraft was damaged by fire after belly landing at RAF Westonzoyland.[34] The
pilot had forgotten to lower the undercarriage during a night asymmetric landing.
The aircraft was classified as a Category 5 accident.

10 July 1953   • Sea Fury F.B.11 • Serial Number VR931 • Number 1834 Naval
Air Squadron • Home Base – RNAS Yeovilton • Somerset

This aircraft was ditched following a rocket projectile attack on Port Quinn Range,
Cornwall.[35] Lieutenant W. T. Alden RN was slightly injured in the incident.

11 July 1953   • Gloster Meteor T.7 • Serial Number WL344 • Number 209
Advanced Flying School • Home Base – RAF Westonzoyland • Bridgwater, Somerset

The aircraft was practising asymmetric roller landings with the port engine throttled
back at Dunkerswell airport, Devon.[36] As the aircraft touched down the trainee pilot
unexpectedly raised both the flaps on the undercarriage, when the weight had just
been taken off the wheels. The undercarriage retracted and the aircraft was severely
damaged as it made a belly landing.

15 July 1953   • Gloster G.41G Meteor F.4 • Serial Number VW300 • Number
209 Advanced Flying School • Home Base – RAF Westonzoyland • Bridgwater, Somerset

On an instrument approach to Westonzoyland this aircraft clipped some trees on
landing.[37] The damage was such that it was eventually struck off charge at No 49
Maintenance Unit (MU), RAF Colerne, on 5 April 1954, as a Category 5 loss.

24 July 1953   • D.H.100 Vampire F.B.5, Serial Number WA438 • D.H.100
Vampire F.B.5, Serial Number VV456 • Number 208 Advanced Flying School • Home
Base – RAF Merryfield • Ilton, near Ilminster, Somerset

There were two simultaneous Vampire crashes on the runway at RAF Merryfield as WA438 and VV456 fatally collided with each other. A flight of three aircraft attempted to land in line astern. Two of the planes then crashed in flames resulting in the loss of Pilot Officer Lane and Pilot Officer Roberts.

4071370 SAC (Senior Aircraftman) Brian Lovell of 'A' Flight was a member of the ground crew engines at RAF Merryfield at the time and an eyewitness to the tragic incident as it occurred. On 4 March 2011, at the age of seventy-eight, he recalled:

They (the aircraft) approached the airfied in formation flying parallel to the second runway, Isle Abbots to Ashill direction. As they passed over the field they peeled off in a turn to port. In doing so the instructor is in the lead with his pupils spaced out in line astern.

On hearing their approach, we as ground crew are ready to receive them by watching them on the final approach. The runway controller in the Black and White Chequered vehicle at the end of the runway has to keep watch too.

The practice was for the lead aircraft to land on the right-hand side of the runway, followed by the second on the left and the third would land on the right. In this sequence each aircraft is safely spaced out on the runway.

The third aircraft became too close to the second on the approach which prompted the runway controller to fire double Verey Shells, one red and one green. The green was meant for the second Vampire to continue to land and the red for the third one to overshoot and go round again, but the second did not follow the green. It lifted up on seeing the red and collided with the third. Both aircraft turned over and plunged to the right of the runway before exploding. We as ground crew could only stand and watch this unfold across the airfield.

The following day the crash crew arrived to remove the wreckage but the remains of the aircraft were too entangled. As I did the airfield tractor towing, I had to go and assist in pulling them apart. The crane was on one side of the wreckage and I and my tractor on the other. The picture is quite vivid in my mind today, seeing those aircraft turn over and explode.

4090854 Pilot Officer Richard Barrie Lane, aged twenty-four, was born in Northampton on 20 February 1929. He is buried at Abingdon churchyard near Northampton and can be found in the family grave.

4095331 Pilot Officer Brian John Roberts, aged twenty-three, was born on 13 June 1930 in Goodmayes, Essex. He is buried at the cemetery in Ilton, in Grave C.1.

8 September 1953 • Gloster Meteor T.7 • Serial Number WA712 • Number 209 Advanced Flying School • Home Base – RAF Westonzoyland • Bridgwater, Somerset

This aircraft crashed at Draycot Peak near Sutton Benger, Wiltshire, while on a night-training flight.[38] The aircraft became overstressed, caught fire and broke up in the air. The pilot was killed during this accident.

2539694 Pilot Officer Ian Douglas Guthrie Somerside, aged twenty-one, was born in Dennistown, Glasgow, on 19 October 1931. He is buried in the cemetery at Westonzoyland in Section 2, Grave 56.

8 September 1953 • D.H.100 Vampire F.B.5 • Serial Number VV564 • Number 208 Advanced Flying School • Home Base – RAF Merryfield • Ilton, near Ilminster, Somerset

This aircraft crashed south of Otterford, Somerset, and not far from the B3170, after the pilot, Pilot Officer G.W. Rippon, aged nineteen and who lived in South Harrow, had successfully baled out after a fracture of the impeller blades caused the engine to explode at about 7,500ft.[39] The aircraft rapidly descended, on fire with black smoke billowing out from behind it, coming to rest in a field belonging to Church Farm just after midday, above the church at Otterford. It left a large crater where the aircraft had impacted. The pilot landed unhurt about a quarter of a mile away from the wreckage.

The wreckage was returned to No 59 MU at RAF Colerne for disposal, where it was struck off charge on 29 September 1953.

Source: *Chard and Ilminster News*, 12 September 1953.

18 September 1953 • D.H.100 Vampire F.B.5 • Serial Number VZ312 • Number 208 Advanced Flying School • Home Base – RAF Merryfield • Ilton, near Ilminster, Somerset

The aircraft went into a spin at 8,000ft and continued spinning until it crashed at Long Forehead Field, Tintinhull. The pilot baled out at 300ft but his parachute failed to deploy as he was far too low. His body landed about 30ft away from the remains of his crashed aircraft.

Brian Pittard recalls visiting the scene shortly after the incident.[40] By the time he had arrived there was no one there. There was a white circle of foam with the jet's pipe in a straight-up position, with wisps of smoke spiralling from the exhaust. The force of the impact had buried most of the aircraft into the ground. Nearby was an oval shape, where an imprint had been left by the pilot's body.

2607893 Pilot Officer William Brian Parry, aged twenty-three, was born on 13 October 1929 at Coniston, Lancashire. He is buried in the cemetery at Ilton and can be found at Grave U.2.

Source: *Western Gazette*.

14 October 1953   • Gloster G.41G Meteor F.4 • Serial Number VT303 • Number 209 Advanced Flying School • Home Base – RAF Westonzoyland • Bridgwater, Somerset

The aircraft was abandoned over the Bristol Channel on a training flight when it went into an inverted spin. The pilot was seen to bale out over the Cardigan Bay area and the Tenby lifeboat was launched to carry out a search, but to no avail.

The body of the pilot was eventually recovered from the River Parrett at Stretcholt, near Pawlett, fourteen days later, when it was spotted by a Water Board employee.

4096470 Pilot Officer Ronald Mills Bent, aged twenty-four, was born on 7 February 1929 at New Plymouth, New Zealand. He is buried in the cemetery at Westonzoyland and can be found at Grave 277.

Source: *Western Gazette.*

27 October 1953   D.H.100 Vampire F.B.5 • Serial Number VV618 • Number 208 Advanced Flying School • Home Base – RAF Merryfield • Ilton, near Ilminster, Somerset

The pilot was on cross-country training in Wales and after refuelling at RAF Valley he took off once more,[41] when the port tank fell off and smashed into some church railings at Rhymney. The aeroplane then went into a steep starboard-turning climb. It reappeared moments later through thick cloud, coming down in a shallow dive. It crashed into the ground at approximately 4.25 p.m. The impact left a large crater in the common between Rhymney and Dowlain, Glamorgan, killing the pilot.

607359 Pilot Officer Derek Victor Reypert, aged twenty-one, was born on 11 July 1922 at Scotton, near Richmond in Yorkshire. He is buried at the cemetery in Ilton and can be found at Grave U.3.

2 November 1953   • Gloster G.41G Meteor F.4 • Serial Number VT305 • Number 209 Advanced Flying School • Home Base – RAF Westonzoyland • Bridgwater, Somerset

This aircraft crashed while attempting a night landing.[42] Both engines had been shut down to simulate an engine failure and subsequently failed to respond to an increase in throttle setting and the aircraft undershot the runway. It was sufficiently damaged to be written off.

19 November 1953   • D.H.100 Vampire F.B.5 • Serial Number WA251 • Number 208 Advanced Flying School • Home Base – RAF Merryfield • Ilton, near Ilminster, Somerset

The pilot was an experienced piston-engine flyer (he had 238 flights recorded on his log) and was on his first solo jet take-off at RAF Merryfield. As the aircraft left the runway, the tail booms scraped the ground. It climbed in a dangerously nose-high attitude to about 30–40ft before stalling. The port wing struck the runway and the aircraft cart wheeled along the runway.[43] The pilot was thrown clear, suffering fatal injuries.

A sequel to this accident occurred as the pilot was rushed to Taunton Hospital by RAF ambulance, some 10 miles away. The ambulance driver, LAC (Leading Aircraftman) John William Burdett was later charged with driving without due care as it was alleged that he had hit two cars in Taunton during his mercy dash. The magistrates dismissed the case in early January 1954.

Eyewitness Brian Lovell remembered on 4 March 2011:

I recall this one having had a mainplane change, air tested and returned to service. On takeoff it lifted too early causing it to stall. It side slipped and cartwheeled to the left. During the cartwheel the cockpit broke away, resulting in the death of the pilot. He had been struck on the head by one of the batteries that are secured in the aircraft's nose cone. The aircraft fortunately missed the 'B' Flight offices, coming to rest standing on one leg of its undercarriage but due to the bent throttle control it was still at full throttle. The fire section finally stopped the engine with CO_2.

2560624 Pilot Officer Martin Jackson, aged twenty, was born on 24 August 1933 at Woolwich, London. He is buried in the churchyard at Kingswood, Surrey.

24 November 1953 • D.H.100 Vampire F.B.5 • Serial Number VV619 • Number 229 Operational Conversion Unit • Home Base – RAF Chivenor • Near Barnstaple, North Devon

The pilot was undertaking a low-level cross-country training sortie.[44] He was trying to fix his position when his aircraft dived into the ground in low cloud, killing the pilot. The accident occurred approximately only a few yards from the Waterloo to West Country railway line near Chard Junction Station and Wiltshire United Dairies Ltd.

As was standard practice in those days, the inquest into the pilot's death was held in RAF Merryfield. Evidence given there by Mr Frederick William Darke reported that he heard the sound of a 'plane quite close, making a screaming noise'. He ducked to the ground and there was an explosion in the field next to him. The plane had crashed about 45 yards from him and the field that it had come down in was ablaze, including the surrounding hedges.

He ran to the crater that the aircraft's impact had left but could see no body in it. He later made the grizzly discovery of part of the pilot's body some 70 yards away from the impact crater.

Flight Lieutenant R. Ramirez said in his evidence to the coroner that the pilot's brief was to carry out a low-level cross-country sortie, but at 250ft above ground level. Where the crash took place would have put the pilot on his authorised route.

607352 Pilot Officer Anthony Corbin Roland Pugh, of Machyulleth, Wales, was aged twenty-one when he died. He is buried in Eglwysfache Cemetery in Glandyfi, Montgomeryshire.

Source: *Chard and Ilminster News*, 28 November 1953.

14 December 1953 • Supermarine Type 358 Seafire F.XVII • Serial Number SP341 • Number 764 Naval Air Squadron • Home Base – RNAS Yeovilton • Near Ilchester, Somerset

Midshipman J.W. Mathews was taking off in this aircraft when it ground looped and ran off the runway.[45] Its undercarriage collapsed causing extensive damage and it was finally struck off charge on 18 January 1954.

1954

4 February 1954   • Prototype Britannia • Serial Number G-ALRX • Filton Airfield, Bristol

On this day this aircraft, the second prototype of its kind, took off from Filton on a test flight. The pilot was Captain A.J. (Bill) Pegg. Flight engineers for the trip were Ken Fitzgerald and Gareth Jones. On board were Dr Archibald E. Russell, chief designer of Bristol Aircraft Division; Dr Stanley G. Hooker, chief engineer of the Bristol Engine Division; and Mr Farnes, the Bristol sales manager. This was not just a routine test flight. On board were also two representatives of the Dutch airline KLM, a potential Britannia customer. G. Malouin of KLM was co-pilot for the flight. Altogether there were thirteen people on the aircraft.

The aircraft experienced an overheating No 3 engine, which was turned off to be allowed to cool down. It was then restarted but it overheated again, exploding and bursting into flames. The pilot turned the aircraft back towards Filton to make an emergency landing. He shut down No 4 engine as a precaution. Suddenly, Nos 1 and 2 engines also failed and for a short while the aircraft was without power. The engineers on board managed to relight the two engines and the aircraft hastily headed towards Filton.

By this time the No 3 engine was well alight and, with no chance of making it back to the airfield, the pilot skilfully made a wheels-up landing on the mud flats of the River Severn near the village of Littleton-on-Severn, not far from the eastern end of the first Severn Road Bridge. He landed successfully and the mud put out the fire which was threatening to explode the fuel tanks.

Just before 8 p.m. that night, the attempt to recover the aircraft was abandoned when a wire hawser rope snapped. The aircraft's wings and most of its fuselage were covered by the incoming tide.

Although the aircraft was recovered the next day, it was a total wreck and ended its days as an instructional airframe. Due to its historical significance the aircraft nose section was saved and is now housed at Kemble, Gloucestershire.

Source: www.bristol-britannia.com.

12 February 1954   • Gloster G.41G Meteor F.4 • Serial Number VT313 • Number 209 Advanced Flying School • Home Base – RAF Westonzoyland • Bridgwater, Somerset

The pilot, Pilot Officer A. Chapman, aged nineteen, unfortunately selected 'undercarriage down' when it was already down. The undercarriage promptly retracted, causing the aircraft to belly land.[46] This accident blocked the runway at Westonzoyland. The aircraft was sent to the Gloster Aircraft Company with a view to repairing it on 22 March 1954. After examination it was declared a Category 5 loss and it was finally taken off RAF charge on 7 May 1954.

12 February 1954   • Gloster Meteor T.7 • Serial Number WH244 • Number 209 Advanced Flying School • Home Base – RAF Westonzoyland • Bridgwater, Somerset

A flight of seven Meteors from the 209 Advanced Flying School took off from Westonzoyland at 10 p.m. for night-flying practice. A separate crash had occurred on the runway involving Gloster Meteor F.4, Serial No VT313 (see p. 47), at Westonzoyland, blocking it.[47] The flight commander was instructed to fly to RAF Merryfield. Fog reduced visibility down to 1,000 yards at Merryfield, so the flight leader decided to return to Westonzoyland, where five of the seven aircraft made a successful landing on the grass beside the blocked runway. Meteors T.7 WH244 and VW430 never returned and both crashed within minutes of each other by flying into the ground.

WH244 hit the top of a clump of trees less than a quarter of a mile from the village of Stocklinch, Somerset, and came down in a ploughed field in front of three houses at Tanway. On impact the aircraft blew up, causing a 'terrific explosion'.

At the inquest at RAF Merryfield the coroner was told that Pilot Officer Fry had flown a total of 270 hours: 170 hours dual and 100 hours solo. Forty-two of these hours were on jet aircraft. This was the pilot's first solo flight at night. He had been identified by his name tab.

579460 Pilot Officer Frederick Earnest Fry, aged twenty-six, was born on 9 August 1927 at Woking, Surrey. He lived in Hatton Hill, Windlesham, Surrey. He is buried at Westonzoyland Cemetery and can be found at Grave 278.

Source: *Chard and Ilminster News*, 20 February 1954.

12 February 1954   • Gloster G.43 Meteor T.7 • Serial Number VW430 • Number 209 Advanced Flying School • Home Base – RAF Westonzoyland • Bridgwater, Somerset

This aircraft was the second plane that was lost in the entry described above.[48]

VW430 crashed at Ashill, close to the Ilminster/Taunton road, approximately 100m from Thickthorn Manor, which was the home at the time of Air Vice-Marshal M.L.Taylor. The aircraft blew up on impact and burning wreckage was strewn across three fields. The inquest at RAF Merryfield was told that the pilot officer had been identified by the contents of the wallet he was carrying at the time.

4019072 Pilot Officer Roy James Tilley, aged twenty-four, was born on 14 February 1929 at Minchinhampton, Gloucestershire. He lived in Stonehouse, Gloucestershire. He is buried at the Westonzoyland Cemetery and can be found in Grave 279.

Source: *Chard and Ilminster News*, 20 February 1954.

16 February 1954   • D.H.100 Vampire F.B.5 • Serial Number VX473 • Number 208 Advanced Flying School • Home Base – RAF Merryfield • Ilton, near Ilminster, Somerset

The pilot took off from RAF Merryfield at 10.20 a.m. and approached Dunkerswell airfield at 10.40 a.m. to carry out a practice landing.[49] In those days, a red-and-white-painted hut existed just before the runway. It was manned by a duty RAF corporal whose job was to warn pilots if they were flying too low on their approach to the airfield.

In this case the pilot was observed to be flying too low and the duty corporal hastily fired a red flare to warn him off. This warning was either not seen or ignored and the aircraft crashed about 100 yards short of the runway and immediately burst into flames. The pilot was thrown clear of the aircraft and ground staff found him in a sitting position trying to beat out his burning clothes. This disaster was followed by another when the service ambulance he was in broke down and he had to be transferred to an ambulance that had been called out from the nearby town of Honiton. Unfortunately, the pilot died of severe burns two days later in Musgrove Park Hospital, Taunton.

2560467 Pilot Officer Robert William Miall, aged nineteen, was born on 6 May 1934 in Brighton, Sussex. He lived at North Acres Street, near Hassocks, Sussex. He is buried in Ilton Cemetery and can be found in Grave C.2.

Source: *Chard and Ilminster News*, 20 February 1954.

12 March 1954   • Gloster Meteor T.7 • Serial Number WL423 • Number 209 Advanced Flying School • Home Base – RAF Westonzoyland • Bridgwater, Somerset

This aircraft failed to return from a training flight over the Bristol Channel during a sortie of aerobatics and circuits and was reported as overdue.[50] It took off from Westonzoyland airfield at 8.28 a.m. Pilot Officer Higgins was the pilot and Flight Lieutenant Pinder was the instructor. No radio message was received from the aircraft indicating any problems. All shipping was put on alert in the Bristol Channel to look out for any sign of the pilots and a message was broadcast over the local BBC station just in case the aircraft had come down in a remote area.

Lieutenant Pinder's body was recovered some time later from the sea and was cremated at the Charing Crematorium in London. At the inquest into his death, P.C. King of Burnham-on-Sea stated that he had seen the body of Flight Lieutenant Pinder washed up on the foreshore at Berrow, at a point opposite Heron House. The cause of his death was never established.

181557 Flight Lieutenant Robin Walter Pinder RAFVR, aged twenty-nine, was born on 23 September 1924 in Willesden, London. He was the only son of Lady Pinder and was married to Jean. He lived in Pedwell, near Street in Somerset.

3512990 Pilot Officer Michael Neale Huggins is listed as missing presumed dead. He was born on 28 March 1927 and was aged twenty-six when he died.

Source: *Western Gazette*, 16 July 1954.

17 March 1954   • Gloster G.41G Meteor F.4 • Serial Number VT309 • Number
209 Advanced Flying School • Home Base – RAF Westonzoyland • Bridgwater, Somerset

This aircraft was being piloted by Air Commodore F. St George Braithwaite. He abandoned his take-off and lowered his undercarriage in an effort to halt the plane.[51] He overran the runway and the starboard engine caught fire at RAF Westonzoyland. The resulting damage was classed as a Category 5 write-off. This same officer was destined to become an air vice-marshall and would later die in another air crash in the Far East in December 1956.

26 March 1954   • Gloster G.41G Meteor F.4 • Serial Number VT171 • Number
209 Advanced Flying School • Home Base – RAF Westonzoyland • Bridgwater, Somerset

This aircraft crashed into the undershoot region at RAF Westonzoyland. Pilot Officer R.H. Farey lost control after entering the slipstream of another aircraft.[52] He successfully escaped from the crash.

2 April 1954   • Supermarine Type 358 Seafire F.XVII • Serial Number SP351 •
Number 764 Naval Air Squadron • Home Base – HMS *Heron* • RNAS Yeovilton, Ilchester, Somerset

After his instructor had briefed the student pilot not to fly below 300ft, this aircraft crashed on high ground during a low-level exercise 4½ miles south-west of Warminster, Wiltshire.[53] The pilot was killed.

The aircraft was reported missing on that Friday but was not found until the following day after a second search of the area had taken place. It appears as if his aircraft hit the top of Cold Kitchen Hill, near Kingston Deverill in Wiltshire, and exploded on impact. The hill is 900ft above sea level, and at the time of the crash rain and mist obscured the top of it. The pilot had only been at RNAS Yeovilton for six weeks before he lost his life.

Sub Lieutenant Alan Munro Agnew was born on 2 April 1954 and was aged twenty-two when he died. He is buried in the RN Cemetery in St Bartholomew's church, Yeovilton and his grave can be located in Appendix 2, Grave 32. Sub Lieutenant Agnew lived at No 43 Broadhurst Gardens, London, NW6. He was the only son of the late Mr Eric Munroe Agnew and Mrs Agnew.

6 April 1954   • D.H.100 Vampire F.B.5 • Serial Number WG797 • Number 202
Advanced Flying School • Home Base – RAF Valley • Holyhead, Anglesey, North Wales

This aircraft experienced engine failure after take-off from RAF Merryfield. The aircraft belly landed near Staples Farm, Staple Fitzpaine in Somerset.[54]

Soon after commencing his return journey to North Wales, the pilot began to experience engine trouble and jettisoned his fuel tanks over the village of Ashill,

Somerset. Looking for somewhere to make a landing, he brought the aircraft down in a wheat field, crashing through a small hedge before coming to a halt. Twenty-two-year-old Pilot Officer E. Dyer stepped out from the cockpit of his aircraft completely unharmed.

Source: *Chard and Ilminster News*, 10 April 1954.

13 May 1954   • Gloster Meteor F.4 • Serial Number RA419 • Number 209 Advanced Flying School • Home Base – RAF Westonzoyland • Bridgwater, Somerset

This aircraft was written off after an undercarriage leg collapsed after a heavy landing.[55] The pilot escaped.

21 June 1954   • Gloster Meteor F.4 • Serial Number RA436 • Number 12 Flying Training School • Home Base – RAF Westonzoyland • Bridgwater, Somerset

After recovering from a loop, the pilot experienced severe vibration and buffeting. The leading edge of the starboard centre section of the wing was missing and because of this the stalling speed had increased to 210 knots.[56] The aircraft returned to base and made a wheels-up landing from an approach speed of some 215 knots. Later it was found that the securing screws that retained the panel were missing. The aircraft had only recently been inspected and declared fit to fly. It was written off by the RAF as a Category 5 loss.

15 July 1954   • D.H.100 Vampire F.B.5 • Serial Number VZ234 • Number 233 Operational Conversion Unit • Home Base – RAF Pembrey • South Wales

Flying Officer W.C. King successfully abandoned his aircraft after engine failure. He was flying out from RAF Pembrey, South Wales, on a training flight. The aircraft subsequently crashed into the Bristol Channel.[57] Flying Officer KING was rescued from his floating dinghy by a New Zealander helicopter pilot, Lieutenant Rex Sherlock, who let down a rope attached to a winch to retrieve him from the sea.

12 August 1954   • D.H.100 Vampire F.B.5 • Serial Number VV464 • Number 9 Flying Training School • Home Base – RAF Merryfield • Ilton, near Ilminster, Somerset

Whilst a flight of Vampires were formation flying over RNAS Yeovilton the pilot of VV464 lost contact with the remainder of the flight. The leader instructed him to rejoin them but, despite being given several courses at different times to rejoin the flight by RAF Merryfield, he failed to do so. The missing aircraft unfortunately crashed into the ground at West Quantockshead in Somerset, cutting a swathe through a plantation of young trees before the aircraft finally exploded. The point at which the pilot crashed was 700ft above sea level.

At the inquest held within RAF Merryfield, witnesses stated that Pilot Officer Pendergast was flying beneath a cumolonimbus cloud which was at about 150ft. It was also raining at the time, which meant that visibility in the Vampire was practically down to nil. A flight lieutenant gave the coroner evidence that the pilot had been on a jet conversion course for sixteen weeks at RAF Merryfield with another two weeks to go before the course ended. He described him as an 'average' pilot who had flown thirty-six and a half hours dual, and twenty-four hours, ten minutes solo. Squadron Leader Cyril Frederick Babcok said he was in the control tower at the time and estimated the crash to have occurred at about 3 p.m. The crashed aircraft had been located by other aircraft. The coroner recorded a verdict of 'Misadventure'. This appears to have been the standard verdict of the time.

4112530 Pilot Officer Trevor John Pendergast, aged twenty-three, was born on 5 April 1935 at Woolwich, London. He lived at No 40, Highfield Road, Chorley in Lancashire. His grave can be found in the cemetery at Ilton in Plot C.3.

Source: *Western Gazette*, 20 August 1954; *Chard and Ilminster News*, 21 August 1954.

20 August 1954   • D.H.115 Vampire T.11 • Serial Number XD530 • Number 9 Flying Training School • Home Base – RAF Merryfield • Ilton, near Ilminster, Somerset

This aircraft first attempted a landing at RNAS Yeovilton but overshot the runway.[58] It then crashed into rising ground 4½ miles east of RAF Merryfield whilst on final approach and during poor visibility. The cause of this crash was never established.

The aircraft first came to earth in a field belonging to Mr W.J. Aplin of Lower Burrow Farm and created a small crater by the force of its impact. It then skidded along the ground for about another 100 yards before bursting through a hedge and finally coming to rest in an orchard.

Witnesses at the inquest held at RAF Merryfield said that the aircraft appeared to be in flames when it crashed and blew up. Evidence given to the coroner by Flight Lieutenant Taylor said that the pilot had 250 hours' flying experience, forty-three of them in jet aircraft. Although it was the pilot's first solo flight in the Vampire T.11, he indicated that he was quite competent.

The coroner (Mr D.J. Cooper) recorded a verdict of 'Misadventure' and observed 'that it was not clear from the evidence what happened to the plane and it was difficult to know why it lost height and crashed, apparently out of control'.

4113239 Pilot Officer George Moreton Carthew, aged 21, was born on 21 November 1932 at Pontnewdd, Monmouthshire. He lived in the Marls, Shirenewton, Chepstow, and his final resting place is in the cemetery at Ilton. He can be found in Grave U.4.

Source: *Chard and Ilminster News*.

21 August 1954   • North American Harvard IIB (AT-16) • Serial Number KF531 • Number 1834 Naval Air Squadron • Home Base – HMS *Heron* • RNAS Yeovilton, Ilchester, Somerset

The engine of this aircraft started to run roughly after some aerobatics. On making its approach to RNAS Yeovilton, with a view to landing, the engine caught fire.[59] The pilot, Lieutenant R. Brewer, baled out at 800ft. The aircraft crashed in flames behind a row of houses at the Mead, Ilchester. There were no casualties from this incident. This officer trained with an Royal Navy Volunteer Reserve (RNVR) squadron at weekends.

31 August 1954 • Gloster G.41G Meteor F.4 • Serial Number VT285 • Number 12 Flying Training School • Home Base – RAF Westonzoyland • Bridgwater, Somerset

Following an overshoot after attempting a simulated double-flame-out approach, this aircraft bounced and skidded to a halt and then sank on the runway. The aircraft was written off but the pilot, Wing Commander H.G. Hastings escaped.[60]

21 September 1954 • D.H.100 Vampire F.B.5 • Serial Number WA247 • Number 9 Flying Training School • Home Base – RAF Merryfield • Ilton, near Ilminster, Somerset

Pilot Officer S.A. Holmes was on his first solo of this type of aircraft. This aircraft's tail boom hit the runway on an overshoot and he lost control. The aircraft ran off the runway and down the long slope towards Ashill Wood, where it caught fire, resulting in it being written off. The pilot escaped. In his book, *Broken Wings, Post-War Royal Air force Accidents*, James J. Halley MBE records that the aircraft ran into a fuel installation and caught fire.[61] Brian Lovell was there at the time and he states that this did not happen, as the fuel installations were well away from the runways.[62]

24 September 1954 • D.H.100 Vampire F.B.5 • Serial Number WA274 • Number 9 Flying Training School • Home Base – RAF Merryfield • Ilton, near Ilminster, Somerset

The engine suffered an explosion on take-off, and the aircraft made a forced landing 2½ miles west of Merryfield in a field belonging to Wood Court Farm – the owner at the time being Mr E. Scriven. The pilot of the aircraft was twenty-nine-year-old Pilot Officer V.W. Wilson of Bakewell, Derbyshire. The pilot, despite suffering severe injuries to his back, managed to drag himself a few feet from the blazing aircraft before collapsing.

Mr Wickham described to a representative of this newspaper how he was standing by his farm buildings and happened to glance upwards and saw a Vampire 'extraordinarily low'. I was waiting for it to come into sight again but it did not and I though it was probably in trouble. 'I waited for an explosion,' Mr Wickham said. 'I ran up to the top of my field, which is on high ground, and, looking in the direction of the plane, saw a cloud of smoke.'

Mr Wickham described how he got into his car, picked up Mr Scott at his garage, and raced to the scene. 'Two people were standing in the gateway, watching it burn,' he went on. 'I ran up across the field on the higher side of the crashed plane, with Mr Scott on the other side. I saw the pilot lying from

6 to 10 feet away from the plane and went up to him to move him, but could not do so alone. I called to Mr Scott and together we dragged the pilot clear of the aircraft by catching hold of his shoulders. We stayed with him until an ambulance arrived.

Mr Wickham added that it was 'sheer determination' on the part of the pilot that he pulled himself clear of the cockpit.

Mr Alex Scott was a former Second World War flight lieutenant and owned the Stewley Lodge filling station, while Gerry Wickham was a local farm owner. Both men received commendations for their bravery. The pilot was injured and conveyed to the hospital in the nearby county town of Taunton.

Source: *Western Gazette*, 1 October 1954.

17 October 1954   • D.H.100 Vampire F.B.5 • Serial Number WA330 • Number 501 (County of Gloucester) Squadron RAF • Home Base – RAF Filton • Bristol

This aircraft dived into the ground on the Quantock Hills close to Holford Combe, Somerset, after control was lost whilst flying in cloud.[63]

91390 Flying Officer Eric Stanley Barwick of 22 Royal Auxiliary Air Force was killed. He was aged twenty-two when he died. He was cremated at Arnos Vale Crematorium, Bristol.

20 October 1954   • D.H.100 Vampire F.B.5 • Serial Number VZ310 • Number 9 Flying Training School • Home Base – RAF Merryfield • Ilton, near Ilminster, Somerset

Squadron Leader R.J. Colston, aged thirty-two and who lived in London, successfully abandoned this aircraft after its controls jammed and it dived into ground in a field near Lyng Court, West Lyng, near Taunton.[64] It burst into flames as it disintegrated, leaving a deep crater at its point of impact. The flames were so intense that a nearby tree caught fire.

Source: *Chard and Ilminster News*, 23 October 1954.

21 October 1954   • Gloster Javelin F.A.W.1 • Serial Number XA546 • Test Pilot • Royal Aircraft Establishment • Home base – Farnborough Airfield • Hampshire

This aircraft was put into an intentional low-level spin eleven minutes after take-off on a pre-delivery flight. It failed to recover from the manoeuvre and crashed into the Bristol Channel near Weston-super-Mare.[65] The pilot was reported to have baled out, but despite an intensive air-sea rescue search he was never found. Flight Lieutenant Ross had reported that he was in trouble before he exited the aircraft, and with a westerly wind blowing it was thought that he might have been blown well inland, which complicated the rescue mission. He was later posted as 'Missing Presumed Killed'.

A naval salvage operation was launched and pieces of the aircraft were recovered soon afterwards, the wreckage lying at a depth of between 4 and 10 fathoms.

153992 Flight Lieutenant Robert James Ross, aged thirty-two, was born on 14 February 1932 in Inverness, Scotland.

4 November 1954 • D.H.112 Sea Venom F.A.W.20 • Serial Number WM546 • Number 809 Naval Air Squadron • Home Base – RNAS Yeovilton • Ilchester, Somerset

This aircraft took off at 11.29 p.m. and was returning to RNAS Yeovilton at 11.50 p.m. in a controlled night descent. It was given instructions to descend but just after midnight, the aircraft crashed into some high ground approximately 1 mile west of the village of Charlton Horethorne in Somerset at Sigwells.[66] The aircraft exploded on impact and started to blaze fiercely, lighting up the sky around it. The force of the crash created numerous other small fires and the pilot, who came from Cornwall, was severely burned in the blaze. His observer was thrown clear and died from multiple injuries. The coroner reminded those present at the inquest of the two men of the hazards that they undertook when flying in the service of their country.

The pilot, Lieutenant Dudley Nicholls Hobbs-Webber was born on 4 June 1931 and was aged twenty-three when he died. His final resting place is shown in Appendix 2. He had only recently been married.

4049145 Flying Officer John O'Boyle RAF, the observer, was born on 14 July 1931 and was aged twenty-three when he died. He is buried in the Worthing Road Cemetery at Basingstoke.

Source: *Western Gazette.*

19 November 1954 • Gloster G.41G Meteor F.4 • Serial Number VW302 • Number 12 Flying Training School • Home Base – RAF Westonzoyland • Bridgwater, Somerset

This aircraft ran out of fuel after instrument failure and was abandoned 6 miles north of Lynmouth, North Devon.[67] The crash was witnessed by some Lynton boatmen, as well as Mr Tom Richards, his brother and seventy-two-year-old uncle; they sailed out some 6 miles to the wreckage in a 23ft launch. They found the pilot floating near the aircraft, and despite getting him back to Lynton Hospital, the pilot died without regaining consciousness.

583850 Flying Officer Donald Harry Butterworth, aged twenty-four, was born in Edmonton, London, on 6 February 1930 and lived in Chingford, Essex. He is buried in the cemetery at Westonzoyland and can be found in Section 2, Grave 280.

28 November 1954 • D.H.100 Vampire F.B.5 • Serial Number VZ177 • Serial Number WE836 • Number 614 (Swansea) Squadron RAF • Home Base – RAF Filton • Bristol

The two aircraft collided over the Isle of Wight and, after flying on for a short distance, one of the aircraft crashed at Burlesdon Bridge, Hamble.[68]

The other aircraft managed to remain in the air and made its way back to RAF Filton. Despite his best efforts, the pilot was forced to bale out successfully. The aircraft came down near some houses at Hallen, Bristol.

2523877 Pilot Officer Nigel Grahame Palmer was killed when he was thrown from the aircraft on impact. He was born on 29 May 1930 and was aged twenty-four when he died. His grave can be found in Ship Lane Cemetery, Farnborough, Hampshire, and the pilot's final resting place can be located in Section 3, Row B, Grave 129.

1 December 1954 • Gloster Meteor T.7 • Serial Number WL467 • Number 12 Flying Training School • Home Base –RAF Westonzoyland • Bridgwater, Somerset

The engine of this aircraft blew up on single-engine overshoot and the aircraft force landed in a field. The aircraft was written off but the pilot escaped unharmed.[69]

10 December 1954 • Supermarine Type 395 Seafire F.XVII • Serial Number SX194 • Number 764 Naval Air Squadron • Home Base – HMS *Heron* • RNAS Yeovilton, Ilchester, Somerset

This aircraft was being piloted by Sub Lieutenant J.M. Kendall RN. It did not have its tail wheel locked down, and because of this made a heavy landing, causing severe damage to the fuselage.[70] It was struck off charge on 22 February 1954.

1955

10 January 1955 • Gloster Meteor T.7 • Serial Number WA666 • Number 12 Flying Training School • Home Base – RAF Westonzoyland • Bridgwater, Somerset

This aircraft dived into the ground just after its initial take-off approximately 1½ miles north–north-east of Westonzoyland, sadly killing both the pilot and instructor.[71]

607182 Flight Lieutenant John William Wills, aged twenty-four, was born on 23 October 1930 at Eastbourne, Sussex. His last resting place can be found at the cemetery in Westonzoyland at Grave 281.

3044553 Flight Lieutenant Alexander Telford Kenworthy, aged twenty-seven, was born on 21 March 1927 in Rochdale, Lancashire. His last resting place can be found at the cemetery in Westonzoyland at Grave 282.

17 January 1955 • D.H.112 Sea Venom F.A.W.20 • Serial Number WM520 • Number 890 Naval Air Squadron • Home Base – RNAS Yeovilton • Ilchester, Somerset

On approaching RNAS Yeovilton, this aircraft suffered engine trouble with the failure of the front engine bearing.[72] As a consequence it undershot the runway.

Commissioned Pilot Tuck had to make an emergency landing in icebound fields beyond the River Yeo. He and his observer, Lieutenant N. Craig escaped unharmed.

Territorials of the 511th Construction Company Royal Engineers had to be brought in to help recover the aircraft. They were used to build an extra wide Bailey bridge which they threw across the River Yeo, dragging the aircraft over it on specially constructed skis. Once they had done this, the aircraft was recovered by the 40ft recovery trailer.

Source: *Western Gazette*, 21 January 1955.

31 January 1955   • D.H.112 Sea Venom F.A.W.20 • Serial Number WM542 •
Number 809 Naval Air Squadron • Home Base – RNAS Yeovilton • Ilchester, Somerset

This aircraft was in a stream landing at RNAS Ford on a flight from Yeovilton.[73] It flew in low and slow and then levelled off, going back up to 50ft. It then half rolled to port and flicked over on to its back, hitting a tree and catching fire. Both of the crew were unfortunately killed during this air accident. These officers are buried in the Royal Naval Cemetery at St Bartholomew's church in Yeovilton village.

Lieutenant Commander (P) Frank Cawood AFC MID, aged thirty-one, was born on 29 September 1923 at Wath, near Ripon, Yorkshire, but lived in Thirsk, Yorkshire. He was also an empire test pilot. His final resting place is shown in Appendix 2.

Lieutenant (O) Colin Edward George Jones, aged twenty-three, was born on 7 May 1931 in Plymouth, Devon, but lived in Bude, Cornwall. His final resting place is shown in Appendix 2.

2 February 1955   • Gloster Meteor T.7 • Serial Number WL408 • Number 12 Flying
Training School • Home Base – RAF Westonzoyland • Bridgwater, Somerset

Both pilots were experienced instructors and were on their monthly staff continuation training flight when the accident occurred. The aircraft took off from the airfield at 8.14 a.m. and at 8.30 a.m. the pilot radioed for permission to enter the low-flying area. The flying conditions were perfect. At about 350ft the aircraft suddenly went into a dive and crashed into an orchard in Durston, Somerset.

In its fatal dive the aircraft passed diagonally over the main road from the northwest, narrowly missing a house and adjoining Fir tree, but cutting the telephone cable and wires on the opposite side and consequently putting the local telephone system out of action.

When the plane first struck the ground it partly demolished an iron and timber shed belonging to Mr E.H. Liddon, forestry contractor, who lives nearby, and then tore through one orchard into another, damaging a number of apple trees. The machine finally hit an Oak tree, exploded and caught fire over an area of about 40 yards.

183367 Flight Lieutenant Iain Hastings, aged thirty-two, was born on 19 August 1922 at Lockerbie, Dumfriesshire, and is buried in the cemetery in Westonzoyland. He can be found at Grave 283. He lived in Burnham-on-Sea.

3507713 Flying Officer John Harold Marvin, aged twenty-five, was born on 26 December 1929 at Loughborough, Leicestershire. He is buried at Shepshed Cemetery in Leicestershire and can be found in Section 93, Grave 8A. At the time of his death he lived in Bridgwater.

Source: *Western Gazette.*

15 February 1955   • Gloster Meteor T.7 • Serial Number WH194 • Number 12 Flying Training School • Home Base – RAF Westonzoyland • Bridgwater, Somerset

Whilst being flown by a Lebanese air force officer, Lieutenant S.E. Balhawane, aged twenty-two, this aircraft crashed near Lympsham, Somerset, after the it went into an uncontrollable and inverted spin during aerobatics practice.[74] Both crew ejected safely from the aircraft. The instructor was Flight Lieutenant Don A. Cooper, aged twenty-four.

28 April 1955   • Gloster Meteor F.4 • Serial Number VZ392 • Number 12 Flying Training School • Home Base – RAF Westonzoyland • Bridgwater, Somerset

This was probably one of the more unusual (and luckiest) collisions between an aircraft and the ground. The Meteor came out of cloud and bounced off the ground of a high hill, near Whitchurch in Somerset.[75] Somehow, the aeroplane managed to stay in the air and the pilot returned himself safely to Westonzoyland, where the aircraft was written off as a Category 5. It was finally taken to No 49 MU (Maintenance Unit) at RAF Colerne for scrapping.

29 April 1955   • Avro 652A Anson T.22 • Serial Number VV358 • 81 Group Communications Squadron RAF • Home Base – RAF Rudloe Manor • Wiltshire

This aircraft crashed 1 mile south-east of Weston-super-Mare when at 50ft its port engine cut out.[76] The pilot, realising that he had a populated area and rising ground ahead of him, opted for a belly landing in a field. The aircraft hit a hedge before finally coming to rest. It was written off on 19 May 1955 and used for spares.

5 May 1955   • D.H.112 Sea Venom F.A.W.20 • Serial Number WM558 • Number 890 Naval Air Squadron • Home Base – RNAS Yeovilton • Ilchester, Somerset • Detached to HMS *Albion*

On the day that WM558 was due to take off, there was water lying in the *Albion's* catapult track. On launching, this was forced up ahead of the aircraft. This water was then ingested into the engine which caused a flame out. The aircraft lost power and crashed into the sea some 800 yards in front of the ship before passing beneath it.[77] Lieutenant Commander Alan Gordon-Johnson, the pilot, and the commanding officer of the squadron, along with his senior observer, Lieutenant Jack Carter, were rescued. For the crew, there would be another occasion when his aircraft crashed into the sea and was forced beneath the ship. (See the incident for 19 May 1955.)

13 May 1955 • D.H.100 Vampire F.B.5 • Serial Number WA300 • Number 501 (County of Gloucester) Squadron RAF • RAF Filton • Bristol

The aircraft overshot a roller landing and then commenced a slow turn to starboard and lost more speed.[78] It then began losing height, before the wings rocked and it rolled over. The aircraft then went into a spin and dived into the ground close to the railway line from Avonmouth to Severn beach, killing the pilot who was the commanding officer of 501 Squadron.

The aircraft bore the distinctive black and yellow triangles of the squadron, one on each side of the tail boom with the RAF roundel located in the middle. The round yellow boar's head badge was proudly displayed on the port side of the aircraft, just below the cockpit.

130954 Squadron Leader Geoffrey Berkeley Mercer was thirty-one years of age when he died. He was born on 7 June 1923.

19 May 1955 • D.H.112 Sea Venom F.A.W.20 • Serial Number WM556 • Number 890 Naval Air Squadron • Home Base – RNAS Yeovilton • Ilchester, Somerset • Detached to HMS Bulwark

The aircraft was towed slowly to the end of the catapult when it was fired during a night launch.[79] It then went straight over the bow and into the sea before passing beneath the ship. The two crew members, Lieutenant Commander Alan Gordon-Johnson, the pilot, and the commanding officer of the squadron, along with his senior observer, Jack Carter, were both rescued from their dinghy. This was the second time that this particular crew had been rescued in similar circumstances within two weeks of each other. (See the incident for 5 May 1955.)

The squadron had been testing the new Mirror Landing Aid that had just been introduced into service in 1954 and was the original invention of Commander H.C.N. Goodhart RN. This gave the pilot a system of coloured lights and did away with the old system of hand-held bats being displayed by the flight deck officer.

29 May 1955 • D.H.100 Vampire F.B.5 • Serial Number VZ121 • Number 501 (County of Gloucester) Squadron RAF • Home Base – RAF Filton • Bristol

This aircraft sank back after take-off and its brakes failed when it landed; it was badly damaged.[80] It veered off the runway and was written off. Pilot Officer J.L.T. Williams escaped unharmed from the accident.

21 June 1955
• Hawker Sea Fury T.20 • Serial Number WG653 • Number 1834 Naval Air Squadron • Home Base – HMS *Heron* • RNAS Yeovilton, Ilchester, Somerset

This aircraft was the last one airborne, in a division of four flying out of Hal Far airfield, Malta.[81] Its starboard wing dropped on take-off before the wheels were fully retracted. The starboard fuel tank exploded and the aircraft crashed through the walls at the end of the runway, killing the pilot.

Sub Lieutenant Jeffrey William Brett Coates RNVR was born on 16 June 1932 and aged twenty-three when he died. He is buried at Capucinni Cemetery, Malta, in Grave 189.

17 August 1955
• North American Sabre F.1 • Serial Number XB808 • Number 147 Squadron RAF • Home Base – RAF Benson • Near Wallingford, South Oxfordshire

This aircraft collided with Sea Hawk WM964 whilst in the landing circuit above RNAS Yeovilton and crashed 3 miles east of Yeovilton, near the village of West Camel.[82] Wreckage from this aircraft fell on the lawn of a house in West Camel, barely 6ft away from the two-month-old baby of Mrs Audrey Davis, who lay sleeping in a pram. Sadly, the pilot was killed. One of the pilots from the two aircraft did manage to eject and was seen floating down in his parachute, but somehow he perished in the process.

582445 Flying Officer Kenneth George Macleod, aged twenty-seven, was born on 11 March 1928. He is buried in St Helen's churchyard, Benson, Oxfordshire. His last resting place can be found at Grave 7.

Source: *Western Gazette.*

17 August 1955
• Hawker Sea Hawk F.B.3 • Serial Number WM964 • Number 811 Naval Air Squadron • Home Base – RN Detachment Lossiemouth • Scotland

Sea Hawk Serial No WM964 collided with RAF Canadair Sabre XB808 of 147 Squadron RAF, whilst on a circuit around RNAS Yeovilton.[83] The Sea Hawk came down 3 miles east of Yeovilton at West Camel, Somerset, and regrettably the pilot was killed. One of the pilots from the two aircraft did manage to eject and was seen floating down in his parachute, but somehow he was killed in the process.

Sub Lieutenant J.M. Margoliouth was born on 12 August 1933 and was aged twenty-two when he died. His final resting place is shown in Appendix 2.

Source: *Western Gazette.*

22 August 1955
• D.H.112 Sea Venom F.A.W.20 • Serial Number WM559 • Number 890 Naval Air Squadron • Home Base – RNAS Yeovilton • Ilchester, Somerset • Detached to HMS *Bulwark*

Commissioned Pilot Clarke and Lieutenant West were rescued when the arrestor hook broke off on landing and their aircraft went off the deck and into the sea.[84] Two days later, the squadron was told that they were banned from deck landings because of a suspected straining of the arrestor hook.

26 September 1955   • English Electric Canberra B.2 • Serial Number WK136 • Number 231 Operational Conversion Unit • Home Base – RAF Merryfield • Ilton, near Ilminster, Somerset

The aircraft took off from RAF Bassingbourne (approximately 3 miles north of Royston, Herefordshire) and crashed near Little Stonham, 3½ miles east of Stowmarket, Suffolk. The tail trim actuator 'ran away' at 20,000ft.[85]

The navigator, Flying Officer D.E. Taylor, and the pilot/instructor, Squadron Leader S.G. Hewitt, successfully ejected in their Martin Baker ejection seats. Pupil pilot Flying Officer Bates managed to use his rumble seat (non-ejection) and successfully escaped from the stricken aircraft.

The only fatality was the pupil navigator, Flying Officer Patrick John Leigh, aged twenty-three, who was born at Chudleigh in Devon. He managed to eject successfully in his Martin Baker seat but did not release from it and was unfortunately killed in the accident. His grave can be found at Trusham Parish churchyard, near Newton Abbot, Devon.

4 November 1955   • Gloster Meteor T.7 • Serial Number WG947 • Number 231 Operational Conversion Unit • Home Base – RAF Merryfield • Ilton, near Ilminster, Somerset

This pilot officer hailed from Ceylon. He took off and at about 150ft above the runway the starboard wing dropped and the plane turned over on to its back, crashing in that position.

An eyewitness at the inquest said:

As the aircraft became airborne with its wheels-up and at a height of about 50ft I noticed it swing to starboard. Initially the swing was not great, but as the aircraft continued to climb the swing became more apparent.

At a height of between 150 and 200 feet the starboard wing dropped; the aircraft turned over on to its back and crashed upside down.

The pilot was heard to shout over the radio, 'I've had it!' just before the plane hit the ground.

607498 Pilot Officer Michael Leonard Jonklass is buried in the cemetery at Ilton in Grave C.4.

Source: *Western Gazette*, 11 November 1955.

28 November 1955 • D.H98 Mosquito T.III • Serial Number HJ970 • Number 233
Operational Conversion Unit • Home Base – RAF Pembrey • South Wales

This aircraft's undercarriage somehow became jammed on landing at Filton, but the aircraft, piloted by Squadron Leader J.A.W. Long, successfully belly landed.[86] It was written off.

7 December 1955 • D.H.112 Sea Venom F.A.W.21 • Serial Number WW152 •
Number 892 Naval Air Squadron • Home Base – RNAS Yeovilton • Ilchester, Somerset

The aircraft was being flown by an American crew of two. The pilot was First Lieutenant P.H. Sallade USMC and his navigator was First Lieutenant N.J. Hale USMC.[87] On a routine flight they suffered engine problems and flew in circles round Dorchester in an effort to find somewhere to land. A witness said that she heard 'peculiar noises' coming from the aircraft as it circled. Eventually it was successfully force landed with its wheels up in a field belonging to Mr W.H. Cooper's Middle Farm, just off the Bridport Road. On landing the aircraft tore up two wire fences before finally coming to rest about 100 yards from the perimeter of a council estate.

From there, the remains of the aircraft were sent to the Aircraft Investigation Unit for examination before being returned to RNAS Yeovilton in January 1956. The aircraft was scrapped in February 1956.

Source: *Western Gazette*, 9 December 1955.

1956

5 January 1956 • D.H.112 Sea Venom F.A.W.20 • Serial Number WM551 •
Number 808 Squadron Royal Australian Navy • Home Base – HMAS *Melbourne*

This squadron was commissioned at RNAS Yeovilton on 23 August 1955. They took part in RAN's (Royal Australian Navy) flying trials for their new aircraft carrier, HMAS *Melbourne*.

The aircraft took off from Yeovilton in poor weather with a destination of RNAS *Culdrose*.[88] Unfortunately it clipped a tree, sheering the top of it off as it made its climb out of the airfield near Limington. It then went on to lose height gradually and hit a chimney stack of a house called Greenleigh in Ilchester at Northover, scattering bricks across the main Ilminster to Shepton Mallet road. The aircraft then crashed into a nearby caravan park at Castle Farm, Ilchester. This site held a total of twelve caravans that were being used as married quarters for men at the nearby RNAS Yeovilton.

Mrs Grace Beard and her small son Geoffrey were killed on the ground and in one of the caravans. Leading Airman Vic Beard was away on a course at the time and therefore not home in the caravan.

Leading Airman Terry McMurtie, his wife Mary and six-month-old son Gerald managed to escape from a second caravan that was almost completely destroyed by this aircraft. They escaped through the only surviving window that was not smashed. Three others on the ground were also injured.

Some houses were damaged too, and by a quirk of fate one of those houses damaged was where Commander Brown RAN had spent Christmas with his family.

The pilot, Lieutenant (P) Peter Haldane Wyatt RN (the squadron instrument rating examiner) was born on 26 March 1930 and was aged twenty-five when he died.

The body of Commander George F.S. Brown RAN (staff officer (aviation) at Australian House) was returned to his native land. HMAS *Melbourne* finally departed for Australia in March 1956.

This was not the first, nor indeed was it to be the last, time that naval aircraft were to crash into caravans being used as naval married quarters. Previously, on 25 January 1955, a Hawker Hunter Mk 4 aircraft had crashed into some caravans whilst making an emergency landing at RNAS Ford, near Littlehampton in Sussex. Chief Petty Officer (Aircrewman) William Ewing and his wife Audrey, together with Petty Officer (Electrician) George Scorer were killed. The wife of Scorer and their child Linda were both injured in the same incident.

Source: *Western Gazette.*

16 January 1956 • D.H.89A Dominie 1 Mk 2 • Serial Number NR739 • Aircraft Trials and Development Unit, Communications Flight • Home Base – RAF Locking • Weston-super-Mare, Somerset

This aircraft swung while taxiing along the runway at Weston-super-Mare.[89] The pilot applied the brakes to correct the swing but they locked on and the tail lifted, which caused the aircraft to nose over. The aircraft was a write-off; it was struck off RAF charge on 26 March 1956. It was then stored locally before being sold on 21 June 1957 to the Hants and Sussex Aviation Company, who were based at Portsmouth. The aircraft was then converted to a Mk 4 and re-registered as G-APKA. Its certificate of airworthiness was granted on 6 May 1958 and was sold that year to Sierra Leone Airways, re-registered as VR-LAE and named RMA *Kassewe.* Its final disposition is not known.

24 February 1956 • English Electric Canberra T.4 • Serial Number WJ871 • Number 231 Operational Conversion Unit • Home Base – RAF Merryfield • Ilton, near Ilminster, Somerset

This aircraft came down 2 miles west of Stilton, Huntingdonshire.[90] The tailplane actuator malfunctioned and resulted in the plane diving straight into the ground, killing the crew of two. A large crater was left in the field where the aircraft fell and wreckage was scattered over a wide area.

3046036 Flying Officer Jason Spokes, aged twenty-seven, is buried in Bassingbourne Cemetery, Royston, Hertfordshire. His grave can be located in Row 11, Grave 8. He was born on 25 September 1928.

924325 Flight Lieutenant Herbert James Brice, aged thirty-six, is buried in St Mary's Parish Cemetery, Old Bletchley, Buckinghamshire. He was born on 22 June 1919.

8 March 1956 • D.H.112 Sea Venom F.A.W.21 • Serial Number WW142 • Number 891 Naval Air Squadron • Home Base – HMS *Heron* • RNAS Yeovilton, Ilchester, Somerset • Detached to HMS *Ark Royal*

During a night interception exercise in the Mediterranean, and flying off of HMS *Ark Royal*, this aircraft was engaging an RAF Shackleton when all communications with it were suddenly lost.[91] An SAR mission was immediately launched and a solitary yellow buoy with a white flashing light was found, but there were no other signs of the missing aircraft. This accident occurred some 40 miles south-west of the island of Sardinia. Both pilot and observer are listed as 'Missing Presumed Killed'.

Lieutenant John Orpin Ealand, the pilot, was born on 24 May 1929 and was aged twenty-six when he lost his life. He lived in Perth, Scotland.

Flying Officer Roy John Mullord RAF, the observer, was born on 6 January 1931 and was aged twenty-five when he died. He lived in Emsworth, Hampshire.

To compound the tragedy, on the very same day a Fairey Gannet A.S.1, Serial No XA337, and also operating from the *Ark Royal* with No 824 Naval Air Squadron, crashed into the sea on take-off and over the starboard bow, killing all three crew.[92] They too were listed as 'Missing Presumed Killed'.

Lieutenant Leslie Moorcroft Tooley, the pilot, was born on 11 January 1929 and was aged twenty-seven when he died. He lived in Burscough, Lancashire.

Sub Lieutenant John Benjamin Claxton, the observer, was born on 12 June 1934 and was aged twenty-one when he died. He lived in Stowmarket, Suffolk.

JX646362 Petty Officer Telegraphist (A) Francis Christopher (Paddy) Ramplin was born on 11 August 1928 and was aged twenty-seven when he died. He lived in Dublin.

12 March 1956 • English Electric Canberra B.2 • Serial Number WD952 • Home Base – RAF Filton • Filton Airport, Bristol

The aircraft was being used as a test bed for the Olympus engine.[93] The port engine failed on take-off at 50ft and the all-black-painted aircraft landed on its belly before hitting an oak tree near Cribbs Causeway in Bristol. Its port wing, undercarriage and rudders were torn off in the incident. The aircraft was damaged beyond repair and written off. It was later broken up at RAF Colerne. The crew were lucky and escaped unharmed from this accident.

This particular aircraft had gained the world height record on two occasions. It reached 63,668ft (19,406m) at 3.17 p.m. on 4 May 1953 over the Somerset town of Taunton (piloted by Wing Commander Walter F. Gibb) and 65,890ft (20,083m) on 29 August 1955 (once more piloted by Wing Commander Walter F. Gibb).

31 May 1956 • D.H.112 Sea Venom F.A.W.21 • Serial Number WW224 •
Number 890 Naval Air Squadron • Home Base – HMS *Heron* • RNAS Yeovilton, Ilchester,
Somerset • Detached to HMS *Bulwark*

The aeroplane was carrying out deck-landing trials on HMS *Bulwark* in the English
Channel at the time of the accident. The catapult failed on the launch of this aircraft.[94]
Despite this, the aircraft managed to climb steeply but the starboard wing dropped
and it crashed into the sea upside down, killing the crew. The accident occurred at
500 15'N, 00 56'W.

Lieutenant Eric Lawson Johnson was born on 13 September 1927 and was aged
twenty-eight when he died.

Lieutenant Gerald Michael Nichols was born on 12 June 1930 and was aged
twenty-five when he died.

4 June 1956 • D.H.112 Sea Venom F.A.W.21 • Serial Number WW262 •
Number 890 Naval Air Squadron • Home Base – HMS *Heron* • RNAS Yeovilton, Ilchester,
Somerset

The aircraft stalled short of the round down during deck-landing trials on
HMS *Bulwark* and struck the port safety net just below the batman position, crashing
into the sea in home waters.[95]

Lieutenant Commander (P) Peter Swinn Brewer, aged thirty-two, was born at
Cottingham, Yorkshire, on 24 March 1924. He was the commanding officer of the
squadron and his body was recovered from the sea.

Lieutenant (O) Ernest Edward John Massee was born on 25 September 1925 and
was thirty when he died. He lived in Catford, London. He was posted as 'Missing
Presumed Killed'.

8 July 1956 • D.H.100 Vampire F.B.5 • Serial Number VV661 • Number
501 (County of Gloucester) Squadron RAF • Home Base – RAF Filton • Bristol

---

During a paired take-off from Filton airfield, the lead aircraft lifted off too early
causing it to swing and strike the runway.[96] VV661 took avoiding action and both
aircraft abandoned take-off. This aircraft then ran through the boundary fence after
the brakes failed and was written off.

3 August 1956 • D.H.89A Dominie • Serial Number X7397 • Home Base –
RNAS Yeovilton • Ilchester, Somerset

The brakes on this aircraft failed whilst it was taxiing along the runway and it nosed
over.[97] The pilot was Lieutenant Commander S.J. Hall with six sea cadet passengers.
There were no casualties. The aircraft was struck off charge and reduced to spares on
13 September 1956.

11 September 1956   • Boulton Paul P.108 Sea Balliol T.21 • Serial Number
WL719 • Flag Officer Flying Training Flight • Home Base – RNAS Yeovilton

The pilot, Commander C.R.J. Coxon, experienced engine failure whilst over the Forest of Dean.[98] He successfully made a wheels-up landing in a field. The aircraft was declared a Category 4 and transported to the Air Accident Investigation Unit, Lee-on-Solent, for repair. It then went to the Aircraft Holding Unit, Lossiemouth, where it was finally struck off charge on 17 March 1964.

16 September 1956   • Bristol Type 173 Mk 2 Prototype • Serial Number G-AMJI
(XH379) • Ministry of Supply • Home Base – Filton Airfield • Bristol

This prototype helicopter (developed later to enter service in the RAF as the Belvedere) first flew on 31 August 1953. During a rearward flight movement during an air display, the nose dropped and hit the ground.[99] The damage it caused led to the helicopter being written off as a Category 4 accident. Two men were injured.

At the time of the crash the aircraft was still painted in the British European Airways livery. The aircraft had been named *Sir Bors* (after one of King Arthur's famous knights of the round table) by BEA and had been returned to the Ministry of Supply on 11 September 1956 on expiration of its lease. It was written off on 16 September 1956 (see plate 9).

1 October 1956   • D.H.112 Sea Venom F.A.W.21 • Serial Number XG679 •
Number 809 Naval Air Squadron • Home Base – HMS *Heron* • RNAS Yeovilton, Ilchester, Somerset • Detached to HMS *Albion*

This aircraft was being manhandled into its flying position when the brakes failed and the aircraft went over the side and into the Mediterranean.[100] Naval Airman P. Shirley was injured in this incident and was rescued from the sea by HMS *Albion*'s SAR helicopter.

29 October 1956   • D.H.112 Sea Venom F.A.W.21 • Serial Number XG636 •
Number 891 Naval Air Squadron • Home Base – HMS *Heron* • RNAS Yeovilton, Ilchester, Somerset

Nine miles off Portland Bill radio contact was lost with this aircraft. It occurred during a night-time glow-worm exercise.[101] Glow worm was a very powerful night illumination flare that lit up a large area of sea surface in order for aircraft to identify and attack their targets.

Sub Lieutenant (P) Ralph Edward Craven was born on 12 November 1934 at Harrogate in Yorkshire. He was aged twenty-one when he died.

Lieutenant (O) Jon Nicholas Lud Holthusen was born on 22 December 1929 and was aged twenty-six when he died in the same incident.

2 November 1956 • D.H.112 Sea Venom F.A.W.21 • Serial Number WW281 •
Number 893 Naval Air Squadron • Home Base – HMS *Heron* • RNAS Yeovilton, Ilchester,
Somerset • Detached to HMS *Eagle*

This aircraft was hit by light flak during the Suez operations (Operation Musketeer)
during an attack on the Almaza airfield. The aircraft lost all its hydraulics but made
a perfect wheels-up landing back on HMS *Eagle*.[102] In doing so, it became the first
aircraft to be saved by the ship's nylon barrier, which prevented it from crashing
over the bow and into the sea. It was declared a total loss. The pilot was Lieutenant
Commander J.F.O. Wilcox. His observer, Flying Officer Olding, was badly wounded
and later had to have his left leg amputated above the knee.[103]

19 November 1956 • D.H.112 Sea Venom F.A.W.21 • Serial Number WW193 •
Number 893 Naval Air Squadron • Home Base – HMS *Heron* • RNAS Yeovilton, Ilchester,
Somerset • Detached to HMS *Eagle*

Whilst being serviced in the hangar, somehow the starboard outer gun of this aircraft
was accidentally fired.[104] Forty-six rounds of 20mm ammunition were expended.
Extensive damage was caused to Sea Venoms WW270, WW282 and Wyvern WP340
was also damaged. Sea Venom WN336 was written off.

FX918121 Naval Airman Clive Arthur Naylor was hit by the cannon fire and
died as a result. He was born on 24 June 1936 and was aged twenty when he lost
his life.

21 November 1956 • D.H.100 Vampire F.B.5 • Serial Number WA121 • Number 229
Operational Conversion Unit • Home Base – RAF Chivenor • Near Barnstaple, North
Devon

This aircraft flew into high ground in cloud approximately 6 miles south-west of
Porlock, Somerset.[105] The pilot was below the recommended safety height for flying
in cloud.

3511270 Flying Officer Charles William Powell was killed. He was born on
30 June 1929 and was aged twenty-seven when he lost his life. He is buried in
St Augustine's churchyard, Heanton Punchardon, North Devon. This churchyard
contains quite a few other military graves due to the proximity of what used to be
RAF Chivenor.

1957

10 January 1957 • Sikorsky S-55 Whirlwind H.A.S.22 • Serial Number WV199 • Number 845 Naval Air Squadron • Home Base – RNAS Yeovilton • Ilchester, Somerset • Detached to HMS *Ocean*

The aircraft entered a hover and after a loss of power ditched into the Mediterranean Sea off the island of Malta and sank.[106] Lieutenant M.C. Rusling, Sub Lieutenant H.C.G. Griffin and Leading Seaman W. Robinson were saved. A definite cause of the accident was never established.

3 February 1957 • D.H.100 Vampire F.B.9 • Serial Number WR260 • Number 501 (County of Gloucester) Squadron RAF • Home Base – RAF Filton • Bristol

The flying elements of the Royal Auxiliary Air Force were about to be disbanded as a result of a defence review. Approximately an hour before the Duke of Gloucester was due to take the final salute of the squadron, a pilot took off without authority. He was not wearing a helmet and had not even secured his parachute and harness.

The adjutant of the squadron tried to stop the pilot from taking off by driving along the runway in his car and positioning himself where he expected the Vampire to take off. Instead the pilot chose to fly off from another runway, using less than half of its length to take off.

Flying underneath the Bristol suspension bridge, the pilot pulled up into a slow roll and entered cloud.[107] He came out of it in an inverted position, rolling slowly and losing height. He then turned to port, levelled his wings and lost more height. Tragically for him, he then hit the steep side of the gorge and caught fire on impact near Pill, about 2 miles away from the bridge. He was killed instantly.

2607762 Flight Lieutenant John Greenwood Crossley RAuxAF was born on 24 November 1928 and was aged twenty-eight when he died. He is buried in the Filton New Cemetery, Bristol, in Grave C.18.

17 February 1957 • Fairey Gannet A.S.1 • Serial Number WN357 • Number 847 Naval Air Squadron • Home Base – HMS *Heron* • RNAS Yeovilton, Ilchester, Somerset • Detached to Nicosia, Cyprus

On patrol off Cyprus at 200ft and flying on the port engine alone, the engine suddenly seized up in flight and it ditched into the sea off Cyprus.[108] The pilot was unable to start the starboard engine in time and the aircraft crashed into the Mediterranean.

The crew, Lieutenant Commander W.G. Martin, Lieutenant C.J.V. Clarke and Telegraphist (A) J.E. Harris were rescued uninjured by the Italian boat MV *Irma*.

3 August 1957   • D.H.112 Sea Venom F.A.W.21 • Serial Number XG619 •
Number 891 Naval Air Squadron • Home Base – HMS *Heron* • RNAS Yeovilton, Ilchester,
Somerset • Detached to HMS *Bulwark*

This aircraft experienced engine failure during its catapult launch and ditched over
the bow of the ship.[109] Sadly, both of the crew lost their lives in this accident.

Lieutenant (P) Brian Wilfred Burt was born on 9 January 1934 and was aged
twenty-three when he died.

Lieutenant (O) Anthony Townend was born on 16 January 1933 and was aged
twenty-four when he died.

6 November 1957   • Prototype Britannia 300 • Registration Number G-ANCA •
Ministry of Supply • Home Base – Filton Airfield • Bristol

> This test aircraft had just completed a flight of 1 hour and 40 minutes and
> carried a crew of 8 along with 7 technicians. Tests included strain-gauge meas-
> urements on the non-standard propeller of the number two engine, and high
> speed upset manoeuvre recovery tests in connection with the US certification.
> The aircraft was returning to Filton.

The aircraft entered the landing circuit for Filton but for some unknown reason a
partial gear extension occurred. It was seen to be jettisoning fuel, which led some
observers to believe that the aeroplane was on fire, though it was not. At 1,500ft they
began a left turn to the base leg. The right wing suddenly dropped and the aircraft
went into a very steeply banked right-hand turn. The Britannia briefly recovered
but banked steeply again and struck the ground in the wood near Downend village,
just outside of Bristol, causing considerable damage to a row of ten houses. A massive fireball was thrown up as the aircraft exploded, and the heat generated from the
explosion was felt by British Telecom engineers as they worked on the roof of the
Frenchay Hospital, some half a mile away from the scene. The wood in which the
aircraft came down is now known as 'Britannia Wood'.

A memorial service was held for the men at Bristol cathedral on Tuesday
19 November 1957.

The names of the fifteen men who lost their lives on that fateful day were:

Ernest Hugh Statham – Bristol's assistant chief test pilot and flying the aircraft.
Squadron Leader Donald Matthew Hunter, RAF Transport Command – co-pilot.
John Kenneth Barker – electronics engineer, Redifon Ltd.
John Edward Burton – section leader, Strain Gauge Department, de Havilland
    Propellers.
Donald Charles Cameron – Bristol's flight engineer.
Albert Edward Ebling – tester, Stain Gauge Department, de Havilland Propellers.
Philip Norman Edward Hewitt – Bristol's senior technical engineer.
Kenneth Graham Lucas – electronics engineer, Redifon Ltd.
Dudley Neville Stephen Moynihan – development engineer, de Havilland Propellers.

Frederick William Mycroft – Bristol's junior technical engineer.
John Harold Parry-Jones – Bristol's systems engineer.
Nigel Morris Thorne – photographer.
William James Todd – Bristol's radio operator.
Bernard Francis Waite – photographer and writer.
Frederick Charles Walsh – electronics engineer, Redifon Ltd.

Aircraft Technician John Dickens counted himself as a lucky man. At the last minute he was asked to step down from the flight to allow a Redifon technician to take his place. At the time, the company was experimenting with flight simulation systems.

Source: www.flickr.com.

7 November 1957   • Hawker Hunter F.4 H.U. • Serial Number XF948 • Number 229 Operational Conversion Unit • Home Base – RAF Chivenor • Near Barnstaple, North Devon

This aircraft suffered an engine fire some 10 miles north of Lundy Island in the Bristol Channel.[110] The pilot, Pilot Officer Colin Ernest Truman, aged twenty-one, ejected at 4,000ft but was never found. On 23 February 1958, the crew of an Anson aircraft reported the wreckage of a Hawker Hunter on the mud flats of the Severn Estuary. This wreckage was never recovered or seen again.

6 December 1957   • D.H.112 Sea Venom F.A.W.22 • Serial Number XG727 • Number 891 Naval Air Squadron • Home Base – RNAS Merryfield • Ilton, near Ilminster, Somerset

The aircraft suffered an engine failure because of a problem with the fuel system and caught fire during night aerodrome dummy deck landings at RNAS Merryfield. It crashed in open countryside about 2 miles west-south-west of the airfield, near to the village of Ashill.[111] Debris was scattered over a radius of about a quarter of a mile. The main part of the aircraft landed in a field no more than 100 yards from buildings at Ashton's Farm and the petrol station, close to the centre of the village.

The crash was spectacular in the way that the night sky was lit up by the blazing plane. The author recalls that, as a ten-year-old, he was walking in total blackness when he heard a crack and above him the aircraft suddenly caught fire, lighting the way for him to see. Within a minute he also heard the sound of the explosion.

The villagers of Ashill heard the sound of the explosion and some saw the aircraft come down. They rushed to the scene. Amongst them was the landlord of the Ashill Inn at the time, Mr C. Nightingale. He and others used torches to try to find the pilot.

After successfully baling out, the pilot made his way to a cottage, which was occupied by Mr and Mrs A.C. Priddle. The *Chard and Ilminster News*, dated 14 December 1957, records: "'He looked very ill and complained of a pain in his back,' said Mrs Priddle. "I was just about to make him a cup of tea when a car arrived to take him back to the station.'"

The pilot, Lieutenant Commander W. George B. Black, a squadron commander at Merryfield, ejected but was injured in the process.[112] The last known location of this aircraft's remains was in the aircraft scrapyard of Staravia Ltd, Ascot.

Source: *Chard and Ilminster News*, 14 December 1957.

13 December 1957 • D.H.112 Sea Venom F.A.W.20 • Serial Number WM555 • Number 890 Naval Air Squadron • Home Base – RNAS Merryfield • Ilton, near Ilminster, Somerset

On landing at Merryfield the starboard tyre burst, followed by the collapse of the starboard oleo.[113] The aircraft, piloted by Flight Lieutenant C.D. Walker RAF, swung off the runway causing the starboard oleo to collapse. The aircraft was written off as it was considered to be uneconomical to repair it.

1958

17 January 1958   • D.H.112 Sea F.A.W.22 • Serial Number XG735 • Number 891 Naval Air Squadron • Home Base – RNAS Merryfield • Ilton, near Ilminster, Somerset • Detached to HMS *Bulwark*

The aircraft climbed steeply after a night launch from HMS *Bulwark* and was approximately 60 miles off Land's End, Cornwall, in the south-west approaches to the UK. It turned to starboard and nose dived into the sea, killing both of its crew.[114]

Lieutenant (E) Thomas Neill Storey was born on 15 April 1931 and was aged twenty-six when he died. He was the pilot of the aircraft.

4084061 Flight Lieutenant Anthony John Kay RAF was born on 1 September 1933 and was aged twenty-four when he died. He was the observer in the aircraft.

12 March 1958   • D.H.112 Sea Venom F.A.W.22 • Serial Number XG728 • Number 891 Naval Air Squadron • Home Base – RNAS Merryfield • Ilton, near Ilminster, Somerset • Detached to HMS *Bulwark*

This aircraft climbed steeply on launch from HMS *Bulwark* and rolled to starboard. It crashed into the sea 500 yards off the ship's starboard bow.[115]

Lieutenant (P) John Keith Jakeman was born on 23 February 1934 and was aged twenty-four at the time of his death.

Sub Lieutenant (O) Phillip Maurice Martin was born on 2 March 1932 and was aged twenty-six at the time of his death.

15 April 1958   • D.H.112 Sea Venom F.A.W.21 • Serial Number XG671 •
Number 893 Naval Air Squadron • Home Base – RNAS Merryfield • Ilton, near Ilminster,
Somerset • Detached to HMS *Ark Royal*

Flying off of HMS *Ark Royal* and in the Mediterranean Sea, the ailerons of this
aircraft jammed.[116] The crew were forced to eject and abandon the aeroplane off
the island of Malta. Lieutenant D.J. Schofield escaped unhurt, but Lieutenant John
Webster was injured. Both men parachuted into the sea and were rescued by the
plane guard destroyer.

1 May 1958   • D.H.112 Sea Venom F.A.W.21 • Serial Number XG609 •
Number 766 Naval Air Squadron • Home Base – HMS *Heron* • RNAS Yeovilton, Ilchester,
Somerset

The crew of this aircraft were both killed when their aircraft appeared to break up in
a straight and level flight after recovering from a rocket practice dive on the Lilstock
Naval Range in West Somerset.[117]

    The aircraft was at about 100ft when eyewitnesses said that the aircraft 'seemed to
explode'. It crashed into the sea half a mile beyond the target near Bridgwater, killing
both of the crew. Both of the crewmen are buried in the Royal Navy Cemetery in
the church of St Bartholomew's in Yeovilton.

    Lieutenant Commander William Alistair Maitland Ferguson DSC, aged thirty-
four, was born on 12 July 1923 at Kirkintilloch, Scotland. His final resting place is
shown in Appendix 2.

    Lieutenant (O) Michael Anthony Moore, aged twenty-seven, was born on
2 January 1931 in Putney, London. His final resting place is shown in Appendix 2.

Source: *Western Gazette.*

9 May 1958   • D.H.112 Sea Venom F.A.W.22 • Serial Number XG732 •
Number 891 Naval Air Squadron • Home Base – RNAS Merryfield • Ilton, near Ilminster,
Somerset • Detached to HMS *Bulwark*

The aircraft lost speed on launch from HMS *Bulwark* and ditched some 300 yards
ahead of the ship.[118] The pilot was killed and the observer, Lieutenant T.A. Davis, was
injured. Lieutenant (P) Henry John Regnart was born on 22 August 1931 and was
aged twenty-six when he lost his life.

    This same aircraft had also been involved in a recent accident on 4 March 1958
when, being flown by a pair of USMC exchange crew, it landed on HMS *Bulwark*
without its nose wheel being extended. It was repaired and flew again until its
fatal accident.

19 May 1958   • D.H.112 Sea Venom F.A.W.21 • Serial Number XG653 •
Number 893 Naval Air Squadron • Home Base – HMS *Heron* • RNAS Yeovilton, Ilchester,
Somerset • Detached to HMS *Ark Royal*

This aircraft lost height on launching from HMS *Ark Royal*.[119] It flew into the sea half
a mile ahead of the ship and broke up. The pilot, Lieutenant John Frederick Carey
of Bexley Heath, Kent and aged twenty-two, escaped. He was rescued from the sea
by the escorting destroyer HMS *Diana*. Unfortunately, his observer lost his life in
the incident.

Sub Lieutenant (O) Michael Harry Goodwin of Palmers Green was born on
12 June 1937 and was aged twenty-one when he died.

23 July 1958   • D.H.112 Sea Venom F.A.W.22 • Serial Number XG689 •
Number 894 Naval Air Squadron • Home Base – RNAS Merryfield • Ilton, near Ilminster,
Somerset • Detached to HMS *Eagle*

During a ground-controlled approach to the ship this aircraft hit the round down and
somersaulted up the deck, bursting into flames as it did so.[120]

Lieutenant (P) Arthur Geoffrey Hamon was born on 4 February 1929 and was
aged twenty-nine when he died.

Sub Lieutenant (O) Alan John Hayward was born on 12 October 1936 and was
aged twenty-one when he died.

25 July 1958   • D.H.112 Sea Venom F.A.W.21 • Serial Number XG625 •
Number 893 Naval Air Squadron • Home Base – HMS *Heron* • RNAS Yeovilton, Ilchester,
Somerset

Just before 3 p.m. and during the form up for a preliminary formation fly-past for the
Duchess of Kent, who was visiting RNAS Yeovilton that day, the aircraft hit rising
ground in low-level cloud at Corfe, near Taunton in Somerset.[121] The aircraft came
down in a field on the top of the Blackdown Hills, on a part known as Corfe Hill.
The parachutes of the two crewmen were found with the aircraft's wreckage.

Lieutenant (P) John Webster, aged twenty-three, was born on 12 April 1935 at
Ilkeston, Yorkshire. It is not known where he was buried but his body was returned to
his relatives for a private funeral.

Lieutenant (O) Brian Christopher Wood, aged twenty-five, was born on 12 March
1933 in London. He is buried in the Royal Navy Cemetery in the church of
St Bartholomew's, Yeovilton village. His final resting place is shown in Appendix 2.

4 September 1958 • Fairey Firefly F.R.5 • Reconstructed as a Fairey Hamble in 1956
• Converted to a Fairey Ringway in 1957 • Serial Number VT403 • Ferry Flight Yeovilton
• Home Base – HMS *Heron* • RNAS Yeovilton, Ilchester, Somerset

The aircraft was going to be delivered to Hal Far in Malta. The aircraft took off from Yeovilton but swung off the runway on take-off due to the tail wheel being unlocked.[122] Further swings were experienced after the aircraft became airborne and the take-off was aborted. The pilot applied severe rudder in order to avoid the air-traffic control tower and parked Sea Venoms. It struck the ground travelling sideways. The undercarriage collapsed and the tip tanks were set alight. The pilot, Mr C.J. Kiss and REM (Radio Electrical Mechanician) H.D. Joyce escaped the aircraft but suffered slight burns. The aircraft was written off.

8 September 1958 • Westland Whirlwind H.A.S.7 • Serial Number XL833 • Number 845 Naval Air Squadron • Home Base – HMS *Heron* • RNAS Yeovilton, Ilchester, Somerset

This aircraft ditched into Aden Harbour after its engine-oil temperature suddenly increased and the aircraft lost power.[123] Lieutenant C. Gill and Sub Lieutenant A.M.D. de Labilliere were rescued by a boat. Although the engine was removed and returned to the UK, the actual airframe of the helicopter was ditched at sea.

8 September 1958 • D.H.112 Sea Venom F.A.W.21 • Serial Number XG620 • Number 809 Naval Air Squadron • Home Base – RNAS Merryfield • Ilton, near Ilminster, Somerset

This aircraft collided with Sea Hawk F.G.A.6, Serial No XE402, which was part of No 804 Naval Air Squadron.[124] The accident occurred over Cyprus during an anti-EOKA operation. Both aircraft crashed into the sea.

Lieutenant Commander A.A. Knight and Lieutenant D.W. Ashby parachuted to safety from the Venom and Lieutenant T.M. Tuke successfully ejected from the Sea Hawk.

25 September 1958 • Supermarine Scimitar F.1 • Serial Number XD240 • Number 803 Naval Air Squadron • Home Base – RNAS Lossiemouth • Scotland

Commander J.D. Russell, the commanding officer of the squadron, took off from RNAS Yeovilton. He was leading his squadron to land on the newly refitted HMS *Victorious*, which was steaming off the Isle of Wight en route to the Mediterranean. On board were selected members of the press to witness the landings.

The two leading aircraft made three dummy runs across the flight deck before Commander Russell made a perfect landing. The aircraft caught the first wire which then broke, scattering waiting flight-deck crew who ran for their lives. The aircraft then continued slowly along the deck and went over the side of the ship, into the sea. Unfortunately, the commander must have been too preoccupied with his post-landing checks to realise that the aircraft had not been successfully wired and he went over the side with his aircraft. A helicopter that was on standby lowered a man on the end of a rope ladder to try to rescue the pilot. The aircraft floated briefly before it quickly sank below the waves, its cockpit still closed. Commander Russell was seen desperately trying to open the cockpit of the doomed aircraft, which opened momentarily before sliding closed again. The commander's legs remained strapped by the leg restraints to the ejector seat and he drowned. Despite an extensive hour-long search, the body of the pilot was not recovered at that time. British *Pathé News* filmed the whole tragic incident as it happened and this can be viewed at http://www.britishpathe.com/record.php?id=35495.

Eventually the wreck was salvaged from 220ft, but as it was brought to the surface it broke in two and only the cockpit area was saved. His body was recovered. Commander John Desmond Russell was born on 6 August 1924 and was aged thirty-four when he died. He was married with two young children and lived in Rustington, Sussex.

6 October 1958   • Percival P-40 Prentice T.1 • Serial Number G-AOOM • Plymouth Aero Club

Patrick Victor Keown-Boyd (aged fifty-nine) and his wife were holidaying with Mr and Mrs Geoffrey Francis Windsor Parker at an inn in Dartmoor. Mr Parker (aged forty-four) was a qualified pilot and also the BOAC manager in a Middle Eastern country. The two friends decided to hire an aircraft from the Plymouth Aero Club and fly to Weston-super-Mare. On the way the men detoured to Mr Keown-Boyd's Pondclose Farm, near Lower Burrow, Kingsbury Episcopi.

One of the first men on the scene of the crash was Mr William Elliot, of Burrow Farm, who had been watching the aircraft circling around as he picked fruit in an orchard opposite his home. He told the newspaper's representative: 'I saw the plane circle around about four times – in fact once I shouted to the men in it because it was so low. Then all of a sudden the engine cut out. It spun around a couple of times and came straight down.'

Both men were trapped in the wreckage and died at the scene in an orchard that lay just before Palmers Lane.

Mr Keown-Boyd is buried in the Kingsbury Episcopi Churchyard and his tombstone records the fact that he lost his life in an air crash. It is not known where Mr Parker is buried.

My thanks go to Patrick Palmer for informing me about this air crash.

Source: *Western Gazette*, 10 October 1958.

1959

30 January 1959   • Westland Whirlwind H.A.S.7 • Serial Number XL837 • Number 845 Naval Air Squadron • Home Base – HMS *Heron* • RNAS Yeovilton, Ilchester, Somerset • Detached to HMS *Victorious*

This aircraft ditched into the Mediterranean Sea off Malta from a 10ft hover.[125] A loud bang had occurred, followed by the engine over-speeding. The aircraft was sonar dipping at the time and practising on the successful wartime 'T'-class submarine HMS *Tally-Ho* (P317). The submarine had detected that the aircraft had crashed and quickly came to the surface and rescued the crew after they had spent about fifteen minutes in the water. From there, all three crew members, pilot Lieutenant Mike F. Barstow, Leading Seaman Colin Gough and the observer, Lieutenant Christopher J. Jarman, were flown to the sickbay on HMS *Centaur*.

25 February 1959   • Westland Whirlwind H.A.S.7 • Serial Number XK945 • Number 845 Naval Air Squadron • Home Base – HMS *Heron* • RNAS Yeovilton, Ilchester, Somerset • Detached to HMS *Centaur*

Whilst in a 30ft hover the engine of this aircraft failed and it ditched into the Mediterranean Sea off Malta.[126] Lieutenant Commander A.G. Cornabe, Lieutenant J.A. Coleman and Lieutenant I.W. Pawe were rescued by helicopter XK942.

26 February 1959   • D.H.112 Sea Venom F.A.W.22 • Converted from F.A.W.21 on 12 November 1958 • Serial Number WW295 • Number 809 Naval Air Squadron • Home Base – HMS *Heron* • RNAS Yeovilton, Ilchester, Somerset • Detached to HMS *Albion*

This aircraft appeared to leave the catapult normally after launching some 30 miles south-east of Jervis Bay, Australia. It then slowly climbed and rolled gently to starboard. Its nose dropped and the aircraft crashed into sea ahead of the ship. The force of the impact caused it to break up and it sank immediately. The crew were not recovered.[127]

Lieutenant (P) Rodney Francis Power Carne was born on 10 November 1933 and was aged twenty-five years when he died.

Lieutenant (O) Derek Ian Douglass was born on 16 October 1934 and was aged twenty-four years when he died.

30 April 1959   • Westland Whirlwind H.A.S.7 • Serial Number XK941 • Controller (Air) • Westland Aircraft Works • Home Base – Westland's Airfield • Yeovil, Somersetl

---

During a test flight to check the standard clutch and in a 6ft hover over the airfield at Yeovil, Somerset, control was lost.[128] This was due to fatigue failure of the starboard lateral control rod. The main rotors struck the ground and the aircraft went over on to its port side a few yards from Bunford Lane. It then caught fire. Fortunately, the pilot, Lieutenant John G. Brigham and Mr Robert K.C. Klitz, his observer, escaped unharmed.[129]

Source: *Western Gazette*.

26 May 1959   • D.H.112 Sea Venom F.A.W.21 • Serial Number WW289 •
Number 891 Naval Air Squadron • Home Base – HMS *Heron* • RNAS Yeovilton, Ilchester, Somerset • Detached to HMS *Centaur*

This aircraft moved forward out of the wire after a normal landing on HMS *Centaur* whilst operating in the Bay of Biscay. This was approximately 150 miles off St-Nazaire, France. The pilot reported having no brakes and the aircraft struck two other parked aircraft before going over the starboard side and into the sea.[130] The pilot was killed and three men on the deck were injured. Sub Lieutenant (O) W. Adams was unhurt.

Lieutenant Commander (P) Charles Raymond Bushe, the squadron's senior pilot, was born on 21 April 1929 and was aged thirty-one when he was presumed to have drowned.

7 June 1959   • D.H.C.1 Chipmunk T.10 • Serial Number WZ880 • Bristol
University Air Squadron • Home Base – Filton Airfield • Bristol

Whilst the pilot of this vehicle was demonstrating a stall, the right wing dropped and the aircraft went into a spin at Winterborne from which it failed to recover.[131] It was approximately 2½ miles east-north-east of RAF Filton at the time. The pilot, Flight Lieutenant Alec Shannon, ordered the cadet with him to abandon the aircraft. The pilot jumped from the stricken aircraft at the last possible moment after trying unsuccessfully to release the cadet student; Cadet Flight Sergeant Francis Devonshire, aged nineteen, was unfortunately killed.

Flight Sergeant Devonshire was a member of the Bristol University Air Training Corps and he worked at the Bristol Aeroplane Company. He lived in St Andrews, Bristol.

25 June 1959   • D.H.112 Sea Venom F.A.W.22 • Serial Number XG696 •
Number 891 Naval Air Squadron • Home Base – HMS *Heron* • RNAS Yeovilton, Ilchester, Somerset • Detached to HMS *Centaur*

With little fuel left in its tanks, this aircraft made a straight-in approach. It struck two parked Sea Hawks, WV844 and WV798, losing the tip tank from its starboard wing. The aircraft then climbed away slowly for 1 mile to give the crew a chance to eject.[132] This they safely did and the aircraft crashed into the Mediterranean.

Lieutenant P.J. Dale and Sub Lieutenant A.R. Bradshaw were both recovered unhurt from their experience.

19 September 1959 • D.H.112 Sea Venom F.A.W.21 • Serial Number XG617 • Number 766 Naval Air Squadron • Home Base – HMS *Heron* • RNAS Yeovilton, Ilchester, Somerset

At an air day at RAF Chivenor in North Devon, two Sea Venoms were descending in line astern intending to complete a fast fly-past. Somehow, as they approached the main runway the two aircraft collided.[133] The pilot of this aircraft, Lieutenant G.P. Carne was involuntarily ejected and survived, but sadly the observer was killed in the accident. The aircraft came down in Braunton Marshes.

Lieutenant (O) Robin William Hart Miller, aged twenty-six, was born on 17 July 1933 at Gillingham, Kent. He lived with his wife in Yeovil. Lieutenant Miller is buried in the Royal Navy Cemetery in the church of St Bartholomew's, Yeovilton village. His final resting place is shown in Appendix 2.

19 September 1959 • D.H.112 Sea Venom F.A.W.21 • Serial Number WW297 • Number 766 Naval Air Squadron • Home Base – HMS *Heron* • RNAS Yeovilton, Ilchester, Somerset

In the same incident as described above,[134] the second aircraft involved, WW297, crashed into a field approximately half a mile away from the power station at Yelland. The pilot, Lieutenant L.F. Hilditch ejected safely, but sadly his observer did not.

FX 114539 Chief Petty Officer (Radio Electrician) David S. Chapman, aged thirty-seven, was born on 28 April 1922 in Leeds, Yorkshire. He lived in Worthing, Sussex, with his wife. His last resting place is not known.

19 September 1959 • Auster J/1N Alpha • Serial Number G-AGVM • Privately Owned

During the Battle of Britain celebrations at Bristol airport, Lulsgate, this aircraft unfortunately crashed. It ended up in an inverted position on the ground, but with its main fuselage clear of it. The pilot and the co-pilot both sustained minor injuries.

The aircraft was repaired and flew again. At one stage (at the RAF Church Fenton Air Show in 1972) this aircraft was part of the Gemini Team from RAF Leeming that performed synchronised aerobatics with other privately registered aircraft.

7 October 1959 • D.H.112 Sea Venom F.A.W.21 • Serial Number WW213 • Number 891 Naval Air Squadron • Home Base – HMS *Heron* • RNAS Yeovilton, Ilchester, Somerset • Detached to HMS *Centaur*

This aircraft broke out of the catapult hold back at full power whilst awaiting launch.[135] It taxied forward and then went over the port side of the ship into the sea. Sadly, both of the crew lost their lives in the incident.

Lieutenant (P) Ian William Ogilvy was born on 2 December 1932 and was aged twenty-six when he died.

Lieutenant (O) Cecil Armstrong Meek was born on 13 June 1930 and was aged twenty-nine when he died.

15 October 1959 • D.H.115 Sea Vampire T.22 • Serial Number XA117 • RNAS Yeovilton Station Flight • Home Base – HMS *Heron* • Ilchester, Somerset

This aircraft ran off the end of the runway during an emergency landing at RNAS Brawdy, Pembrokeshire.[136] The emergency was caused by a rough running engine due to turbine-blade fractures. The plane was considerably damaged and finally struck off charge as a write-off on 26 February 1960. The pilot, Captain Basil Charles Godfrey Place VC, DSC was unhurt. He eventually reached the rank of rear admiral and was made the admiral commanding reserves.

Godfrey Place won the Victoria Cross in 1943, at the age of twenty-two, as captain of the midget submarine X7. During a bold attack on the battleship *Tirpitz*, the most important unit of the German fleet at that time, midget submarines X7 and X6 exploded four charges underneath the ship as she lay at anchor in Kaafjord, Norway. This caused severe damage to the ship and rendered her unfit for sea until April 1944.

After the war, he continued his naval career but never held another submarine appointment. In 1950, he transferred to the Fleet Air Arm, training as a pilot and qualifying as such in 1952. Later that year he saw active service in the Korean War, flying the Sea Fury in 801 Squadron from HMS *Glory*.

He retired in 1970 and died on 27 December 1994, aged seventy-three. He is buried in the Corton Denham Cemetery in Somerset.

Source: *Independent on Sunday*, 30 December 1994.

30 December 1959 • D.H.115 Vampire T.11 • Serial Number XE830 • Number 1 Flying Training School • Home Base – HMS *Heron* • RNAS Yeovilton, Ilchester, Somerset

The pilot was detached to RAF Linton on Ouse for training. The accident occurred during night-flying training. At the end of a circuit of roller landings the aircraft was at about 300ft when it stopped climbing.[137] It went into a left-hand diving turn from which it never recovered. It crashed about 1½ miles away from the RAF station. There was some evidence that the pilot was disorientated and was having trouble with his instrument flying.

Lieutenant (P) Myles Hastings Atkins, aged twenty-two, was killed. He was born on 18 January 1937 and was cremated at the City of London Crematorium.

1960s

1960

19 January 1960 • Percival P.56 Provost T.1 • Serial Number WV664 • Number 766 Naval Air Squadron • Home Base – HMS *Heron* • RNAS Yeovilton, Ilchester, Somerset • Detached to Number 1 Flying Training School

This aircraft dived from cloud into the ground near Pocklington, Yorkshire, whilst on a training sortie.[1] It was thought that the pilot had probably become disorientated.

Midshipman Alan Lambert Varney was born on 27 January 1941 and was aged eighteen when he died. He is buried in the churchyard of Newton-on-Ouse parish church.

20 January 1960 • D.H.112 Sea Venom F.A.W.21 • Serial Number XG658 • Number 766 Naval Air Squadron • Home Base – HMS *Heron* • RNAS Yeovilton, Ilchester, Somerset

The aircraft was flying on exercise out of RNAS Yeovilton and was making an emergency landing during a snow storm, close to RAF Transport's command terminal station at Lyneham, Wiltshire.[2] It came in too low and hit a narrow strip of woodland. The aeroplane ploughed across a field before exploding and catching fire in another piece of woodland. Wreckage was scattered about over a wide area.

Lieutenant (P) (AE) Anthony William George Kemsley, aged twenty-four, was born on 3 June 1935 in Gillingham, Kent. He is buried in the Royal Navy Cemetery in the church of St Bartholomew's, Yeovilton village. His final resting place is shown in Appendix 2.

Lieutenant (O) John Edwin Stanley Munday, aged twenty-three, was born on 11 February 1936 in Tavistock, Devon. It is not known where he is buried.

10 February 1960 • D.H.112 Sea Venom F.A.W.22 • Converted from F.A.W.21 on 12 November 1958 • Serial Number WW147 • Number 894 Naval Air Squadron • Home Base – HMS *Heron* • RNAS Yeovilton, Ilchester, Somerset • Detached to HMS *Albion*

Immediately after a catapult launch from HMS *Albion*, this aircraft ditched about 3 cables (about 185m in today's measurements) ahead of the ship. There were no signs that the pilot had suffered any loss of control.[3] The two crewmen lost their lives in this incident.

Lieutenant G. Stanley. No other details are known. His name is not recorded on the Roll of Honour or on the Fleet Air Arm Roll of Honour.

Lieutenant J.S. Sturgeon. No other details are known. His name is not recorded on the Roll of Honour or on the Fleet Air Arm Roll of Honour.

24 February 1960   • D.H.112 Sea Venom FA.W.22 • Serial Number XG686 • Number 891 Naval Air Squadron • Home Base – HMS *Heron* • RNAS Yeovilton, Ilchester, Somerset • Detached to HMS *Centaur*

The engine of this aircraft ceased to function when it was some 750ft away from the ship and it crashed into the sea. The crew safely ejected off of Ceylon (Sri Lanka).[4] Lieutenant R.L. Wilkinson and Sub Lieutenant C.L. James were both saved.

15 March 1960   • D.H.112 Sea Venom F.A.W.22 • Converted from F.A.W.21 on 16 September 1958 • Serial Number XG614 • Number 894 Naval Air Squadron • Home Base – HMS *Heron* • RNAS Yeovilton, Ilchester, Somerset • Detached to HMS *Albion*

While operating off HMS *Albion*, the aircraft collided with Sea Venom XG723 off Malta and crashed into the Mediterranean Sea.[5] Lieutenant (X) R.W.N. Riley and Sub Lieutenant (O) J.D. Brown both successfully ejected, although both suffered injuries as a result of the ejection.

15 March 1960   • D.H.112 Sea Venom F.A.W.22 • Serial Number XG723 • Number 894 Naval Air Squadron • Home Base – HMS *Heron* • RNAS Yeovilton, Ilchester, Somerset • Detached to HMS *Albion*

While operating off HMS *Albion* the aircraft collided with Sea Venom XG614, 7 nautical miles south-east of Hal Far, off Malta, and crashed into the Mediterranean Sea.[6]

Sub Lieutenant (P) Richard John Loe was born on 18 October 1938 and was aged twenty-one when he died.

Sub Lieutenant (O) Alexander Gordon Smyth was born on 1 February 1938 and was aged twenty-two when he died.

26 April 1960   • Fairey Gannet Aircraft Early Warning Mk 3 prototype • Serial Number XJ440 • Test Flight for Bristol Siddley • Home Base – RAF Filton • Bristol

The purpose of the test flight XJ440 was on was to assess the Double Mamba oil system for oil leaks in a single-engine configuration; at the time, it was classified as secret. When the aircraft was on its final return leg to Filton and in single-engine flight, the engine stalled in its final circuit, 1 mile short of Runway 10.[7] The aircraft spun into the ground at Cribbs Causeway with its undercarriage down. Attempts were made by passers-by to rescue the crew but the fiercely burning aircraft prevented them from doing so. The bodies of the crew were not removed from the aircraft until approximately an hour after the accident.

The test pilot, Mr Richard Hazelhurst, aged thirty-seven, of Westbury-on-Trym, was killed along with his crew, Mr Peter Field, aged thirty-four, and Mr Eric Potter, aged thirty-five. It is not known where they are buried.

7 May 1960   • D.H.100 Vampire F.B.5 • Serial Number WA445 • 3 Civil Anti-Aircraft Co-operation Unit (CAACU) • Home Base – Exeter Airport • Exeter

On completion of an army co-operative exercise the aircraft landed back at Exeter airport.[8] It had been making mock shallow dives on gun positions at Westonzoyland, Somerset. The ground crew informed the pilot that during the sortie a bird had entered the port air intake. The pilot was unaware of any bird strike taking place. The aircraft was eventually written off because of this accident.

14 May 1960   • Supermarine Scimitar F.1 • Serial Number XD242 • Number 803 Naval Air Squadron • Home Base – RNAS Lossiemouth • Scotland

Whilst in flight, the pilot had shut down one engine to conserve fuel. He attempted to overshoot from his approach to Yeovilton, Somerset, but the aircraft failed to gain height and speed, and crashed on to the airfield.[9] The pilot, Lieutenant I.B. Macleod, escaped from the aircraft but suffered severe injuries. The ejection seat fired when it was being removed from the wreckage. The wreckage itself ended its days at Aberporth for missile trials and was tested to destruction.

7 July 1960   • Vickers Varsity T.1 • Serial Number WJ914 • RAF Technical College • Home Base – RAF Locking • Weston-super-Mare, Somerset

The Varsity was flying an inspection visit to RAF Oakington, Cambridgeshire.[10] A Vampire T.11 from nearby RAF Oakington, Serial No XD549, with a two-man crew flying a training mission, suddenly approached beneath them and clipped the wing of the Varsity. The wing came off and the aircraft dived into the ground, coming to rest in a cornfield behind Redhouse Farm, Hardwick. Both aircraft crashed between the villages of Comberton and Hardwick, narrowly missing them. All six on board the Varsity and the two aircrew of the Vampire jet were killed.

The Royal Show at Cambridge happened to be taking place on that day, and air-traffic control at Cambridge immediately diverted an Automobile Association aircraft that was traffic spotting. It was overhead very quickly and reported two separate burning wrecks.

500035 Flight Lieutenant Zenon Waclaw Kaye, aged thirty-eight, was the captain of the aircraft. He was born on 28 January 1922 and was buried in the St Mary the Virgin churchyard, Newport, Essex. His final resting place can be found at Grave 536.

182956 Flight Lieutenant William Henry Jackson, aged thirty-eight, was the co-pilot of the aircraft. He was born on 17 February 1922 and was buried in the St Mary the Virgin churchyard, Newport, Essex. His final resting place can be found at Grave 537.

3040526 Flight Sergeant Walter Leslie Hannant, aged thirty-four, was an air signaller. He was born on 21 October 1925 and was buried in the St Mary the Virgin churchyard, Newport, Essex. His final resting place can be found at Grave 538.

571574 Flying Officer Lewis Stanley Roy Utton, aged forty, was the engineering officer. He was born on 23 March 1920 and is buried in the Hawkwell churchyard at Hawkwell in Essex. He was based at RAF Debden.

2608346 Flight Lieutenant Brian Walker, aged twenty-six, was born on 20 February 1934 and was a passenger in the aircraft. He is buried at the Quantock Road Cemetery at Bridgwater, Somerset. His final resting place is in Section A, Grave 364.

40540935 Flight Lieutenant Malcolm Beauchamp White, aged twenty-seven, was the navigator. He is buried at Immingham parish churchyard, Grimsby, Lincolnshire, and can be found in Plot 177. He left behind a widow, Barbara, and twins, Peta and Christopher.

7 July 1960   • D.H.115 Vampire T.11 • Serial Number XD549 • Number 5
Flying Training School • Home Base – RAF Oakington

This Vampire T.11 from RAF Oakington, Serial No XD549, with a two-man crew flying a training mission, suddenly approached Varsity WJ914 (see details in preceding entry) beneath them and clipped the wing of the Varsity.[11] The wing came off and the aircraft dived into the ground near some council houses in a bean field.

4230326 Pilot Officer Joseph Jarvis Ball, aged twenty-one, was born on 11 March 1939. He came from Pretoria, South Africa, and was the pilot. He is buried at the Long Stanton Cemetery in Cambridge and his grave can be found in Section B, Row E, Grave 2.

2614268 Flying Officer Albert John Lakeman, aged twenty-four, was born on 1 November 1945 and came from Exeter. He was the instructor. Flying Officer Lakeman is buried at the Long Stanton Cemetery in Cambridge and his grave can be found in Section B, Row E, Grave 1.

19 July 1960   • D.H.C.1 Chipmunk T.10 • Serial Number WP836 • 3 Air
Experience Flight • Home Base – RAF Locking

This aircraft was parked when it was struck by a civilian Miles Messenger aircraft G-AKBM.[12] The damage it sustained caused it to be written off and it went to No 6 Air Experience Flight at White Waltham for ground instruction as 7655M.

14 September 1960 • D.H.112 Sea Venom F.A.W.21 • Serial Number WW205 •
Number 894 Naval Air Squadron • Home Base – HMS *Heron* • RNAS Yeovilton, Ilchester,
Somerset • Detached to HMS *Albion*

On a night approach, the port wing dipped of this aircraft and the drop tank hit the deck. The aircraft missed the wires and went over the port side and into the South China Sea.[13]

Lieutenant (P) Nicholas Albert Croad was born on 3 October 1934 and was twenty-five when he died.

Lieutenant (O) Robin John Edwards was born on 26 August 1937 and was twenty-three when he died.

16 September 1960 • Vulcan B.2 • Serial Number XH557 • A&AEE Boscombe Down

The aircraft was on a delivery flight from Boscombe Down to Filton. As the Vulcan bomber landed in moderate rain it began to aquaplane along Runway 10. The drag parachute was deployed but no drag was felt. The pilot decided to abort the landing. With full power applied to all four of the aircraft's powerful Bristol Siddeley engines and at about 600 yards from the end of the runway, the aircraft managed to get airborne again some 50ft from the end of the runway and an overshoot was executed.

At the end of the runway, and serving the A38, nestled behind some chain-link fence, lay the aptly named Runway Garage. The inappropriateness of its position was soon proved as the aircraft narrowly missed the garage, its engine blast all but destroying the four petrol pumps that were located there. It also hit a street light, bursting four of its eight starboard tyres. As the aircraft managed to climb, the deployed brake parachute fell away. Two cars on the A38 were spun around by the blast from the engines and iron railings on the other side of the road were torn up. The aircraft also narrowly missed the Proteus Engine test bed that was located in the Rolls-Royce East Works. After this incident the location of the garage was wisely moved.

The aircraft was piloted by Flight Lieutenant Wareham of the Handling Squadron, Boscombe Down, and his co-pilot was Mr T.P. Frost (chief test pilot, Bristol Siddeley Engines).[14] The crew were Flight Lieutenant M.H. Pasking (navigator), Flight Lieutenant J.J. Denn (air engineering officer), Mr Stubbs (Bristol Siddeley AEO in training) and Mr Robinson (Avro servicing crew).

Source: Collier, D., *UK Flight Testing Accidents 1940–71* (Air Britain Historians Ltd, 2002).

17 September 1960 • D.H.110 Sea Vixen F.A.W.1 • Serial Number XJ515 • Number 892 Naval Air Squadron • Home Base – HMS *Heron* • RNAS Yeovilton, Ilchester, Somerset

Whilst on a NATO exercise approximately 50 miles north of the Shetlands, this aircraft hit the round down of HMS *Ark Royal* late in the evening and skidded along the deck on its main wheels and nose.[15] The aircraft then burst into flames before it disappeared over the port side of the ship. A ten-hour intensive search for the missing crew took place in the darkness, with the searchlights of HMS *Ark Royal* and the cruiser HMS *Gambia* assisting. Small boats were also launched to help with the search, but despite the best efforts of all concerned, both of the crew were listed as 'Missing Presumed Killed'.

Lieutenant (P) Harold Bond was born 26 July 1933 and was aged twenty-seven when he died.

Lieutenant (O) Daniel Coutts Marjoribanks was born on 28 April 1935 and was twenty-five when he died.

9 November 1960   • De Havilland Canada 1 Chipmunk 22 • Registration Number
G-AORV • Military Serial WB725 • Privately Owned

The Sudanese pilot Omar Eisa, aged twenty-two, was flying from Weston-super-Mare
to Exeter airport. No one witnessed what happened on the Quantock Hills, but some
forestry workers heard the noise of the crash. They made a search and found the plane
in an isolated spot known as the Slades. This is a clearing at a height of about 1,000ft
and owned by the Forestry Commission. It is about 3 miles to the south-west of Over
Stowey village. Workers found that the aircraft had hit a tree and killed the pilot, who
was still inside the aircraft.

Source: *Western Gazette.*

1961

6 January 1961   • D.H.110 Sea Vixen F.A.W.1 • Serial Number XJ573 • Number
893 Naval Air Squadron • Home Base – HMS *Heron* • RNAS Yeovilton, Ilchester,
Somerset

This aircraft became low on the final stages of a very steady night approach to
HMS *Ark Royal*.[16] It was waved off and banked to port but, unfortunately, the port
wing of the aircraft struck an engine box at Fly 4 and the aircraft crashed into the sea.
    The alarm to search the area came just as the 108 Minesweeper Squadron panto-
mime, *Snow White*, was about to start. The urgency of the rescue mission was so great
that these sailors carried out their task, some still dressed in the costumes that they
would have worn on stage.
    Lieutenant (P) Norman Leslie Dudgeon was born on 12 June 1930. He was thirty
when he died.
    Sub Lieutenant (O) Anthony James Russell was born on 26 July 1940. He was
twenty when he died.

Source: *The Times,* 7 January 1961.

9 January 1961   • Auster A.O.P.9 • Serial Number WZ716 • LAS – Army Air Corps
• Home Base – Middle Wallop

Five Auster aircraft were on a spotting exercise from Middle Wallop to Exeter. The
group met with heavy fog and one Auster, piloted by a sergeant, successfully landed in
a field next to the stopgate garage on the Ilminster to Honiton Road near the A30/
A303 junction.[17] Shortly afterwards another aircraft landed beside him.
    Once the heavy mist had cleared, the first aircraft, through necessity, made a down-
wind take-off. The aircraft clipped the top of a hedge and just managed to clear the

road before it crashed, cartwheeling down a field several times before it stopped. The pilot, Captain Peter Munden suffered head injuries and the man with him, Captain Terence Parsons, suffered a broken thigh.

Due to this incident the aircraft was written off. Its last known location was on the scrap dump at the Bicester Army Depot on 20 March 1961.

Source: *Western Gazette.*

11 January 1961   • Westland WS-55 Whirlwind H.A.R.10 • Serial Number XJ762 • Westland Aircraft Works • Home Base – Westland's Airfield • Yeovil, Somerset

During recovery from a practice auto-rotation at Yeovil, Somerset, the engine of this helicopter failed at 100ft. The aircraft struck the ground heavily, breaking off the tail cone. The tail cone doubled back on the main body of the aircraft and ended up with the tail rotor parallel with the cockpit. As a result of this accident the aircraft was written off. The two crew members of the aircraft escaped without injury. The pilot was Squadron Leader L.C.E. de Vigne DSO, DFC, AFC and Mr R. Mills was his flight test observer.[18]

8 February 1961   • D.H.110 Sea Vixen F.A.W.1 • Serial Number XJ583 • Number 892 Naval Air Squadron • Home Base – HMS *Heron* • RNAS Yeovilton, Ilchester, Somerset • Detached to HMS *Victorious*

A drop tank caught fire after the starboard oleo leg collapsed when landing on HMS *Victorious*, while operating off Malaysia.[19] The two crew, Lieutenant P. Marshall and Sub Lieutenant M. Maddox escaped injury. The aircraft was returned to the UK on HMS *Hermes* and was later allocated to Arbroath as A2507.

9 February 1961   • D.H.110 Sea Vixen F.A.W.1 • Serial Number XJ527 • Number 892 Naval Air Squadron • Home Base – HMS *Heron* • RNAS Yeovilton, Ilchester, Somerset • Detached to HMS *Hermes*

This aircraft crashed into the sea 25 miles off Horsborgh Lighthouse, Tengah, Singapore.[20] Both of the crew, Lieutenants G.W.G. Hunt and J.S. Morris safely ejected after a fire started in the starboard engine. The aircraft was not recovered.

1 March 1961   • Ashton 3 • Serial Number WB493 • Bristol Siddeley Engines • RAF Filton • Bristol

The chief test pilot of Bristol Siddeley, Mr T.P. Frost was testing his aircraft and landed back at Filton airfield.[21] The aircraft he was flying was a prototype jet airliner, although it first appeared almost a year after the de Havilland Comet. It was never intended for commercial use, but was designed purely for experimental reasons.

The port undercarriage leg light had indicated to the pilot that it was unlocked, yet a visual airborne inspection had confirmed to the pilot that all was well. When he landed, the leg suddenly folded which caused overstressing to the port wing and it slewed to port. It was classified as a Category 5.

1 May 1961 • Westland Whirlwind H.A.S.7 converted to H.A.S.9 • Serial Number XN260 • Number 848 Naval Air Squadron • Home Base – HMS *Heron* • RNAS Yeovilton, Ilchester, Somerset • Detached to HMS *Bulwark*

This aircraft crashed into trees in the Kota Belud training area of North Borneo.[22] Sub Lieutenant D.A. Creamer and three Royal Marines escaped without injury, and another Royal Marine received slight injuries. Parts of it were salvaged and what was left was blown up.

This event occurred before the confrontation with Indonesia began. This particular loss happened during a big South-East Asia Treaty Organisation exercise given the code name 'Pony Express'. This exercise was the biggest in the six-and-a-half-year existence of SEATO. It involved sixty ships, from six nations, carrying out coastal bombardment followed by an assault from sea and air. Under battle conditions 6,000 men landed on the North Borneo coast. Forty-two Commando Royal Marines, Australian infantry and US marines formed the assault force. Attacks on shipping were made by British and US submarines, while RAF bombers from Singapore acted as enemy aircraft.

26 May 1961 • Westland Whirlwind H.A.S.7 • Serial Number XM683 • Number 848 Naval Air Squadron • Home Base – HMS *Heron* • RNAS Yeovilton, Ilchester, Somerset • Detached to HMS *Bulwark*

This aircraft ditched into the Celebes Sea off Brunei, 1 mile from HMS *Bulwark*, after power loss and intermittent engine cutting.[23] The pilot, Lieutenant R.M. Edmonds, was rescued by the ship's SAR helicopter. This particular helicopter was powered by the 750hp Alvis Leonides Major 155 engine, and was the second squadron loss within the same month.

20 June 1961 • D.H.110 Sea Vixen F.A.W.1 • Serial Number XJ566 • Number 892 Naval Air Squadron • Home Base – HMS *Heron* • RNAS Yeovilton, Ilchester, Somerset • Detached to HMS *Victorious*

After being waved off during a night ground-controlled approach to HMS *Victorious* while operating off Singapore, the aircraft turned to port and entered the water with 70° of bank and 200 yards off the port beam.[24] Both of the crewmen lost their lives in this accident.

Lieutenant (P) Thomas Gilbertson was born on 25 April 1933 and was aged twenty-eight when he died.

Sub Lieutenant (O) Robin Trenholm Nelson was born on 16 March 1941. He was aged twenty when he died.

20 July 1961   • D.H.110 Sea Vixen F.A.W.1 • Serial Number XJ569 • Number 899 Naval Air Squadron • Home Base – HMS *Heron* • RNAS Yeovilton, Ilchester, Somerset

The aircraft stalled and spun in from 20,000ft during a low-speed flying test.[25] The aircraft crashed near Ridge Hill Farm (between Sydling and Cerne Abbas, Dorset). The crew, consisting of Lieutenant Commander (P) John E. Kelly and Lieutenant (O) David Ashby, ejected safely, although Lieutenant Commander Kelly suffered injuries that prevented him from flying in an aircraft that had ejector seats. He converted to helicopters and successfully flew them for another ten years before retiring from the Royal Navy. For Lieutenant Ashby, this was his second ejection from a fighter aircraft. Previously he had made a successful ejection from a Sea Venom.

25 July 1961   • D.H.112 Sea Venom F.A.W.22 • Serial Number XG672 • Airworks, Yeovilton • Home Base – HMS *Heron* • RNAS Yeovilton, Ilchester, Somerset

The aircraft had been in a formation take-off from RNAS Yeovilton on a short runway with no wind.[26] It failed to take off and ploughed through two caravans and into the house of a former Sea Venom pilot, Lieutenant Commander Nigel de Winton in Yeovilton village.

Mrs Marigold de Winton was at home at the time with her two children. She snatched them up and they ran for their lives as the aircraft burned fiercely and ignited the thatched roof of her house. Mrs Christine Marks, a mother of four children, was rescued from one of the caravans, although her condition at the time of rescue was critical.

The pilot, Mr Arthur Percy Jennings, aged thirty-two, and who lived in the High Street, Wincanton, was killed. His body was recovered from the scene about an hour afterwards.

Source: *Western Gazette.*

27 October 1961   • D.H.110 Sea Vixen F.A.W.1 • Serial Number XJ519 • Number 892B Naval Air Squadron • Home Base – HMS *Heron* • RNAS Yeovilton, Ilchester, Somerset • Detached to HMS *Victorious*

This aircraft broke out of the catapult hold back and went over the side of HMS *Victorious* while operating in Subic Bay, Philippines.[27] Both of the crew were rescued and Sub Lieutenant (P) R.O. Sutton was unhurt. The observer, Lieutenant J.S.D. Robinson was slightly injured.

21 November 1961 • Westland Whirlwind H.A.S.7 • Serial Number XN301 • Number 848 Naval Air Squadron • Home Base – HMS *Heron* • RNAS Yeovilton, Ilchester, Somerset • Detached to HMS *Bulwark*

Approaching HMS *Bulwark* as she lay in Hong Kong Harbour, the pilot came in at too low a level and was affected by the downwash of a preceding aircraft. The aircraft struck the edge of the deck and fell away over the port side and into the harbour.[28] Lieutenant D.W. Shrubb, Petty Officer B.F. Surtees and Marine J. Tennent were all safely recovered to the ship.

14 December 1961 • Hawker P.1127 • Prototype Kestrel/Harrier • Serial Number XP836 • Hawker Aircraft Limited • Home Base – Dunsfold, Surrey

The aircraft suddenly experienced a 100mph speed loss coupled with an unexpected air frame and engine roughness. At the same time the plane underwent violent lateral rocking. The pilot had no options and he told his escorting aircraft that he was going to try to make an emergency landing at RNAS Yeovilton.

The aircraft smashed into a Dutch barn on the approach and destroyed 180 tons of hay, scattering wreckage over a wide area. Both the barn and the prototype aircraft were soon burning furiously.

The test pilot, Mr A.W. 'Bill' Bedford successfully ejected from the aircraft at a height of 200ft. A navy helicopter, which happened to be Admiral Percy Gicks' VIP helicopter, was soon on the scene. After a medical check up at the Yeovilton sickbay where it was ascertained that he had no injuries, Mr Bedford was returned to Dunsfold.

After the crash it was discovered that the front fibreglass left-hand exhaust nozzle on this aircraft had torn off, causing an uncontrollable roll to port when its flaps were extended. Later aircraft were fitted with steel exhaust nozzles.

Source: *Western Gazette.*

1962

1 May 1962 • D.H.110 Sea Vixen F.A.W.1 • Serial Number XJ528 • Number 890 Naval Air Squadron • Home Base – HMS *Heron* • RNAS Yeovilton, Ilchester, Somerset • Detached to HMS *Ark Royal*

During a night-interception exercise (Exercise Sea Devil, a SEATO exercise) the pilot felt a severe blow or explosion whilst flying at the height of 2,000ft.[29] Both crew then ejected as the aircraft fell out of control. The aircraft crashed into the South China Sea off the Philippines and was not recovered. Lieutenants R.H. Burn and D.H. Ross were safely picked up by the USS *Caliente.*

9 May 1962   • D.H.C.1 Chipmunk T.10 • Serial Number WG420 • Bristol
University Air Squadron • Home Base – Filton Airfield • Bristol

Pilot Peter Michie, a student at Bristol University and member of the University Air Squadron, was on a solo aerobatics sortie in a Chipmunk. Whilst flying upside down at the apex of a loop, the aircraft suddenly experienced complete engine failure at 4,000ft.[30]

The pilot rolled the aircraft up the right way and made a successful forced landing in a field beside the River Severn, near Oldbury-on-Severn. No injuries or damage to the plane was caused in this incident. Due to his limited amount of flying hours at the time (ninety) he was awarded an Air Commodores Green Endorsement in recognition of the feat.

This incident is included because of the historical significance of the Belvedere helicopter recovering the downed plane in an airlift.

Mr Michie has written a book called *Mayday, Mayday, Mayday, Charlie Juliet*, in which the following anecdote appears and is reproduced here with his permission:

> About 10 minutes later an English Bobby (policeman) appeared from what must have been a nearby road. He was pushing his bicycle and had the bottom of his trousers in classic English bicycle clips. I was very pleased to see him but it seemed that he did not reciprocate this feeling as his opening words to me were: 'You can't park that plane here sir!'
>
> When I protested that I had to make a forced landing because of engine failure, his response was, 'Show some respect for the law, young man!'

2 June 1962   • D.H.C.1 Chipmunk T.10 • Serial Number WK516 • Bristol
University Air Squadron • Home Base – Filton Airfield • Bristol

This aircraft struck high-tension cables during a practice forced landing at Thornbury, Bristol. It hit the ground heavily and was damaged beyond repair.[31] Fortunately both of the crew came away without any injuries. The wreck of this aircraft was last sighted at No 71 MU Bicester on 4 April 1963.

17 June 1962   • D.H.C.1 Chipmunk T.10 • Serial Number WP976 • Bristol
University Air Squadron • Home Base – Filton Airfield • Bristol

During high winds, the pilot lost control over this aircraft while landing at Filton airfield.[32] The aeroplane bounced and then crashed through the boundary fence, coming to rest in an inverted position in a field. The pilot was slightly injured in the accident.

20 June 1962 • Westland Whirlwind H.A.R.10 • Serial Number XP392 • Westland Aircraft Works • Home Base – Westland's Airfield • Yeovil, Somerset

This aircraft was being flown by the Westland's test pilot, Squadron Leader L.C.E. de Vigne DSO, DFC, AFC.[33] It suffered a fuel flow failure whilst at 25ft during a dress rehearsal prior to a sales demonstration for the Spanish air force in Spain. It force landed on uneven ground and rolled on to its side. Fortunately there were no casualties. The damaged sustained by the helicopter was such that it was declared a Category 5 loss.

12 July 1962 • Scout A.H.1 • Serial Number XR493 • Westland Aircraft Works • Home Base – Westland's Airfield • Yeovil, Somerset

This helicopter was being flown by the production test pilot, Mr J.L. Barnes.[34] At 1,500ft the tailplane and tail rotor broke away in flight. The helicopter rolled to starboard and pitched down, but the pilot managed to make a successful forced landing on the airfield. Although no one was hurt in the incident, the helicopter was declared a Category 4, but later saw service with the Army Air Corps. It was also to be involved in some more incidents before going to the Army Air Corps (see 6 May 1963).

17 July 1962 • D.H.98 Mosquito B.35 converted to TT.35 • Serial Number VP191 • 3 Civil Anti-Aircraft Co-operation Unit (CAACU) • Home Base – Exeter Airport • Exeter

This aircraft abandoned its take-off at RAF Locking, Weston-super-Mare.[35] It overshot the runway and went into a hedge, tearing off the undercarriage. The aircraft was written off. Mainly used for target-towing duties, this aircraft had the distinction of being one of the last three Mosquitos in RAF service. The other two were eventually withdrawn from service in 1963.

25 July 1962 • Hawker Sea Hawk F.G.A.4 • Serial Number WV919 • Fleet Requirements Unit • Home Base – Hurn Airport • Bournemouth

The seat inner-tube of this aircraft was believed to have been incorrectly locked, which caused an involuntary ejection.[36] The aircraft crashed into the sea near Bleadon, Weston-super-Mare, and burst into flames. The pilot, Mr A. Rhodes, from Christchurch, sustained injuries to his ankles. The wreckage was recovered and removed by the Mobile Aircraft Repair Transport & Salvage Unit, which was based at Lee-on-Solent, near Portsmouth.

Some internet sites show this aircraft as having crashed at Hurn airport on this date. This is incorrect.[37] On 13 March 1962, this aircraft burst both of its main tyres on landing at Hurn and this is probably why some internet sites have the wrong information recorded.

23 August 1962   • D.H.110 Sea Vixen F.A.W.1 • Serial Number XJ493 • Number 766 Naval Air Squadron • Home Base – HMS *Heron* • RNAS Yeovilton, Ilchester, Somerset

A false fire-warning signal was given in the cockpit of this aircraft and the pilot attempted to abort take-off.[38] The runway arrester gear failed to hold the plane and the aircraft crashed through a hedge and into the nearby River Yeo, killing both the pilot and his observer. The aircraft ended up with its tail boom submerged in the river and its nose embedded in the river bank. The aircraft was recovered with the help of the Territorial Army, who had to build a Bailey bridge to get the aircraft back on to the right side of the river. The aircraft was later used for ground instruction at Arbroath.

Lieutenant (P) Richard Hugh Eyton-Jones, aged twenty-four, was born on 2 March 1938 in Littlehampton, Sussex. He lived in Martock with his new bride. He is buried in the Royal Navy Cemetery in the church of St Bartholomew's, Yeovilton village. His final resting place is shown in Appendix 2.

Acting Sub Lieutenant (O) David Graeme Scott, aged twenty-two, was born on 1 October 1939 and lived in Great Malvern, Worcestershire. He also is buried in the Royal Navy Cemetery in the church of St Bartholomew's, Yeovilton village, and his last resting place lies next to his pilot.

Source: *Western Gazette*, 31 August 1962.

4 September 1962   • D.H.110 Sea Vixen F.A.W.1 • Serial Number XJ603 • Number 892 Naval Air Squadron • Home Base – HMS *Heron* • RNAS Yeovilton, Ilchester, Somerset • Detached to HMS *Hermes*

On a night-time approach to HMS *Hermes*, which was sailing just off Malta, this aircraft hit the round down.[39] It skidded up the angled deck and then plunged over the ship's side and into the sea, killing the crew.

Lieutenant (P) Edward Revel Mason was born on 19 June 1938 and was twenty-four when he died. He lived in Shortlands, Kent.

Lieutenant (O) Robin Gilbert Lunn was born on 16 March 1939 and was twenty-three when he died. He lived in Yeovilton.

29 October 1962   • D.H.110 Sea Vixen F.A.W.1 • Serial Number XJ562 • Number 890 Naval Air Squadron • Home Base – HMS *Heron* • RNAS Yeovilton, Ilchester, Somerset • Detached to HMS *Ark Royal*

The port engine of this aircraft failed to relight after a double generator failure at night.[40] The crew, Lieutenant G.P. Dobie and Sub Lieutenant R.M. Gravestock were picked up from the sea by a Wessex helicopter. This was the first time that a Wessex 1 SAR had been used in the auto-hover mode to effect a rescue.

3 December 1962 • Avro 698 Vulcan B.1 • Serial Number XA894 • Home Base –
RAF Filton • Bristol

The Vulcan was being used as a test bed for the Olympus 22R engine, which was
to power the TSR2. The engine was run to full power on maximum reheat when
an LP turbine disc failed, puncturing two fuel tanks and starting a fire which rapidly spread.[41] The core of the disc continued across the airfield, bouncing every 150ft
towards a parked Bristol Type 188. It eventually ran out of momentum just short of
the stationary aircraft.

The fire destroyed the Vulcan and a brand-new fire engine that was parked close
by. Luckily there were no serious injuries to the engineers or fire crew. The fire was
so intense that it was allowed to burn itself out. This aircraft was replaced by another
Vulcan, XA903, in May 1963.

Source: Aviation-Safety.net.

1963

28 January 1963 • D.H.110 Sea Vixen F.A.W.1 • Serial Number XJ585 • Number
893 Naval Air Squadron • Home Base – HMS *Heron* • RNAS Yeovilton, Ilchester,
Somerset • Detached to HMS *Centaur*

The Sea Vixen was flying from HMS *Centaur* and 16 miles south of the Lizard, south-
west Cornwall.[42] It was making a night carrier-controlled approach landing when
it hit the round down. It caught fire and skidded along the deck, damaging aircraft
XJ572, XN648, XN657 and XN658 parked on Fly 1. The aircraft then crashed into
the sea over the bow, killing the crew.

Lieutenant Commander (P) Derek Frederick Fieldhouse, aged thirty-six, was
born on 11 April 1926 at Maidstone in Kent. The body of the pilot, Lieutenant
Commander Fieldhouse, was recovered and he is buried in the Royal Navy Cemetery
in the church of St Bartholomew's, Yeovilton village. His final resting place is shown
in Appendix 2.

His observer, Lieutenant (O) Stacey Naylor Swift, aged thirty-four, was born on
23 January 1929 at Hendon, Middlesex. He lived in Barton St David, near Somerton,
Somerset. His body was not recovered from the sea.

14 March 1963 • Hunting (later B.A.C.) Jet Provost T.3 • Serial Number XN504 •
Home Base – HMS *Heron* • RNAS Yeovilton, Ilchester, Somerset • Detached to Number
1 Flying Training School

Lieutenants Ward and Pinney successfully abandoned this aircraft approximately
half a mile north of Rufforth, when engine power was lost in the circuit on a

landing approach.[43] The crew ejected when they realised that they would not reach the runway.

28 April 1963 • Piper PA-23-250 • Registration Number G-ASCR • Privately Owned

This private aircraft, built in 1962, was damaged beyond repair when it crashed at Worlebury, Somerset. No other details are known.

6 May 1963 • Westland Scout A.H.1 • Serial Number XR493 • Westland Aircraft Works • Home Base – Westland's Airfield • Yeovil, Somerset

This helicopter, piloted by the chief test pilot, Mr M.M. Reed, and with Mr A.I. Ives, the flight test observer, suffered an engine failure in the circuit around Westland's airfield.[44] The pilot made a successful forced landing for which he was awarded a Green Endorsement in his log book. Although there were no casualties, the helicopter was declared a Category 4.

This same aircraft and with the same crew had forced landed in a field near Yeovil on 9 April 1963. At that stage it was repaired as a Category 3.

After a career with the Army Air Corps, the aircraft eventually received a civil Serial No of G-APVM before going to the Oman as 8040M. It ended its days in the Royal Air Force of Oman Museum at Seeb, Oman.

10 May 1963 • Westland Scout A.H.1 • Serial Number XP851 • Number 651 Squadron Army Air Corps • Home Base – Middle Wallop

During winching trials at RNAS Yeovilton and whilst on loan to the Ministry of Aviation, this helicopter suffered a sudden engine failure. After making a forced landing in a field next to the airfield, it managed to roll itself upside down in the soft ground. The pilot escaped unhurt but the aircraft was later written off.

31 May 1963 • D.H.110 Sea Vixen F.A.W.1 • Serial Number XN695 • Number 892 Naval Air Squadron • Home Base – HMS *Heron* • RNAS Yeovilton, Ilchester, Somerset • Detached to HMS *Hermes*

The aircraft was descending with another Sea Vixen down towards HMS *Hermes* from 40,000ft to 500ft for a night glow worm towed-target attack.[45] It continued to descend and flew into the Pacific Ocean, exploding on impact 15 miles west of Okinawa, Japan, killing both of the crew.

Lieutenant (P) Christopher John Bynoe was aged twenty-two when he died.

The age of Sub Lieutenant (O) Paul Austin is not known.

28 June 1963   • D.H.110 Sea Vixen F.A.W.1 • Serial Number XN703 • Number 892 Naval Air Squadron • Home Base – HMS *Heron* • RNAS Yeovilton, Ilchester, Somerset • Detached to HMS *Hermes*

The pilot was undertaking deck-landing practice with this aircraft on HMS *Hermes* off Singapore having just joined the squadron.[46] After the first roller landing the aircraft pulled up steeply, stalled and crashed into the sea. The SAR helicopter was on the scene in one and a half minutes, followed by a sea boat, but there was no trace of the two crewmen. Large amounts of small pieces of wreckage were recovered.

Sub Lieutenant (P) David Edward Arthur Phillips was born on 25 November 1938 and was aged twenty-four when he died.

Sub Lieutenant (O) Michael Dennis Cooper was born on 25 May 1941 and was aged twenty-two when he died.

29 August 1963   • D.H.110 Sea Vixen F.A.W.1 • Serial Number XN710 • Number 890 Naval Air Squadron • Home Base – HMS *Heron* • RNAS Yeovilton, Ilchester, Somerset • Detached to HMS *Ark Royal*

This aircraft suffered fuel-transfer problems during a sortie off of the east coast of Malaya.[47] It was diverted to Tengah, Singapore, but the crew were forced to eject with unusable fuel on board and with a double flame out. It crashed into the jungle and was not recovered due to the inaccessibility of the site. Lieutenant David John Dunbar-Dempsey and Sub Lieutenant W. Hart were both unhurt and picked up by the ship's Wessex V SAR team.

5 September 1963   • Wasp H.A.S.1 • Serial Number XS476 • Westland Aircraft Works • Home Base – Westland's Airfield • Yeovil, Somerset

Whilst being flown by a production test pilot, Mr J.O. Matthews, this helicopter suffered an engine failure.[48] The aircraft was then force landed into a nearby field. There were no injuries sustained by the pilot but the helicopter was declared a Category 4.

The aircraft became part of the Royal Navy's helicopter fleet, finally ending up in the RN Observer School by July 1974. It finished its career as a ground instruction airframe at RNAS Portland with Serial No of A2656. It met its last moments on the Portland fire dump in February 1981.

20 September 1963   • Supermarine Scimitar F.1 • Serial Number XD213 • Number 803 Naval Air Squadron • Home Base – HMS *Hermes*

After taking off, a hydraulic failure occurred and the port oleo leg remained locked down and it failed to lower on approach to RNAS Yeovilton.[49] The pilot was unable to get the leg of the aircraft down manually and as it was deemed to be overweight for a safe landing. The pilot, Sub Lieutenant A.J. Middleton, aged twenty-three, was ordered to abandon it. He was unable to steer his aircraft out to sea and the aircraft crashed in a field near East Chaldon, Weymouth, in Dorset. After his successful ejection the pilot found himself uninjured and surrounded by a herd of very curious cows.

1964

12 January 1964   • Slingsby T.31B Cadet TX3 • Serial Number WT874 • 621 Gliding School • Home Base – RAF Locking • Weston-super-Mare

The RAF versions of this Slingsby Type 31 were used for air cadet training and designated as the Cadet TX3 (a two-seater training glider). This particular aircraft was written off in a flying accident at RAF Locking, Somerset.[50] Later it was rebuilt and became a civilian glider with the designation of BGA1255, crashing once again at Bardney, Lincolnshire. Again it was written off on 30 May 1971.

28 January 1964   • Supermarine Scimitar F.1 • Serial Number XD249 • Number 800 Naval Air Squadron • Home Base – HMS *Heron* • RNAS Yeovilton, Ilchester, Somerset

Whilst ferrying this aircraft from RNAS Yeovilton to RNAS Lossiemouth, Scotland, the aircraft developed a hydraulic leak. The starboard undercarriage was partially lowered and could not be locked by using the emergency system. The aircraft crashed into the Moray Firth off Lossiemouth, Morayshire.[51] The pilot, Lieutenant P.E.H. Banfield ejected into the sea and was injured in the process. He was successfully rescued by an SAR helicopter.

20 February 1964   • D.H.110 Sea Vixen F.A.W.1 • Serial Number XJ523 • Number 766 Naval Air Squadron • Home Base – HMS *Heron* • RNAS Yeovilton, Ilchester, Somerset

During a radar-controlled night approach to RNAS Yeovilton, the aircraft flew into the ground 6 miles short of the runway, about 50 yards from the farmhouse at Summerways Farm, Thorney, close to Kingsbury Episcopi in Somerset.[52] The aircraft exploded on impact and burst into flames. The aircraft was finally sold as scrap on 23 September 1964 at Lee-on-Solent to H.H. Bushell and Company, Birmingham.

Sub Lieutenant (P) George Alexander Steenson, aged twenty and from Glasgow, died from multiple injuries received when he ejected too close to the ground for his parachute to open. He is buried in the Royal Navy Cemetery in the church of St Bartholomew's, Yeovilton village. His final resting place is shown in Appendix 2.

1 The grave of Pilot Dale Carlson at Sherborne.

2 The memorial stone at Hare Lane.

3 The sad and shattered remains of VF309. *(Courtesy of Brian Lovell)*

4 The remains of VF309 covered in foam. *(Courtesy of Brian Lovell)*

5 Where VF300 came to earth can still be seen.

6 The grave of Pilot D.J. Roberts at Ilton cemetery.

7 The remains of WA274 with a fire engine in the background. *(Courtesy of Brian Lovell)*

8 The remains of WA274 covered in foam. *(Courtesy of Brian Lovell)*

9 Bristol 173 G-AMJI captured at the moment of impact. *(Courtesy of Mike Openshaw and Phil Addison)*

10 Chipmunk WG420 being airlifted by an RAF Belvedere. *(Courtesy of Peter Michie)*

11 De Havilland D.H.110 Sea Vixen F.A.W.2 Serial No XS590 on display at the Fleet Air Arm Museum during April 2011. Here the wings are folded as if the aircraft is within a ship's hangar. *(Author's collection, with acknowledgements to the Fleet Air Arm Museum)*

12 Wessex 5 helicopters land in a jungle clearing. *(Author's collection)*

13 Wrington poplars.

14 The remains of Harrier XZ493 at RNAS Yeovilton. *(Courtesy of Brian Pittard)*

Lieutenant (O) Eric Sneddon, aged twenty-two and from Stoke-on-Trent, also died from multiple injuries. His body was recovered from the aircraft. He is buried in the Royal Navy Cemetery in the church of St Bartholomew's, Yeovilton village. He was born on 27 February 1941. His final resting place is shown in Appendix 2.

Source: *Western Gazette*, 28 February 1964.

20 April 1964   • Slingsby T.31B Sedbergh TX.1 • Serial Number XN154 • 618 Gliding School • Home Base – RAF Manston • Kent

This aircraft (a glider) was written off in a flying accident at Locking, Somerset.[53] It was sent to the RAF Gliding and Soaring Association as GSA333, later becoming BGA1465.

11 July 1964   • D.H.110 Sea Vixen F.A.W.1 • Serial Number XJ605 • Number 892 Naval Air Squadron • Home Base – HMS *Heron* • RNAS Yeovilton, Ilchester, Somerset • Detached to HMS *Centaur*

HMS *Centaur* was exercising with other ships in the Malacca Straits off Penang.[54] It was night time. Six minutes after being launched it was reported that the aircraft was spinning uncontrollably and the crew ejected. Radar contact was then lost. Unfortunately, the aircraft was not found and both of the crew were listed as 'Missing Presumed Killed'.

The pilot was Lieutenant (P) Geoffrey Malcolm Lewis Terdre. His date of birth is not shown on the Roll of Honour.

His crewman was Sub Lieutenant (O) Malcolm John Jackson. His date of birth is not shown on the Roll of Honour.

25 November 1964   • D.H.110 Sea Vixen F.A.W.1 • Serial Number XN708 • Number 890 Naval Air Squadron • Home Base – HMS *Heron* • RNAS Yeovilton, Ilchester, Somerset

At the time of the accident 890 Squadron was disembarked from HMS *Ark Royal*. This aircraft was carrying out a Lepus flare night attack (the flare reportedly had a strength of several million candle power) on the frigate F91 HMS *Murray* and failed to pull out of a dive.[55] The accident occurred in Lyme Bay, Dorset, Portland Light, bearing 220° at 23 miles. The two crew members were unfortunately killed in the accident.

The pilot was Lieutenant (P) Michael John Wavell Durrant.

Lieutenant (O) Basil Anthony Last was born on 13 December 1936 and was aged twenty-seven when he died.

1965

22 January 1965 • D.H.110 Sea Vixen F.A.W.1 • Serial Number XN698 • Number 893 Naval Air Squadron • Home Base – HMS *Heron* • RNAS Yeovilton, Ilchester, Somerset • Detached to HMS *Victorious*

The pilot misjudged his approach to HMS *Victorious* while operating this aircraft in the China Sea off Okinawa in the Sea of Japan.[56] He attempted to go round again but the aircraft stalled as it lifted off the deck. The starboard wing struck two aircraft parked in Fly 1 and it then crashed into the sea, killing both of the crew.

Lieutenant (P) Elson Spencer Billett was the pilot of this aircraft.

Lieutenant Commander (O) J.A. Sanderson was born on 31 January 1933 and was aged thirty-one when he died.

10 February 1965 • D.H.110 Sea Vixen F.A.W.1 converted to F.A.W.2 • Serial Number XN709 • Number 890 Naval Air Squadron • Home Base – HMS *Heron* • RNAS Yeovilton, Ilchester, Somerset • Detached to HMS *Ark Royal*

The aircraft was launched from HMS *Ark Royal* before it had developed full power. It lost height and ditched into the Moray Firth 20 miles north-north-east of Lossiemouth and 200 yards ahead of the ship.[57] The pilot, Lieutenant B.L. Friend was slightly injured and survived the crash. Unfortunately, his observer did not.

Lieutenant (O) Victor John Blyther was born on 1 February 1941 and was aged twenty-four when he died.

26 February 1965 • D.H.110 Sea Vixen F.A.W.1 • Serial Number XJ483 • Number 890 Naval Air Squadron • Home Base – HMS *Heron* • RNAS Yeovilton, Ilchester, Somerset • Detached to HMS *Ark Royal*

This aircraft was damaged when it landed heavily on HMS *Ark Royal* while operating in the Moray Firth.[58] The port undercarriage leg collapsed. The crew were Lieutenants A. Munro and W.M. Hodgkins. From there, the aircraft went to HSA Chester for damage assessment and conversion to F.A.W.2. It was decided that it was uneconomical to convert and these attempts were abandoned. It was then sent to RNAS Yeovilton for use as spares.

8 March 1965 • D.H.110 Sea Vixen F.A.W.1 • Serial Number XJ478 • Number 766 Naval Air Squadron • Home Base – HMS *Heron* • RNAS Yeovilton, Ilchester, Somerset

---

On a downwind turn in the landing circuit, this aircraft stalled and dived into a field near the village of Limington, Somerset.[59] The aircraft burst into flames on impact and heavy smoke was still coming from the wreckage for about an hour after the incident. The severely burnt bodies of the two crewmen were removed from the wreckage. The site of the crash was three fields away from the nearest house.

Acting Sub Lieutenant (P) Anthony William Sambrook Sturgess, aged twenty-one, came from the Old Vicarage, Barton Turf. He is buried at Barton Turf churchyard, Norwich, in Norfolk.

Sub Lieutenant (O) Hugh Ian Robert Preus, aged twenty-two, came from Munster Road, Fulham. He was born on 4 January 1943. He is buried in the Royal Navy Cemetery in the church of St Bartholomew's, Yeovilton village. His final resting place is shown in Appendix 2.

Source: *Western Gazette*, 12 March 1965.

26 March 1965 • Hawker Hunter F.4 converted to T.7 • Serial Number WV319 • Instrument Training Flight • Home Base – HMS *Heron* • RNAS Yeovilton, Ilchester, Somerset

---

This aircraft suffered an engine failure on take-off from RNAS Yeovilton and crashed next to the main A303 road in a field at Tintinhull at 12.30 p.m.[60] Both of the crew successfully ejected. Sub Lieutenant Philip J. Searle and Lieutenant Commander Michael W. Haddock were slightly injured. Only two weeks previously the aircraft had been fitted with the latest Martin Baker ejection seats.

An eyewitness, Mrs Jesse Rogers of Townsend, Tintinhull, lived only 200 yards from the scene of the crash. She was reported to have been in her garden when she heard the spluttering sound of an aircraft passing overhead. Next she saw the flash of the aircraft as it hit the ground and exploded. Mrs Rogers had experienced all of this before. On 21 August 1954, a North American Harvard aircraft had crashed just 50 yards from her back door at the Mead, Ilchester.

Source: *Western Gazette*, 2 April 1965.

21 April 1965 • D.H.110 Sea Vixen F.A.W.1 • Serial Number XJ577 • Number 893 Naval Air Squadron • Home Base – HMS *Heron* • RNAS Yeovilton, Ilchester, Somerset • Detached to HMS *Victorious*

Both of this aircraft's engines caught fire immediately after a boost launch from HMS *Victorious* while operating in the East China Sea off Okinawa.[61] The pilot, Lieutenant (X) K.R. Alderson ejected safely. Unfortunately, his observer was found dead below the surface of the sea in a parachute that had failed to deploy.

Sub Lieutenant (O) John Eric Rainsbury was born on 21 June 1944 and was aged twenty when he died. He was buried at sea with full military honours.

31 May 1965 • D.H.110 Sea Vixen F.A.W.1 • Serial Number XN648 • Number 766 Naval Air Squadron • Home Base – HMS *Heron* • RNAS Yeovilton, Ilchester, Somerset

The pilot of this aircraft lost control in a spin from 23,000ft and crashed near Flat Tor on Dartmoor.[62] The aircraft made a large crater in the soil at its impact site, and it is now filled with water. A careful walk around the site will still reveal pieces of metal and fibre glass, all that remains of the wrecked aircraft in Grid Square SX6181. Sub Lieutenants D.J. Cotterill and M.R. Kenwood safely ejected.

8 September 1965 • D.H.110 Sea Vixen F.A.W.2 • Serial Number XP953 • Number 899 Naval Air Squadron • Home Base – HMS *Heron* • RNAS Yeovilton, Ilchester, Somerset • Detached to HMS *Eagle*

The pilot lost control of the aircraft while on approach to HMS *Eagle*, which was operating in the Mediterranean off the island of Malta.[63] The port wing struck the deck as it missed the wires. It then climbed steeply away to port and off the angled deck, entering the sea in an inverted position.

Sub Lieutenant (P) Raymond Matthews was born on 30 November 1942 and was aged twenty-two when he died.

Lieutenant (O) Andrew Philip Rayment was born on 12 July 1939 and was aged twenty-six when he died.

1966

3 January 1966 • Westland WS-58 Wessex H.U.5 • Serial Number XT462 • Number 845 Naval Air Squadron • Home Base – HMS *Heron* • RNAS Yeovilton, Ilchester, Somerset

This aircraft was written off when an unsecured main rotor broke up during a ground run at Culdrose, Cornwall.[64] All of the blades detached and the tail was severed. One large piece of the rotor blade passed through the whole length of the hangar. Sub Lieutenant C.W. Warne was injured during this incident.

9 February 1966 • D.H.110 Sea Vixen F.A.W.1 • Serial Number XJ567 • Number 766 Naval Air Squadron • Home Base – HMS *Heron* • RNAS Yeovilton, Ilchester, Somerset

The aircraft experienced a Master Reference Gyro failure whilst undertaking a formation recovery with a 'buddy' aircraft, from which it had become separated. This meant it had no blind-flying capability and this event occurred during a particularly wet and stormy night.

The aircraft came down somewhere near Manor Farm, about 1 mile east of Sparkford, Somerset, as it made a night instrument approach to RNAS Yeovilton.[65] The aircraft had buried itself into the soft wet field and had the nose and starboard wing down. The tail boom had snapped off and inverted itself on top of the wreck. The pilot, Sub Lieutenant P.M. Latham, was found in a nearby field, safe but injured.

Unfortunately, the observer, Lieutenant (O) Anthony Daniel Stevens, aged twenty-seven, was found dead in the wreckage. He is buried in the Royal Navy Cemetery in the church of St Bartholomew's, Yeovilton village. His final resting place is shown in Appendix 2.

17 March 1966 • D.H.110 Sea Vixen F.A.W.2 • Serial Number XS581 • Number 893 Naval Air Squadron • Home Base – HMS *Heron* • RNAS Yeovilton, Ilchester, Somerset

This aircraft was disembarked from HMS *Victorious* to RNAS Yeovilton. It was lost off Portland Bill, Dorset, whilst carrying out a night glow-worm attack with the frigate HMS *Zulu* (F124).[66]

At that time it was a requirement that naval aircraft would attack enemy surface vessels in defence of the fleet. To achieve this, a division of four aircraft would attack a friendly ship, at night, to simulate a night attack. The ship would tow a target about 1,000 yards behind it, producing a white plume of water that was easily identifiable from above. The division would then form up in line astern, the observer controlling. Each aircraft would carry four 3in flare rockets. They would fire the rockets to light up the target and then they would attack it. The theory was simple but in reality several aircraft were lost during these glow-worm attacks.

This particular aircraft attacked the towed target with 2in rockets and then crashed into the sea approximately 1,000 yards from the ship.

Lieutenant Commander (P) Simon Scott Thomas, aged thirty-one, is buried in the Royal Navy Cemetery in the church of St Bartholomew's, Yeovilton village. His final resting place is shown in Appendix 2.

The final resting place of Lieutenant (O) John William Harvey is not known.

22 March 1966 • D.H.110 Sea Vixen F.A.W.1 • Serial Number XN701 • Number 890 Naval Air Squadron • Home Base – HMS *Heron* • RNAS Yeovilton, Ilchester, Somerset • Detached to HMS *Ark Royal*

On a sortie out of the Naval Aircraft Support Unit from Changi airfield in Singapore, the aircraft went into a steep dive over the South China Sea to release a 1,000lb variable timed bomb.[67] The bomb prematurely exploded at the release point in the dive, killing the crew.

Lieutenant (P) James Forsyth Patrick. No other details are known about this officer.

Lieutenant (O) Colin Lightfoot was born on 1 December 1937 and was aged twenty-eight years when he died.

24 March 1966   • D.H.110 Sea Vixen F.A.W.1 • Serial Number XJ522 • Serial Number XJ513 • Number 766 Naval Air Squadron • Home Base – HMS *Heron* • RNAS Yeovilton, Ilchester, Somerset

Sea Vixen XJ522 was involved in a mid-air collision with Sea Vixen XJ513.[68] During a pre-arranged mass fighter tactics exercise between a dozen aircraft, both Vixens targeted the same Hunter aircraft, Serial No VL704. Both collided at approximately 25,000ft. Fortunately, they were heading in the same direction at the time but the nose of aircraft XJ522 came down heavily upon the tail boom of aircraft XJ513. This caused sufficient damage for the pilot to order 'eject' in Sea Vixen XJ522. Sea Vixen XJ513 was flown by two US navy officers, Lieutenant Charles Hussey and Lieutenant Ralph Magnus. They managed to land safely at RNAS Yeovilton.

Lieutenant (P) Ian MacKechnie and Sub Lieutenant (O) Edward Hughes successfully ejected from Sea Vixen XJ522 and were picked up by some forestry workers who had witnessed the crash. They were then taken to nearby Collihole Farm, where they were eventually collected by a Whirlwind SAR helicopter from RAF Chivenor and transported to Exeter Hospital for treatment. The aircraft crashed into a field near Christow, Teign Valley, Devon.

10 May 1966   • D.H.110 Sea Vixen F.A.W.1 • Serial Number XJ520 • Number 890 Naval Air Squadron • Home Base – HMS *Heron* • RNAS Yeovilton, Ilchester, Somerset • Detached to HMS *Ark Royal*

The aircraft was operating in the Indian Ocean off Beira, Mozambique, during a blockade patrol from HMS *Ark Royal*.[69] There was a failure of a gearbox, which led to a fuel leak and loss of the port engine, followed by the starboard engine. An unsuccessful attempt was made to refuel from a Scimitar.

The observer's seat failed to eject, so the hatch was jettisoned and the observer then separated himself from his seat. The aircraft was rolled twice but the observer was stuck half in and half out of the cockpit. The pilot waited as long as he could and was forced to eject at a very low altitude. The observer was killed when the aircraft struck the water. The pilot, Lieutenant (P) A.L. Tarver, who was slightly injured, was awarded the George Cross for his attempts to save his observer.

Lieutenant (O) John Michael Stuchbury sank with the aircraft.

This was the first of two aircraft to be lost that day from this same aircraft carrier. A Fairey Gannet A.E.W., Serial No XL475, was making a night landing on to HMS *Ark Royal* but missed the wires with its hook. As a consequence, the aircraft struck the deck very hard. The lower part of the nose wheel oleo broke off and the aircraft fell over the port side; however, the crew were saved.

8 July 1966   • D.H.110 Sea Vixen F.A.W.2 • Serial Number XP958 • Number 899 Naval Air Squadron • Home Base – HMS *Heron* • RNAS Yeovilton, Ilchester, Somerset • Detached to HMS *Eagle*

The aircraft was carrying out a night ground-controlled approach on to HMS *Eagle* whilst in the Strait of Johore, Malaysia.[70] The pilot had probably been distracted by a hydraulic failure which could have led him to experience disorientation on the final downward turn. Radar contact was suddenly lost. The aircraft's wreckage was eventually located in shallow water in the Straits of Jahore with the crew still aboard.

Sub Lieutenant (P) Nicholas de Lacy Parrett was cremated at the Mount Vernon Crematorium, Singapore.

Lieutenant (O) Timothy Martin Woodford was born on 31 August 1936 and was aged twenty-nine when he died. His final resting place is not known.

5 August 1966
• D.H.110 Sea Vixen F.A.W.2 • Serial Number XS586 • Number 893 Naval Air Squadron • Home Base – HMS *Heron* • RNAS Yeovilton, Ilchester, Somerset • Detached to HMS *Victorious*

After the catapult launch of this aircraft from HMS *Victorious*, the pilot reported that there was a loss of response to the controls, probably due to the launch speed being too slow. The aircraft stalled and the starboard wing dropped. The nose pitched up and the crew ejected at 200ft in a near-vertical bank.[71] The aircraft then crashed into the sea 40 miles south of the island of Gan in the Indian Ocean. Lieutenants C.R. Hunneyball and W. Hart were both injured in the ejection process but were safely rescued.

28 August 1966
• Auster J5-G Cirrus Autocar • Registration Number G-AMZV • Weston Airways Limited • Home Base – Weston Aerodrome • Weston-super-Mare

At about 0930 hrs on the 28th August, 1966, the aircraft took off from Weston Aerodrome for a local pleasure flight. Prior to the take-off the pilot asked for the passengers to be well strapped in as the flight was to include a stall turn. About five minutes after take-off the aircraft was seen to the north of the aerodrome flying in an easterly direction at about 800 feet. After making a slight dive it pulled up into a climbing turn to the left; during the turn the bank increased and the aircraft became inverted. By this time it was heading westwards and it continued to fly in this direction, still inverted, for some 200 to 500 yards. The wings were level and it lost height with the engine spluttering until at about 200 feet the nose was seen to rise and fall sharply; the aircraft then fell to the ground inverted with the nose about 45 degrees down. The pilot and the three passengers were killed instantly. There was no fire.

The sixty-three-year-old pilot was Mr L.A. Lisle and at the time of the accident he was the manager of Weston Aerodrome. His adult passenger was Mr R. Nunn, aged sixty-one, and two boys, Robert David Budd, aged ten, and Steven Paul Baker, aged nine. The adult passenger and the two boys all came from Knowle in Bristol.

Source: Board of Trade Civil Accident Report No EW/C/0146.

14 September 1966 • B.A.C. Jet Provost T.4 • Serial Number XP616 • Number 1 Flying Training School • Home Base – HMS *Heron* • RNAS Yeovilton, Ilchester, Somerset

---

The pilot was on a familiarisation flight in this aircraft with the RAF and detached to Linton-on-Ouse. In bad visibility, Sub Lieutenant (P) Derek Clark Breen, aged twenty-one, flew his aircraft into the ground during a navigational exercise.[72] He crashed on Rievaulx Moor (known locally as 'Roppa Moor'), Newgate Bank, which is approximately 4½ miles to the north-west of Hemsley, Yorkshire. The resulting fireball from the crash set fire to the moor and it took emergency services some two and a half hours to extinguish it. The location of his burial site is not known.

15 September 1966 • D.H.110 Sea Vixen F.A.W.1 converted to F.A.W.2 • Serial Number XJ606 • Number 893 Naval Air Squadron • Home Base – HMS *Heron* • RNAS Yeovilton, Ilchester, Somerset • Detached to HMS *Victorious*

This aircraft found itself running low on fuel off the Philippines and was diverted to the airfield at Cubi Point. Both of the engines flamed out in the landing circuit but the crew, Lieutenant D.B. Knowles and Sub Lieutenant W.W. Burgher, successfully ejected, although Sub Lieutenant Burgher was slightly injured in the process.[73]

The aircraft crashed on to a road and struck a passing US navy bus. Unfortunately, the driver of this vehicle was badly burned and later died from his injuries.

29 September 1966 • Hawker Hunter F.4 converted to T.8C • Serial Number XF983 • Number 759 Naval Air Squadron • Home Base – HMS *Goldcrest* • RNAS Brawdy • Pembrokeshire, South-West Wales

---

This aircraft crashed on take-off, following an engine fire. The instructor was killed because he ejected too low for the parachute to deploy properly.[74] The student pilot, Sub-Lieutenant P. Lewis was injured during the ejection process. The aircraft crashed into a field next to the farmhouse at Rhosgranog Farm in Llandcloy.

Lieutenant (P) David John (Pete) Starling, aged twenty-five, was born on 13 October 1940. He is buried in the RN Cemetery at Yeovilton village, Somerset. His final resting place is shown in Appendix 2.

1967

3 January 1967 • D.H.110 Sea Vixen F.A.W.2 • Serial Number XS588 • Number 892 Naval Air Squadron • Home Base – HMS *Heron* • RNAS Yeovilton, Ilchester, Somerset • Detached to HMS *Hermes*

This aircraft made a bad landing approach to HMS *Hermes* and was waved off.[75] It landed on the angled deck in a nose-up attitude. The engine consequently stalled and as a result the aircraft crashed into the Mediterranean Sea. This occurred about 50 yards from the ship off the island of Malta. Lieutenant (P) D.R. Gregory, the pilot, was injured, but sadly his observer was killed.

Lieutenant (O) Peter Bellinger Brodie was born on 16 June 1940 and was twenty-six when he died.

23 January 1967 • D.H.110 Sea Vixen F.A.W.1 converted to F.A.W.2 • Serial Number XJ564 • Number 892 Naval Air Squadron • Home Base – HMS *Heron* • RNAS Yeovilton, Ilchester, Somerset • Detached to HMS *Hermes*

On launching from HMS *Hermes*, the ship suddenly carried out a high-speed turn. The instrument panel of the aircraft collapsed into the pilot's lap, probably due to the failure to secure it properly after maintenance, and the aeroplane rotated to a critical nose-up attitude. The crew ejected just ahead of the ship near Gibraltar.[76]

Sadly, Lieutenant (P) James Robin Smith was killed in the incident. He was born on 23 December 1941 and was aged twenty-five when he died. He came from Loughton, Essex. His observer, Lieutenant (O) P.S.J. Love, was safely rescued by the plane guard Wessex.

Unfortunately, the disaster did not end there. Another SAR Wessex helicopter, Serial No XS883, crashed and was also lost when it dashed to the rescue. Lieutenant John Edward Betterton was killed and Naval Airman D.P. Hodgson received injuries in the accident. Naval Airmen J. Bauld and A.R. Chadwick fortunately escaped without any injuries.

30 January 1967 • D.H.110 Sea Vixen F.A.W.2 • Serial Number XS585 • Number 893 Naval Air Squadron • Home Base – HMS *Heron* • RNAS Yeovilton, Ilchester, Somerset • Detached to HMS *Victorious*

The pilot over-rotated this aircraft during a night launch from HMS *Victorious* while in the South China Sea, 70 miles west of Subic, Philippines.[77] The aircraft rolled to starboard, where the pilot, Lieutenant (P) A.C. Selman successfully ejected. The observer did not eject in time and was killed.

Lieutenant (O) Richard Anthony Brown was born on 9 March 1941 and was twenty-five when he lost his life.

6 June 1967 • Westland Scout A.H.1 • Serial Number XV120 • Number 10 Flight • Home Base – RAF Filton • Bristol

Just before 9 a.m., the screaming engine of a helicopter that had taken off on a communications flight to Castle Martin, Pembrokeshire, announced a helicopter in trouble. A high-pitched engine noise, above a fog-shrouded Long Cross housing estate in Filton, could plainly be heard. The helicopter could be seen to have an orange glow through the thick mist and was shedding pieces of metal. It came down and crashed into a telegraph pole some 30 yards from the nearest houses.

The aircraft broke up on impact and blazed furiously, killing the three occupants, despite the best efforts of a local scrap dealer, Mr Stanley Brown, to drag the injured clear. Women from the housing estates ran to the blazing wreck with pans of water in an effort to help extinguish the flames, but to no avail.

455563 Captain Norman Wallace Royal Army Pay Corps, aged twenty-eight years, was the pilot. He came from Southend.

74286 Brigadier George Butler DSO, MC was aged forty-nine. He is buried in the St Michaels and All Angels churchyard, Cornwood, South Devon. He came from Tidworth.

23994261 Lance Corporal John Kirton Carr, REME, aged nineteen, is buried in the Tidworth Military Cemetery. He lived in Oadsby, Leicestershire.

8 August 1967 • Wessex H.A.S.1 converted to H.A.S.3 • Serial Number XP137 • Westland Aircraft Works • Home Base – Westland's Airfield • Yeovil, Somerset

The production test pilot, Mr R.R. Crayton was conducting a test flight.[78] Near the village of Rampisham, Dorset the flotation bags of the aircraft suddenly inflated. This was thought to be caused by a powerful BBC transmitter aerial that was located nearby.

The pilot assumed that he had suffered engine failure and promptly went into auto-rotation. He flared too high in order to miss cars in the village and made a very heavy landing. The helicopter rolled to port and the rotor blades struck the ground. All four of the crew suffered slight injuries in this accident and the aircraft was declared a Category 4. It was repaired and entered service with the Royal Navy.

Eventually it went to a registration of A2633 and was last sighted as a wreck on the Lizard Peninsula at Predannack, Cornwall, in the Fleet Air Arm Fire School in March 2011.

12 September 1967 • D.H.C1 Chipmunk T.10 • Serial Number WP838 • RAF Bristol University Air Squadron • Home Base – Filton Airfield • Bristol

Chipmunk Serial No WP838 crashed 2 miles south-west of Portishead, Somerset, after it had collided with Chipmunk WK610 at 3,500ft when flying in formation.[79] It crashed into a hillside and caught fire, though it quickly burnt out. The aircraft was successfully abandoned by both of the crew.

12 September 1967 • D.H.C1 Chipmunk T.10 • Serial Number WK610 • Bristol University Air Squadron • Home Base – Filton Airfield • Bristol

Chipmunk Serial No WK610 collided with Chipmunk WP838 when flying in formation. It dived into marshland just south of Walton-in-Gordano.[80] It is believed that most of the wreckage of this aircraft is still fairly intact, as she was never recovered from the marshy land, which is now a nature reserve. The aircraft was successfully abandoned by both of the crew.

21 September 1967 • H.S. Kestrel F.G.A.1 • Serial Number XS693 • Bristol Siddeley Engines • RAF Filton • Bristol

During a flight from Filton to Boscombe Down, the engine suddenly surged and was badly damaged when the pilot failed to close the HP cock quickly enough. He was unable to relight the engine and was forced to eject at 200ft, at High Post near Stonehenge, Wiltshire, when he realised he had insufficient height to reach the airfield at Boscombe Down.

The aircraft was one of only three that remained in the UK after the nine original aircraft were split up between the UK, USA and Germany for evaluation. This aircraft was later fitted with the wings from XS694 and is now preserved in Langley, Virginia, USA.

21 September 1967 • Vickers 808 Viscount • Serial Number EI-AKK • Aer Lingus • Dublin

On approach to Filton and during foggy conditions, the pilot misaligned his aircraft with the runway, which he then attempted to correct. In doing so the starboard wingtip and the No 4 propeller hit the runway. The pilot attempted an overshoot but this was not possible due to obstructions in the aircraft's path some little way ahead. The pilot then selected to make a wheels-up landing. The aircraft hit a tree and crashed through a hedge before coming to rest in a field. One side of the aircraft was ripped open; the starboard wing had snapped and a propeller had been broken off on the port engine.

Ten people were injured during the incident, but only three of them, including an air hostess, were deemed sufficiently serious enough to be detained in hospital. The Viscount carried four crew members and seventeen passengers. The aircraft was a write off. This was the first major crash at the airport since it had opened in 1956.

Source: *The Times*, 22 September 1967.

7 December 1967 • Westland Whirlwind H.C.C.12 • Serial Number XR487 • Queen's Flight • Home Base – RAF Benson

During a flight from Benson to Yeovil, the main rotor hub and blade detached itself due to fatigue failure of the drive shaft. The helicopter crashed at Brightwalton, near Newbury, Berkshire, killing four people. The crashing helicopter narrowly missed a house by some 100 yards and came down in a field near Malthouse Farm, Brightwalton.

150493 Squadron Leader Jack Harry Liversidge DFC, AFC was the captain of the helicopter. He was aged forty-nine when he died and was cremated at the Headington Crematorium, Oxford.

4110362 Flight Lieutenant Ronald Fisher was the navigator. He was aged thirty-six when he died and is buried in St Helen's churchyard, Benson, Oxfordshire, in the RAF section, Row 2, Grave 67.[81]

Air Commodore John Blount DFC, aged forty-eight, was the captain of the Queen's Flight when he was killed. His name is not recorded on the Armed Forces Roll of Honour. He was a retired air officer in the RAF Reserve of Officers, from which the captain of the Queen's Flight is always selected.

609039 Squadron Leader Michael William Hermon, Queen's Flight engineering officer. He was aged thirty-two when he died and was cremated at the Headington Crematorium, Oxford.

The royal family had never flown in this particular aircraft because of the rule that any aircraft carrying them had to have more than one engine. The Duke of Edinburgh, however, had often piloted this helicopter. This aircraft was one of two Whirlwind Mk 12s in the flight. This was first fatal crash of the Queen's Flight since its formation in May 1937, having successfully completed 911 journeys involving 1,200 hours' flying time.

Source: *The Times*, 8 December 1967.

1968

26 January 1968   • Hawker Hunter T.8 • Serial Number XL582 • Heron Flight Yeovilton • Home Base – HMS *Heron* • RNAS Yeovilton, Ilchester, Somerset

---

After taking off from RNAS Yeovilton, a loud bang was heard when the aircraft had reached about 900ft. The engine rapidly wound down and a fire warning was given.[82]

Lieutenant Commander Peter Richard Sheppard AFC, aged thirty-four, of Dowlish Wake, Somerset, and Lieutenant Robin Frank Shercliff, aged twenty-six of Worthing, Essex, both safely ejected but were injured in the process. The aircraft came down in an open field 1 mile south of Somerton, Somerset.

Some internet sources attribute this crash as happening at Lee-on-Solent, but this is not so.

Source: *The Times*, 27 January 1968.

16 February 1968   • D.H.110 Sea Vixen F.A.W.1 converted to F.A.W.2 • Serial Number XJ516 • Number 893 Naval Air Squadron • Home Base – HMS *Heron* • RNAS Yeovilton, Ilchester, Somerset

---

This aircraft crashed on its approach to RNAS Yeovilton during a pairs landing.[83] Its port wing dropped and then the aircraft turned over. Fortunately the crew of the aircraft, Lieutenant (P) Charlie E. Beilby and Sub Lieutenant (O) John Sydney Maurice Chandler, both successfully ejected before the aircraft crashed south of the runway. Both of the crew were injured in the ejection process.

9 April 1968   • D.H.110 Sea Vixen F.A.W.2 • Serial Number XS579 • Number
899 Naval Air Squadron • Home Base – HMS *Heron* • RNAS Yeovilton, Ilchester,
Somerset • Detached from HMS *Eagle*

The pilot of this aircraft likely suffered from disorientation as he made a glow-worm attack upon RAF Reliant's splash target in the South China Sea.[84] The aircraft failed to pull out from a 20° dive and was lost. Sadly, both of the crew lost their lives.

Lieutenant (P) Hedley James Williams was born on 22 January 1940 and was twenty-eight when he died.

Lieutenant (O) Cresswell Swann. No other details are known about this officer.

24 July 1968   • D.H.110 Sea Vixen F.A.W.1 converted to F.A.W.2 • Serial
Number XJ489 • Number 899 Naval Air Squadron • Home Base – HMS *Heron* • RNAS
Yeovilton, Ilchester, Somerset

Number 899 Squadron were disembarked from HMS *Eagle* and operating out of RNAS Yeovilton. On the second run of a dummy-landing circuit the aircraft suddenly side-slipped and crashed into marshy ground, exploding on impact.[85] This occurred alongside the Braunton toll road about half a mile west of the airfield at RAF Chivenor, North Devon. Wreckage covered a fairly limited area. Pieces of the engine and wings were scattered in a roadside dyke and some wreckage was strewn across the road.

Lieutenant (P) Frederick Robert Duncan Booth, aged twenty-six, is buried in the Royal Navy Cemetery in the church of St Bartholomew's, Yeovilton village. His final resting place is shown in Appendix 2.

Lieutenant (O) Donald Robert McKenzie is buried in the Royal Navy Cemetery in the church of St Bartholomew's, Yeovilton village. His final resting place is shown in Appendix 2.

Source: *Western Gazette*, 26 July 1968.

30 July 1968   • D.H.110 Sea Vixen F.A.W.2 • Serial Number XS578 (probably)
• Assumed to be Number 899 Naval Air Squadron • Home Base – HMS *Heron* • RNAS
Yeovilton, Ilchester, Somerset

The Times, dated 31 July 1968, reported a near miss that could easily have had horrific consequences. While two children, Linda Winnall, aged nine, and her brother Christopher, aged five, were playing at holding a tea party in the garden of their house in Smallways Lane, Chilton-upon-Polden, a piece of aircraft debris some 4ft long fell into the garden of a neighbour, smashing a cast-iron boiler.

Linda ran in and told her mother, Mrs Maureen Winnall, what had happened. They both went out into the lane outside the house, just as another piece of wreckage, several inches long and smothered in oil, landed a few feet away from the child.

An RNAS Yeovilton spokesman later confirmed that the pilot of the Sea Vixen on a routine flight felt a severe thump at 23,000ft in the rear half of the port drop tank. It called up another aircraft to inspect it. This aircraft confirmed that parts of the aircraft were indeed missing. The aircraft was minus its undercarriage 'D' door and fairing; also a part of its tank was missing. The Sea Vixen returned safely to Yeovilton. The aircraft was being crewed by Sub Lieutenants O.G. Walters and D.J. Hughes.

It was nothing unusual for military aircraft to lose parts while flying and records indicate it was a somewhat regular occurrence. The wonder was that no one was killed or injured from these falling pieces. Other aircraft of the same type that lost parts in flight were: XJ476 lost its nose-wheel panel in flight on 25 August 1969; XJ477 lost its canopy panel at night on 29 March 1965; XJ480 also lost its panel in flight on 11 November 1965. There were many other incidents.

1 October 1968   • English Electric Canberra B.2 • Serial Number WH715 • Empire Test School • Home Base – RAF Boscombe Down • Wiltshire

This aircraft, with only the pilot on board, came down just before 2 p.m. on the A358 at Viney Bridge, and exploded on impact.[86] It came out of cloud on an asymmetric approach. The crashing plane wreaked havoc on Rivermead Garage, whose owner, Mr Ron Meecham, was unfortunately working there at the time. He was very badly burned but survived. Mr Arthur Hoskins from Axminster, a builder employed at the nearby South Western Electricity Board Depot at Viney Bridge was also very badly burned, but he too survived. He had called at the garage for petrol when the accident happened. Another tragedy occurred when fifty-five-year-old Charlie Penman, a foreman at the nearby Crewkerne textiles factory, rushed to the crash to render assistance. He died of a heart attack as he reached the pilot's ejector seat.

It is generally acknowledged that the pilot, a Frenchman who was training to be a test pilot, stayed with the aircraft until the last possible moment in order to minimise the crash. His unselfish actions enabled the plane to just miss the Severalls Park and Park View housing estates. The crashing aircraft ended up no more than 50 yards from an occupied caravan. The force of the crash pushed a road sign 10ft down into the ground, broke a major water main and forced the closure of the road for over five hours.

The pilot ejected too late and was found still strapped into his badly smashed-up ejector seat. Had he not stayed with his aircraft there was a chance that it could have hit the occupied Crewkerne textiles factory and the death toll would have been extremely high.

Capitane Depui was nearing the end of his year long course and would have returned to France and be promoted to the rank of Major. It was acknowledged by his peers that this very talented officer, had he lived, would probably have gone on to attain one of the highest ranks within the French air force.

Source: *Western Gazette.*

25 November 1968 • Fairey Gannet A.E.W.3 • Serial Number XL451 • Number 849 Naval Air Squadron • Home Base – HMS *Heron* • RNAS Yeovilton, Ilchester, Somerset • Detached to HMS *Hermes*

On launching from the ship, the port wing of this aircraft suddenly folded up and it plunged into the sea.[87] This air crash occurred off Okinawa, Japan, killing the crew. They were: Acting Sub Lieutenant (P) Gordon Louttit Still, Lieutenant (O) Thomas Winston Tracey and Sub Lieutenant (O) Nicholas J. Broadway, aged nineteen.

30 November 1968 • D.H.C.1 Chipmunk T.10 • Serial Number WB573 • RAF South Wales University Air Squadron • Home Base – RAF ST Athan • South Wales

This aircraft flew into a hill called Dunkery Beacon, the highest hill in Exmoor, during bad weather, 3 miles south of Porlock whilst on a ferry flight to Swansea.[88] The pilot escaped but the aircraft was written off.

1969

9 January 1969 • D.H.110 Sea Vixen F.A.W.1 converted to F.A.W.2 • Serial Number XJ559 • Number 766 Naval Air Squadron • Home Base – HMS *Heron* • RNAS Yeovilton, Ilchester, Somerset

On a practice single-engine approach to the runway, the aircraft developed a power failure.[89] The jet plunged into a field of marshy ground approximately half a mile from the A372 road near Catsgore, Ilchester, and scattered wreckage over two fields near Kingsdon, Somerset. Sub Lieutenant (P) David Hansom, aged twenty, and Sub Lieutenant (O) Martin Granger-Holcombe, aged twenty-four, both safely ejected from 700ft. Both were rescued by a helicopter from RNAS Yeovilton and taken to Yeovil District Hospital suffering from minor back injuries.

Source: *Western Gazette*, 10 January 1969.

15 January 1969 • Sikorsky WS-61 Sea King H.A.S.1 • Serial Number XV372 • Westland Aircraft Works • Home Base – Westland's Airfield • Yeovil, Somerset

This aircraft was being piloted by Mr J.L. Barnes, test pilot for Rolls-Royce (Bristol Engine Division).[90] The helicopter was on an engine test flight when it force landed near West Harptree on the Mendip Hills, following a double engine failure, due to ingestion of ice dislodged from the windscreen. The starboard sponson collapsed on touchdown, the main rotor struck the ground and the aircraft rolled over. The aircraft was flying from Bristol to Yeovil at the time. The pilot and crew escaped without injury and the aircraft was then allocated to ground instruction use. It was classified as a Category 5 loss.

13 February 1969   • Meteor T.7 • Serial Number WL350 • Fleet Requirements Unit • Home Base – Hurn Airport (now Bournemouth Airport) • Bournemouth

The aircraft had left Hurn airport and flew to RNAS Yeovilton to carry out some routine manoeuvres which it successfully accomplished. It then flew back towards Hurn airport but unfortunately developed problems on the return leg and entered a flat spin. The aircraft came to earth near Hedge End Farm, Turnworth, Dorset. The crew could not eject because the hood failed to jettison correctly and in good time. This was caused by insufficient air flow over the hood.

The aircraft was being flown by Flight Lieutenant R.V. Patchett RAF (on his last flight from the Central Flying School) and Lieutenant R.E.M. Wooley RN. On the day of the accident Lieutenant Wooley was being given his final test as an instructor on this aircraft type.

A Dorset farmer, John Tory, ran half a mile from his farm to the scene of the crash and managed to pull both men from the Meteor's cockpit, but unfortunately they had been killed. Mr Tory was later awarded the Queen's Commendation for Brave Conduct for his efforts to save the two pilots.

On Saturday 15 September 2009, a stone memorial was placed at the spot where the two men died.

5017081 Flight Lieutenant Robert Valen Patchett's home airfield was RAF Rissington, Gloucestershire. He was born on 29 August 1937 and was aged thirty-one when he lost his life. He is buried in the Public Cemetery at Station Road, Bourton, Cheltenham, and can be found at Grave 419.

Lieutenant Robert Wooley had only just retired from the Royal Navy and left to become an instructor at FRU Hurn airport. It is not known where he is buried.

Source: www.airfieldinformationexchange.org.

31 March 1969   • Hawker Hunter F.4 converted to T.8 • Serial Number WW661 • RNAS Yeovilton Station Flight • Home Base – HMS *Heron* • Ilchester, Somerset

This aircraft crashed about 100 yards from some cottages at the Mead, Ilchester. It suffered a compressor failure after rolling from a ground-controlled ascent at 150ft.[91] The aircraft was flying a routine air-experience sortie, doing touch and goes on the airfield, when the engines failed. There was a loud bang followed by severe vibration and both of the crew safely ejected. Residents in the nearby village of Ilchester saw two parachutes floating down but thought that they were part of a display being put on to celebrate the commissioning of No 892 Naval Air Squadron, flying Phantom aircraft, at RNAS Yeovilton. This squadron was commanded at the time by Lieutenant Commander Brian Davies.

Midway through the same day, a Sea Venom F.A.W.21, WW207, being flown by Mr John Steele, who was working for Airwork Services Ltd based at Yeovilton, made a crash-landing on a bed of foam with one wheels up on the airfield. It caused minor damage to this aircraft.

The Hawker Hunter was being flown by Lieutenant Keith Alfred Harris, aged thirty, of Bradford Abbas, with his crewman being Sub Lieutenant Owen S. Barwood, a twenty-one-year-old Australian. Both men escaped unhurt from the incident.

Source: *Western Gazette.*

1 May 1969   • D.H.110 Sea Vixen F.A.W.1 converted to F.A.W.2 • Serial Number XJ521 • Number 766 Naval Air Squadron • Home Base – HMS *Heron* • RNAS Yeovilton, Ilchester, Somerset

The pressure instruments of this aircraft failed during combat training because the two pitot heads had broken off. A pitot head is a measuring instrument consisting of a combined pitot tube and static tube that measures total and static pressure and is used in aircraft to measure airspeed.

As a precautionary measure, the student navigator was ordered to eject at 16,000ft over the Bristol Channel, which he did. Unfortunately, during this ejection process the observer somehow broke his arm. His body was later recovered from the sea, where he was found drowned by a passing merchant ship, just north of the town of Minehead in Somerset. Both his body and parachute were recovered at the scene.

The pilot, Sub Lieutenant (P) N.F. Charles, skilfully managed to return the aircraft to RNAS Yeovilton, where a safe landing was made.

Sub Lieutenant (O) Ian Scott Sutton, aged twenty-one, was born on 20 November 1947. He is buried in the Royal Navy Cemetery in the church of St Bartholomew's, Yeovilton village. His final resting place is shown in Appendix 2.

Source: *Western Gazette.*

17 May 1969   • Westland WS-58 Wessex H.U.5 • Serial Number XT774 • Number 845 Naval Air Squadron • Home Base – HMS *Heron* • RNAS Yeovilton, Ilchester, Somerset • Detached to HMS *Bulwark*

Whilst sailing off Dhekelia, Cyprus, this helicopter was delivering an under-slung load of a trailer to the ship. It suddenly lost power and landed heavily on the deck, collapsing the port undercarriage.[92] It rolled on to its port side and scattered the wreckage of its rotor blades across the deck, killing one of the ground crew and injuring Able Seaman Willis. As part of an exercise being run by HQ (UK) Commandos, the author was on Dhekelia beach delivering a message to the beach master when the news came in over the radio that a helicopter had crashed on board and all movement to the ship was to cease immediately.

088936 Able Seaman Aneuryn Brian Hughes was born on 13 February 1950 and was aged just nineteen years when he was killed.

28 May 1969   • Supermarine Scimitar F.1 • Serial Number XD214 • Airwork FRU
• Home Base – Hurn Airport (now Bournemouth Airport) • Bournemouth

---

Whilst landing at RNAS Yeovilton, the nose wheel of this aircraft collapsed and a
fire started in the nose-wheel bay.[93] The aircraft was later declared a write off and
scrapped at RNAY Fleetlands, Hampshire.

5 June 1969   • D.H.110 Sea Vixen F.A.W.2 • Serial Number XS584 • Number
893 Naval Air Squadron • Home Base – HMS *Heron* • RNAS Yeovilton, Ilchester, Somerset

---

Both the pilot and observer were unfortunately killed in an air crash involving this
vehicle off Hartland Point, Devon.[94] They were flying a night low-level sortie from
Yeovilton under the control of a Gannet A.E.W. when their aircraft suddenly disappeared from its radar. XS584 had flown into the sea. A second Sea Vixen in the
vicinity reported a flash and an explosion.

Lieutenant (P) Ronald James Badenhorst, aged twenty-eight, was born on
28 December 1940 in South Africa. The sea is his grave.

Lieutenant (O) Roger Stuart Cox, aged twenty-three, was born on 26 December
1945 in Norwich, Norfolk. The sea is his grave.

2 August 1969   • Morane Saulnier Commodore MS.893 • Registration Number
G-AWAB • Privately Owned

The pilot intended to fly from Lansdown Racecourse to Thruxton, Wiltshire,
and thence to Denham, Buckinghamshire. Before leaving home he checked
with Thruxton that the weather there was suitable for landing. According to a
witness, by the time the pilot arrived at his aircraft visibility had fallen to about
150 metres due to low cloud rolling across the airstrip. A short time later, when
the pilot was heard starting and running up the engine, visibility had deteriorated to about 50 metres. The aircraft was heard taxiing down the shorter grass
strip then back-tracking along grass 'runway' 25 (elevation 770 feet AMSL) to
the north-eastern end, a total distance of approximately 700 metres.

Shortly afterwards, between 1025 and 1030 hrs and without a further power
check being heard, the aircraft took off and climbed away in cloud towards the
south-west. A few minutes later the aircraft was heard returning towards the
airstrip, its engine faltering or cutting out several times. It crashed into a steep
tree-covered slope some 100 feet below and 150 metres south-east of the take-
off point. Because of the low cloud which enveloped Lansdown plateau no one
saw the aircraft crash. There was no fire but the pilot was killed instantly.

The pilot was forty-three-year-old Mr Thomas Wynne Brailsford. He had a total
flying experience of 299 hours before he crashed.

Source: Board of Trade Accident Investigation Report, September 1970.

7 October 1969 • D.H.112 Sea Venom F.A.W.21 • Serial Number WW186 • RNAS Yeovilton Station Flight • Home Base – RNAS Yeovilton • Ilchester, Somerset

The aircraft, piloted by Lieutenant Peter Shepherd, made a nose and starboard wheels-up landing on the runway.[95] It was initially repaired, but again on 29 October it experienced a hydraulic failure. On 11 November it once more experienced problems with a warning light. Shepherd ejected and landed in a cornfield, damaging his ankles. The aircraft was struck off charge during December 1969 and ended up being used for fire-fighting training on the RNAS Yeovilton dump.

1970s

1970

19 January 1970   • Vickers 701 Viscount • Serial Number G-AMOA • Cambrian Airways • Cardiff, Wales

This aircraft made an exceptionally heavy landing at Bristol Lulsgate airport (now known as Bristol International). The aircraft had actually broken its back but this was only noticed because it was on a sloping apron and it suddenly rolled backwards. The brakes were fiercely applied to stop the roll and it was only then that the aircraft suddenly dipped down and remained in that position. Up until that moment there had been no indication that there had been anything wrong with the aircraft, despite the heavy landing. The crew of four and the fifty-nine passengers escaped unhurt. The flight was due to have gone on to Rhoose airport (later to be renamed Cardiff airport), but as it was the plane was declared a write-off and finally scrapped in 1971.

3 May 1970   • McDonnell-Douglas Phantom F.G.1 • Serial Number XV566 • Number 892 Naval Air Squadron • Home Base – HMS *Heron* • RNAS Yeovilton, Ilchester, Somerset • Detached to HMS *Ark Royal*

This aircraft disappeared whilst under radar control as a target for low-level A1 intercepts in the English Channel, at approximately 8.25 a.m. It was suspected that the pilot became disorientated due to the prevalent weather conditions. Radar contact was lost 30 miles north of Alderney.[1] The aircraft crashed into the sea and both of the crew were killed.

Lieutenant (P) Alexander Stewart was born on 16 January 1941 and was aged twenty-nine when he died. Although his body was never recovered, there is a brass plaque that commemorates him in the Royal Naval Cemetery and it is recorded in Appendix 2.

Lieutenant (O) Phillip John Coombes was born on 6 August 1943 and was aged twenty-six when he died. The sea is his last resting place.

6 May 1970   • Fairey Gannet A.E.W.3 • Serial Number XR433 • Number 849 Naval Air Squadron • Home Base – NASU Brawdy (HMS *Goldcrest*) • St David's, South Wales

Whilst carrying out a night-time flying exercise and on a ground-controlled ascent night approach to RNAS Yeovilton, a fire was reported.[2] The aircraft crashed into a field about a mile from Yeovilton and on the outskirts of the village of West Camel. It burnt out, killing its crew of two.

Sub Lieutenant (P) Stuart Clive I'Anson, aged twenty-four, was born on 20 February 1946 at Hazel Grove in Cheshire. He is buried at Brawdy Cemetery in South Wales and can be found in Row 3, Grave 38.

Sub Lieutenant (O) John Richard Holland, aged twenty-two, was born on 6 December 1947 in Lewisham, London. He is buried at Brawdy Cemetery in South Wales and can be found in Row 3, Grave 39, next to his fellow crew member.

Source: *Western Gazette*, 15 May 1970.

10 May 1970   • D.H.110 Sea Vixen F.A.W.1, converted to F.A.W.2 • Serial Number XN702 • Number 893 Naval Air Squadron • Home Base – HMS *Heron* • RNAS Yeovilton, Ilchester, Somerset • Detached to HMS *Hermes*

This aircraft was badly damaged during a deck landing accident on board HMS *Hermes* when its nose oleo collapsed.[3] The pilot was Lieutenant Michael J. Beveridge. The aircraft was off loaded and transferred by lighter to Limassol Harbour, Cyprus, on 27 May 1970 and on the following day was then towed to MU RAF Akrotiri. The aircraft was finally struck off charge on 20 July 1970.

26 August 1970   • D.H.110 Sea Vixen F.A.W.1, converted to F.A.W.2 • Serial Number XN686 • 'A' Squadron A&AEE • Home Base – Boscombe Down

During low-speed handling tests at 135 knots, it appears as if the flaps were not lowered and control of the aircraft was lost at 5,000ft.[4] The aircraft then spun but at an insufficient recovery height. Flight Lieutenant Richard H.G. Statham RAF and Flight Lieutenant David C. Allardyce RAF both ejected safely but suffered minor injuries as their aircraft crashed into the sea off Burnham-on-Sea.[5] This conflicts with other sources, which quote this aircraft as crashing in open ground near Shepton Mallet.[6]

15 September 1970 • D.H.110 Sea Vixen F.A.W.1, converted to F.A.W.2 • Serial Number XJ561 • Number 766 Naval Air Squadron • Home Base – HMS *Heron* • RNAS Yeovilton, Ilchester, Somerset

This aircraft made a safe and arrested wheels-up landing on a bed of foam at RNAS Yeovilton after its starboard undercarriage door had blown off during its flight.[7] It was badly damaged and it was not considered economical to repair the aeroplane. The aircraft was transferred to the fire section. At the time of the incident the aircraft was being flown by Lieutenant Commander Peter Richard Sheppard with an unknown RAF observer.

13 November 1970 • D.H.110 Sea Vixen F.A.W.2 • Serial Number XP955 • Number 899 Naval Air Squadron • Home Base – HMS *Heron* • RNAS Yeovilton, Ilchester, Somerset • Detached to HMS *Eagle*

This aircraft was taxiing with its wings folded when its starboard wing fold joint hit the tip of the nose of Sea Vixen XN706.[8] It then appeared to over-rotate on the catapult launch and its port wing dropped. The crew ejected as the aircraft crashed into the sea off the port bow. The ship was off the coast of Morayshire at the time.

Flying Officer Geoff M. Hamlyn RAF ejected safely, but the pilot was killed.

Lieutenant (P) Bruce Nelson Harrison was born on 21 October 1944 and was aged twenty-six when he died.

1971

2 March 1971 • Percival P.57 Sea Prince T.1 • Serial Number WP312 • RN Detachment • Home Base – RAF Church Fenton

During a navigation exercise, this aircraft collided at 4,000ft with a Jet Provost T.5A, Serial No XW300, of No 1 FTS over Church Fenton, North Yorkshire, in cloudless sky conditions. WP312 crashed 2 miles south-east of Selby Railway Station, killing its pilot. XW300's crew of two were also tragically killed in this accident.[9] Both aircraft came out from RAF Linton-on-Ouse.

The pilot of WP312, Commander David John Dunbar-Dempsey was born on 19 July 1933 and was thirty-seven when he died. His final resting place can be found at St Bartholomew's Royal Navy Cemetery, Yeovilton. He was the senior naval officer at RAF Linton-on-Ouse at the time. Details are shown in Appendix 2. His name is recorded in the Fleet Air Arm Roll of Honour as DunbarDempsey.

507722 Flight Lieutenant Elwyn David Bell RAF was South African and he was one of the two men killed in the Jet Provost. He was aged twenty-nine when he died and was cremated at the York Crematorium. The name of the other crewman of the Jet Provost is not known.

19 May 1971 • McDonnell-Douglas Phantom F.G.1 • Serial Number XT862 • Number 767 Naval Air Squadron • Home Base – HMS *Heron* • RNAS Yeovilton, Somerset

Both engines of this aircraft flamed out in a recovery from a steep climb. The aircraft entered a spin at 31,000ft and the aircraft crashed into the sea approximately 25 miles from Newquay, Cornwall.[10] Commander (P) William Hawley ejected at 6,000ft and Lieutenant Peter Stephen Jonathan Love ejected at 5,000ft. Both men were successfully recovered by helicopter. Lieutenant Love suffered slight injuries.

28 June 1971   • McDonnell-Douglas Phantom F.G.1 • Serial Number XV565 •
Number 892 Naval Air Squadron • Home Base – HMS *Heron* • RNAS Yeovilton, Ilchester,
Somerset • Detached to HMS *Ark Royal*

This aircraft was flying from the US Naval Air Station at Cecil Field and spun at low
level during air combat drills. The crew, Lieutenant D.A. Hill and Lieutenant Martin
Joseph William Granger-Holcombe, ejected as their aircraft crashed into the Atlantic
Ocean off Florida, USA.[11] Both of the crew were safely recovered by an SAR helicopter from the US Naval Air Station, Jacksonville.

6 July 1971   • D.H.110 Sea Vixen F.A.W.1 converted to F.A.W.2 • Serial
Number XN687 • Number 890 Naval Air Squadron • Home Base – HMS *Heron* • RNAS
Yeovilton, Ilchester, Somerset

The aircraft took off with another to take part in a mid-morning interception exercise.
It was armed with eighteen 2in rockets with dummy warheads. As it climbed away from
the airfield the port engine caught fire and rapidly spread to the rest of the aircraft.[12]
It crashed near Charleton Horthorne, Somerset, barely 250 yards from the bungalow
home of Mr and Mrs Henry Gooding, who were not at home at the time.

The aircraft plunged to earth on the edge of a field belong to Mr Michael Hole, of
Golden Valley Farm. The aircraft disintegrated on impact and left a large crater in the
ground. The force of the crash was such that many pieces of wreckage were scattered
across five fields, four of which were growing barley.

Lieutenant N.E. (Mike) Todd, aged thirty and of Wearne, near Langport, and
his observer, Flying Officer Geoff Hamlyn, aged twenty-four of Troubridge Park,
Ilchester, both ejected safely but suffered some minor injuries. For Flying Officer
Hamlyn this was the second ejection he had experienced in eight months. On
13 November 1970 he ejected from another Sea Vixen F.A.W.2, Serial No XP955 (see
entry for this date) over the Moray Firth, Scotland.

Source: *Western Gazette.*

22 December 1971   • Lynx (P) • Serial Number XW835 • Westland Aircraft Works •
Home Base – Westland's Airfield • Yeovil, Somerset

The chief test Pilot of Westland's, Squadron Leader W.R. Gellatly, was flying this helicopter at the time of the accident.[13] The No 2 engine exploded, caused by a turbine
blade failure because of a fractured oil feed pipe. Both engines caught fire and the aircraft force landed in a field 5 miles west of Yeovil. The fire was put out on the ground.
There were no casualties and despite the fire the aircraft was only a Category 3.

1972

10 January 1972   • McDonnell-Douglas Phantom F.G.1 • Serial Number XT876 • Number 767 Naval Air Squadron • Home Base – HMS *Heron* • RNAS Yeovilton, Somerset

Both crew ejected at 15,000ft after loss of control at altitude, and entered a spin at 30,000ft, some 27 miles north-west of St Mawgan.[14] The aircraft crashed into the sea off Trevose Head, Cornwall. Commander (P) Simon Idiens' parachute malfunctioned and there is a possibility that it failed to deploy. The other member of crew, Lieutenant S.C. O'Connor, survived. The aircraft and pilot were not found.

As a lieutenant commander, Simon Idiens formed and headed up an aerobatic team called 'Simon's Sircus' which was composed of pilots from No 892 Naval Air Squadron in 1968. Public performance was obviously in his blood because he was one of the founding members of the famous aerobatic team affectionately nicknamed 'Fred's Five', a Mk 1 Sea Vixen unit provided by No 755 Naval Air Squadron and commanded by Lieutenant Commander Peter Reynolds RN. This team was prior to 'Simon's Sircus'.

Commander Idiens was born on 4 February 1933 and was aged thirty-eight when he died.

25 March 1972   • Jodel DR 1050 Ambassadeur • Registration Number G-AYEA • Privately Registered • Owners – the Zeta Group

The aircraft was on a private flight from Winkleigh, Devon to Elstree. About 10 minutes after departure it encountered low cloud and diverted to the north of its track. It was forced to climb into the cloud to avoid hitting high ground on Exmoor and disappeared over Bridgwater Bay at 1730 hours. Two days later wreckage from the aircraft was washed ashore on the Somerset coast. The report concludes that there was insufficient evidence to establish the reason why the aircraft struck the water but adverse weather conditions would have presented the pilot with difficulties which were probably the main casual factors in the accident.

The pilot, Mr Christopher H. Roberts, aged thirty-eight, and his three small children, Justin aged eight, Leon aged six and Crispin aged four, were killed. On 27 March, the wreckage of the aircraft was washed up near Brean Down and one of the children's bodies, still wearing a partially inflated lifejacket, was recovered from it. Three days later, the body of the pilot and another child were washed ashore in the Minehead and Lilstock areas. The body of the third child was not recovered.

Source: Aircraft Accident Investigation Bulletin 5/1973.

29 June 1972   • Fairey Gannet A.E.W. Mk 3 Prototype • Serial Number XL474 •
Number 849 Headquarters Flight • Home Base – RNAS Lossiemouth • Scotland

This aircraft stalled and crashed on its approach to RNAS Yeovilton during a demonstration flight for the RN Staff Course at that airfield.[15] The flaps failed to lower and the aircraft came to grief during an attempted recovery from the stall near the small village of Podimore, about 1½ miles from Ilchester and half a mile from the airfield. A rescue helicopter was quickly on the scene.

The plane was burning fiercely when the rescuers landed but that did not deter LAM (Leading Air Mechanic) Peter Hammond and Leading Air Mechanic Tony Wareing from attempting a rescue.

Lieutenant Commander (O) John E. Nash was injured and rescued, but the flames were too intense for the hand-held extinguishers that the two men used to have any real affect on the fire. Despite not being dressed in protective clothing, the two men reached for the pilot but could not release him. Several unsuccessful attempts were made but each time they were beaten back by the ferocity of the flames. Brian Pittard has a picture of the crash site that shows the radar dome with men standing around it. The remains of the aircraft were hidden behind a recovery lorry.

Another helicopter arrived with fire fighters dressed in protective clothing and at last the pilot was released. This rescue helicopter flew directly to Yeovil in an attempt to save the injured pilot and, with great skill, the pilot of the helicopter made a perfect landing on the roundabout on Princes Street, just some 50m from the main entrance to the hospital. This helicopter was piloted by Lieutenant Ken Armfield-Michie with a crew consisting of Leading Radio Electrical Mechanicians Peter Moorhead and Colin Kemp. On board, Surgeon Lieutenant Nick Irish and two medical assistants desperately fought to keep the pilot alive. Sadly, their efforts were in vain and the pilot subsequently died.

Lieutenant (P) Anthony Ernest Trudgett was born on 23 October 1940 and was aged thirty-one when he lost his life. He was married with two children and lived in Lossiemouth.

LAMs Hammond and Wareing were subsequently awarded the MBE for gallantry, receiving their awards at Buckingham Palace in 1973. Part of their citation read: 'London Gazette: "These repeated efforts, with complete disregard for their own safety, showed the highest standards of gallantry."'

Source: *Western Gazette.*

30 July 1972   • De Havilland D.H.82 Tiger Moth • Serial Number G-ANMO •
Weston-super-Mare Airfield

Four aircraft were performing at the Barnstormers Air Display when a low-level mid-air collision occurred at about 150ft with Stampe SV.4C G-AYGR whilst performing a flour-bombing routine. Both aircraft meshed together and fell to earth but all aboard survived.

The pilot of this aircraft during this incident was Colin Goodman and his passenger, a Blue Eagles Team pilot, were badly injured. This aircraft was repaired but was later involved in another accident on 2 October 2005 at Andrewsfied in Essex (see AAIB Report 3/2006). The aircraft is still flying today and regularly takes part in air displays. Its last known location was at White Waltham, Berkshire.

30 July 1972   • Stampe SV.4C • Serial Number G-AYGR • Weston-super-Mare Airfield

Four aircraft were performing a display at the Barnstormers Air Display when a low-level mid-air collision occurred with Tiger Moth G-ANMO whilst perform-ing a flour-bombing routine. This aircraft had belonged to the Rothman's display team and had been used in this part of the display. Both aircraft meshed together and fell to earth but all aboard survived. Pilot Barry Tempest escaped with a large bruise and concussion. His split helmet testified as to how close he had come to disaster.

28 August 1972   • Westland WS-58 Wessex H.U.5 • Serial Number XT454 • Number 845 Naval Air Squadron • Home Base – HMS *Heron* • RNAS Yeovilton, Ilchester, Somerset

This helicopter crashed after flying into power lines near Callington, Cornwall, and went down into a thick copse on the side of a valley at Bicton Wood.[16] Lieutenant Commander R.F. Shercliff and Sub Lieutenant M.D. Wavell were both injured in this accident.

This same aircraft, whilst disembarked from HMS *Bulwark* and parked at RAF Luqa in Malta, had only the year before sustained damage when the island was hit by a freak hurricane on 31 October 1971.

27 September 1972 • Westland WS-58 Wessex H.U.5 • Serial Number XS490 • Number 845 Naval Air Squadron • Home Base – HMS *Heron* • RNAS Yeovilton, Ilchester, Somerset • Detached to HMS *Albion*

On taking off, the helicopter yawed to starboard and its tail rotor blade hit XS485, which was parked on the deck. The aircraft ditched into the cold sea off Norway.[17] Lieutenant Commander N.C.H. James, CPO (Chief Petty Officer) E.P. Martin and ten Royal Netherland Marines were all rescued by SAR and the ship's sea boat.

In January 1974, this aircraft was located at the Air Medical in Seafield Park, where it was used for ground instruction. It was moved to Lee-on-Solent later on that year before being finally scrapped in 1980.

21 November 1972   • Westland Lynx – First Naval Prototype • HU • Serial Number XX469 • Originally G-BNCL • Final Serial Number of A2657 • Westland Helicopters Limited • Home Base – Westland's Airfield • Yeovil, Somerset

The tail shaft break joint of this aircraft disconnected at about 100ft and caused a loss of tail rotor thrust.[18] The aircraft descended rapidly, yawing as it did so. It then struck the ground at Yeovil airfield, Somerset, and rolled over and on to its port side. The pilot, John Morton, and his flight engineer, Mr Peter Wilson-Chalon, were both taken to hospital. Mr Morton was detained with head injuries.

This was the first version of the Lynx with a folding tail. It was also one of the first of two prototypes to complete a roll with pilot John Morton at the helm in August 1972. These aircraft carried full instruments to measure the stress. This aircraft was finally allocated to Westland's as A2657 and broken up at Heysham, Lancashire, in 1991. The other aircraft to complete the roll was XW837, piloted by Roy Moxam.

Source: *Western Gazette*, 24 November 1972.

1973

10 April 1973   • Vickers Vanguard 952 • Serial Number G-AXOP • Flight IM 435 • Invicta International Airlines

The Vanguard airliner left from Bristol Lulsgate airport on a £16.50 day trip to the beautiful Swiss city of Basel. Among the excited passengers were sixty-three people from the Ladies' Guild of Axbridge, forty from the village of Congresbury, including the Congresbury Ladies' Skittle Team from the Plough Inn, five members from the Cheddar's Mothers' Group, and others from the local villages of Wrington and Yatton.

Basel air-traffic control lost touch with the pilot of the flight as it made its approach for landing at 10.10 a.m. The pilot became disorientated when he handed over the plane to his co-pilot for landing, and as a consequence the co-pilot's final approach was based on the wrong landing beacon. As a result, the plane crashed into a wooded hillside near Basel, somersaulted and broke up. To add to the heartache and uncertainty, a casualty list was not immediately forthcoming so many people did not know for quite some time if their loved ones were safe or dead. Added to the confusion was the fact that whole families were on board the aircraft, many bearing the same forename or initials.

On 11 April, during a House of Commons debate, as shown in Hansard, the Member of Parliament for Weston-super-Mare, Mr Jerry Wiggin MP, asked Minister Mr Michael Heseltine MP, 'Does the Minister have any information on when a list of the dead will be available and will he say whether the flight recorder has been recovered?' The minister's reply to this question was:

I am sure that the whole House understands my hon. Friend's deep feelings. The House will sympathise with the people whose anxieties arise from the delay in notification. There has been great difficulty in effecting rescue operations and in finding the dead and identifying them and there has been a delay which, although regrettable, is in these circumstances understandable. The lists of the dead and the survivors are being published as soon as they are available.

The plane carried a total of 139 passengers and six crew members that day.

A total of 108 people died, including four of the crew. The presence of so many groups of women impacted heavily on small towns near Bristol, where a lot of those killed came from.

The Somerset Records Office holds the list of casualties in Papers A\BAF/1/18/1, belonging to the former Conservative MP for Weston-super-Mare and as such they are held as closed records and cannot yet be accessed by members of the public. These Wiggins records will not be available for perusal until 2012.

Lists of survivors and casualties were and still are somewhat confused, local papers only carrying details about those that were locally affected. In consequence, it has been difficult to ascertain who actually lost their lives in that disaster. Using all the casualty lists that I have found there is still a discrepancy.

AAIB Aircraft Accident Report 11/75 says of the incident:

> At 0913.27 hrs, ie shortly before the controller's last call regarding its position to the south of the field, the aircraft brushed against the wooded ridge of a range of hills in the Jura during the overshoot and climb procedure initiated shortly before, approximately 16 km south of Basel airport, almost exactly along the extended centre line of runway 16. It crashed in the vicinity of the hamlet Herrenmatt, in the parish of Hochwald/SO, somersaulted and parts of it caught fire.
>
> The accident happened in daylight. During the approach manoeuvres the aircraft was almost continually in cloud, the cloud base was low, visibility greatly reduced by driving snow and the wind was blowing with light turbulence from the north.

The aircraft disintegrated, except for the tail section, where most of the survivors were found.

> PROBABLE CAUSE: A loss of orientation during two ILS approaches carried out under instrument flight conditions. The following factors contributed to the occurrence of the accident:
> 1) inadequate navigation, above all imprecise initiation of final approach as regards height and approach center-line;
> 2) confusion of aids; and
> 3) insufficient checking and comparison of navigational aids and instrument readings (cross and double checks).
> The poor reception of ht medium wave beacons and technical defects in LOC receiver No. 1 and glide slope receiver no.2 made the crew's navigational work more difficult.

Although the official report blamed pilot error, and in particular the training of the captain, reporter John Dodson writing for the *Telegraph's Sunday Magazine*, No 71 dated 29 January 1979, wrote an article entitled 'The plane that was lured to destruction'. He suggested, 'a phenomenon causing interference to aircraft radio-compass indications, and it appeared that the investigation commission had either overlooked this information, or failed to grasp its relevance'.

The article surmises that 'current passing along a cable can act like a radio transmitting aerial'. The article further suggests that it was these transmissions from a power line belonging to Electricitie de France (EDF) that interfered with the aircraft's electronics, giving it false readings and causing it to crash. It then goes on to offer evidence from other pilots who had experienced this same phenomenon at Basel and other airports, as the downed airliner had over Basel.

On 17 April, a Vanguard airliner flew into Bristol airport containing the coffins of the 106 victims. From there the sad cargo was transported to the RAF station at Locking, near Weston-super-Mare, and placed upon trestle tables in the gymnasium. Throughout the day hearses arrived to collect their tragic cargos.

At Axbridge, a service for sixteen victims was held and thirteen of them were buried side by side. At Cheddar a service for eleven victims was held. At Yatton, four women from the same family were buried. Eight victims were buried at Redhill, near Axbridge. Amongst those killed were:

Pilot – Captain Anthony Dorman – Age: 34
Co-pilot – Captain Ivor Terry – Age: 47
Cabin Crew – Jill Manning
Cabin Crew – Joy Sadler

These thirteen victims are buried next to each other in a plot east of St John the Baptist church and are all marked by the same type of granite headstone in the village of Axbridge, Somerset:

Douglas Besley – Age: 49
Diane Chard – Age: 28
Florence Fowler – Age: 47
Joan Dorothy Furber – Age: 34
Winifred Caroline Glover – Age: 55
Brenda Grace Margaret Hopkins – Age: 38 (Group Leader of Axbridge Ladies' Guild)
Mary Elizabeth Lane – Age: 38
Majorie June Maunders – Age: 35
Marion Mayled – Age: Not known
Kay Newman – Age: 27 (This lady was the 107th victim of the air crash. She died on 17 April 1973, in Basel Hospital)
Gerald Frank Robertson – Age: 61 (Manager of Gough's Caves, Cheddar)
Mary Joan Sandford – Age: 48
Douglas Urch – Age: 57

It is not known where the following victims from Axbridge were buried or cremated:

Mrs Barbara Brooks – Age: 51 (This lady was the 108th victim of the air crash. She died on 22 April 1973 at Basel Hospital)
Mrs E. Brooks
Mrs P. Churcher
Mrs J. Cole
Mrs P. Curry

Mrs Gladys Fish
Mrs Queenie Fowler (Landlady of the Lamb Hotel, Axbridge)
Mrs Kathleen Jenkins (Lived in Weston-super-Mare and was cremated)
Mrs M. Long
Mrs M. Squires
Mrs R. Stacey
Mrs B. Toomer
Mrs Daisy Young (Cheddar)
Miss Alison Young – Age: 21

The Axbridge Ladies' Guild funded a carved wooden font cover, designed and made by local man Russell Wallace in keeping with the church's interior, as a permanent memorial to those persons who lost their lives in the tragedy (thanks to survivor, Mrs Joan Young, for this information).

Twenty persons from Congresbury lost their lives in this disaster. Initially a seventeenth-century sun dial memorial was donated to the village to commemorate these villagers, but alas such is the honour of thieves these days that it was stolen after two years. The following are interred in St Andrews churchyard, in the old part:

Kathleen Mary Attwell – Age: 66 (The Plough Inn)
Raymond Noel Batt – Age: 49
Beryl Gertrude Batt – Age: 41
Rose Evelyn Clark – Age: 74
Evelyn Maud Davis – Age: 71
Linda Jane Davis – Age: 20
Ivor James Gill – Age: 50
Maija Luisa (Marie) Gill – Age: 48
John Michael Gill – Age: 22
Aileen Gladys Gill – Age: 47
Hazel Mary Gill – Age: 9
Myrtle Florence Reakes – Age: 53
Sylvia Jean Roynon – Age: 43
Ellen Mary Roynon – Age: 11
Grace Louisa Searle – Age: 58
Irene Weaver – Age: 48
Florence Durman – Age: 71 (Buried at Pitminster)

The following were cremated:

William Alfred Price – Age: 63
Dorothy Marie Price – Age: 61
Agnes Eleanor Rawlings – Age: 59 (Ashes to Micheldean)

From Cheddar there were four survivors from the crash, but eighteen people were lost:

Mrs Jean Baker (Cheddar Mothers' Group)
Mrs E. Brooks

Mrs Majorie Edwards (Cheddar Mothers' Group)
Mrs Doris Gould
Mrs G. Heritage (Cheddar Mothers' Group)
Mr V. Hughes
Mrs A.M. Isgar
Mr Roy Keen
Mrs M.B. Lane
Mrs H. Lane
Mrs Angela Latham
Mrs Marlene A. Maunders
Mrs Phyllis Maunders
Mrs Kay Newman
Mrs Payne
Mrs D. Young

Some of the victims came from the village of Wrington, about 10 miles south of Bristol. In the recreation ground, behind Silver Street, a row of Lombardy poplar trees were planted in memory of each person who lost their life in the disaster (see plate 13).

There is a plaque on the outer wall of the social club in the playing fields that commemorates the people who lost their lives, but they are not named.

The following lost their lives and are buried in Wrington churchyard:

Kathleen Mary Board – Age: 32
Joan Brooks – Age: Not known
Jean Bull – Age: Not known
Arleen Mary Cleeves – Age: 35
Miss Katrina Joy Coles – Age: 18
Mabel Hester Maria Coles – Age: 52
Josephine Edna Brooks – Age: 49
Nancy Frappell – Age: 55

Others who were lost locally were:

Mrs V. Avery – Not known
Mr Baker – Not known
Miss Jennifer Batt – Fishponds, Bristol
Mrs B.E. Bridge – Westbury-sub-Mendip
Mrs R. Bridge – Westbury-sub-Mendip
Mrs G. Carver – Draycott
Mrs E.B. Chard – Claverham
Miss Jennifer Cole – The Bungalow Inn, Redhill
Mr Collins – Cheddar
Mrs Louisa Davis – Wedmore
Miss A. Hale – Cheddar
Mrs S. Halford – Westbury-sub-Mendip
Mrs M. Harse – Redhill
Mrs A.F. Holford – Draycott

Mrs Hilda Hunt – Bristol
Mrs K. Jenkins – Weston
Mr Colin Jones – Bishopsworth Road, Bristol
Mrs Shirley Jones – Age: 36 – Bishopsworth Road, Bristol
Master Andrew Jones – Age: 13 – Bishopsworth Road, Bristol
Mrs M. Long – Not known
Mrs A. McKenzie – Butcombe
Miss C.A. McKenzie – Butcombe
Mrs Margaret Moore – Weston-super-Mare (Buried in Uphill church, on the hill)
Mrs Moore – Weston-super-Mare (Sister-in-law of the above)
Mrs Patricia Palmer – Redhill
Miss Myrtle Stacey – Bristol
Mrs Shirley Surridge – Bristol
Mr David Surridge – Bristol
Mrs Olive Venn – Bristol
Mrs Myrtle Wheeler – Not known
Master Andrew Wheeler – Age: 7 (Son of the above)
Master Mark Wheeler – Age: 13. (Son of the above)

The Swiss report also made reference to the fact that the training record of the captain had highlighted his 'dubious' basic training. The report said that the captain had made nine attempts before finally managing to pass the British Instrument Rating Test. It went on to say, 'It is certain that repeated failure to pass a test of this kind indicates a lack of suitability on the part of the candidate.'

A total of thirty-nine people survived the initial accident. According to *The Times*, dated 13 April 1973, these people were:

Stewardess D. Axton; Mrs Ivy Besley; Master David Besley; Mrs Jennifer Bowen; Master Jonathan Bowen; Mrs Barbara Brooks (this lady was the 108th victim of the air crash); Mrs M. Carpenter; Mrs Marilyn Carver; Mrs Pam Churches; Mrs A. Clarke; Mrs Sylvia Cole; Miss Susan Dyer; Mrs Eileen Edginton; Miss Brenda Fish; Mr B. Gillow; Mrs Shireen Hart; Mrs I. Hooper; Mrs Thelma Hughes; Mrs J. Ibbs; Mr N. Ibbs; Mr B. Jones; Mrs Hazel Lane; Mrs Mary Long (later listed as having died in the crash); Stewardess E. Low; Mrs Kay Newman (later died in hospital on 17 April 1973); Mrs F. Patch; Mrs Alice Rodgers; Mrs Myrtle Sampson; Mrs K. Scott; Miss Lena Simmonds; Mr Horace Stacey; Mrs Toomer; Mr Fred Tjolle; Mrs Maud Wharton; Master Stephen Wharton; Mrs Anne Rose White; Mrs K. Whinstone; Mrs Jean Worsley; Mrs Joan Young

A D.C.10 aircraft was supplied by Sir Freddie Laker, at his own expense, to bring back the survivors of this disaster to RAF Lyneham. Civilian and RAF ambulances met the flight to ferry the injured to hospital, while coaches were laid on to return the remainder back to their homes. This D.C.10 was the first of such aircraft to land at Lyneham.

On 10 April 1974, about 150 relatives and Swiss officials gathered at the site at Hochwald, near Basel to witness the unveiling of a memorial to those 108 people who lost their lives in this disaster exactly a year ago to the day. The memorial consists of a limestone block surmounted by angel's wings in bronze. It stands by a path that runs across the crash site.

Sources: The Basel Vanguard accident, *Flight International*, September 1975; Vanguard hearing: crew records and equipment faults cited, *Flight International*, November 1974 (p. 666); Swiss Federal Department of Transport and Power No 1973/12 – 800.

17 July 1973 • McDonnell-Douglas Phantom F.G.1 • Serial Number XT871 • Number 892 Naval Air Squadron • Home Base – RN Detachment • RAF Leuchars, Scotland • Squadron moved from RNAS Yeovilton • Detached to HMS *Ark Royal*

This aircraft experienced a port engine problem on launch from HMS *Ark Royal* and crashed off the ship's bow near the Isle of May in the Firth of Forth.[19] The crew, Lieutenant (P) John Cameron Gunning and Lieutenant R.C. O'Connor ejected safely. They were both picked up by a Wessex SAR. The aircraft was later salvaged by the Accident Investigation Unit.

9 September 1973 • Western 0.65 Balloon (Hot Air) • Registration Number G-AZOO • Privately Owned

The aircraft took off from the Royal Naval Air Station at Yeovilton. The accident occurred when the rip panel of the balloon opened in flight at about 1,000ft agl soon after take-off. Although attempts were made to arrest the rate of descent by continuous operation of the burner and jettisoning equipment, the pilot was unable to prevent the balloon from making a heavy landing.

The three persons on board were injured and the balloon was damaged.

Flight Lieutenant Gavin Turnbull of RAF Cottismore suffered some spinal injuries. Lieutenant Terry Adams of Lossiemouth escaped with no injuries. Mrs Helen Ashby, aged twenty-seven, was not so lucky and she suffered from multiple injuries and was detained in hospital.

Source: *Western Gazette*, 14 September 1973.

6 November 1973 • D.H.110 Sea Vixen F.A.W.2 • Serial Number XP954 • Fleet Requirements and Air Direction Unit (FRADU) • Home Base – RNAS Yeovilton • Ilchester, Somerset

This aircraft had a port and starboard fire indicated on the centralised warning panel while it was in the circuit above Ashington.[20] The pilot, Mr Ian Kilgour, aged thirty-two years, came from Somerton, as did his navigator, Mr E.C.A. Welch. Both men safely ejected from 2,500ft. The aircraft crashed in a cultivated field 2 miles south of the airfield, and about 100 yards from some farm buildings. They were rescued by an SAR helicopter from Yeovilton and taken directly to the sickbay with minor injuries.

An eyewitness was Mr William Jolliffe, of Magnolia Cottages, Ashington, who was clearing leaves from his drive when he first heard the aircraft. 'I did not take any particular notice until I heard three distinct bangs. In my ignorance I thought the aircraft had gone through the sound barrier,' he said later.

'Then I saw the aircraft coming towards me and only a few feet from the ground. The next second it ploughed into the ground and there was a terrific explosion.'

Source: *Western Gazette*, 9 November 1973.

1974

16 January 1974   • Westland Sea King Mk41 • Registration Number 89-61 •
Westland Aircraft Works • Westland's Airfield • Yeovil, Somerset

This aircraft was intended for use with the Federal German Navy. On a test flight at 12.18 p.m. over Yeovil airfield, something went wrong:

> The helicopter was undergoing a test flight in strong and gusty wind conditions with a pilot and four Observers. Whilst carrying out a low level circuit on Yeovilton airfield, airspeed fell off markedly and a high rate of descent developed with the helicopter heading down-wind. The pilot applied maximum power but unintentionally raised the collective pitch lever too far and an over pitched condition was reached at too low a height to permit a safe recovery. The helicopter touched down in a field adjacent to the airfield boundary, still heading down wind, struck a building and crashed. The crew of five escaped unhurt.

The aircraft was being piloted by Mr Don Farquarson and his crew consisted of Mr Ian Pavey, Mr Terry Miller, Mr Oluf Runge and Mr Michael Peronne. The aircraft crashed at Higher Farm, Preston Plucknett, next to the airfield during gale-force winds.

Source: AAIB Report 2/75, ref. EW/C476 and *Western Gazette*.

19 February 1974   • Westland WS-58 Wessex H.U.5 • Serial Number XT477 •
Number 845 Naval Air Squadron • Home Base – RNAS Yeovilton • Ilchester, Somerset •
Detached to HMS *Hermes*

This aircraft crashed during a test flight when its engine computer failed.[21] The pilot became disorientated and it crashed into 60 fathoms of a fjord near Harstad in Norway. During the recovery process on 9 May 1974, the aircraft was lost when it sank in 115m of water.

489903 Captain John Robert Greig of the Army Air Corps was born on 4 April 1936 and was thirty-seven when he lost his life.

Do64823Y Acting Leading Electrical Mechanic (Air) David Alan Evans was born on 18 June 1945 at Woodford, Essex, and was twenty-eight when he was unfortunately killed in this air crash.

1975

7 June 1975   • Victa Airtourer 115 • Registration Number G-AWOZ • Operator –
Spencer Aviation

This aircraft came down near Chew Magna, Somerset, and tragically both the pilot and his passenger were killed. It was flying at low level and was performing as part of an air display, attempting a loop the loop, when the accident occurred. The two men killed were Mr James Hamilton, aged fifty-six, an electrical engineer of Tunbridge Close, Chew Magna, and Mr Stanley Sharp, aged fifty-four, a lecturer at Bristol University, of Stepsend, Dundry, near Bristol. Mr Sharp is buried at Dundry.

Catherine Soper from Chew Magna recollected in 2011:

I remember seeing the aircraft flying lower than seemed safe in an upside-down position which alarmed me. It was at the annual Summer Fair held in Chew Magna and was held in Farmer Flowers Field off Tunbridge Road. I had been talking to Jim Hamilton's wife whilst waiting to see the air display; her husband was one of the two men on board and she seemed quite anxious about the display.

It was as I was leaving the field to go across the road to my home that the plane came over almost directly above me and although I did not see the actual crash it was obvious that it had come down and because I had left my 11 year old son with some friends at the fair, I had some panicky minutes before it became clear that the crash had happened some little distance from the crowds who had a few moments previously been enjoying a lovely afternoon with villagers and friends at what had been a very happy event.

Her son, who was eleven years old at the time, remembers:

I recall watching the display with a friend, I can remember thinking he was flying very low, and watching in amazement as he didn't make the turn and crashed into the ground. My memories are then of the crowd running to see if they could help – the plane having come down in the next field.

David Young was playing cricket for Chew Magna on that fateful day. He recalls:

One of our team was an air traffic controller at the nearby Bristol airport in the days when it was not that busy. We watched the low flying aircraft and he remarked that he knew it was going to be there. They both watched as the aircraft attempted a loop the loop, and when it got to the top of the loop it was flying inverted. In a calm tone the air traffic controller remarked that 'he's going to crash.' We watched in horrified fascination as the aircraft disappeared towards the Flower's Field area on that lovely summer's day. We did not see the crash happen.

Simon Ford also remembers:

As a 14 year old resident of Tunbridge Close, Chew Magna, I attended the annual village fete which was held in Dick Flower's farm grounds on Tunbridge Road. The highlight of the fete was to be an air display given by my neighbour Jim (Hammy) Hamilton and his co-pilot, a Mr Sharp of Dundry.

Jim was completing a 'loop the loop' manoeuvre and didn't have enough height, unfortunately hitting the ground at the bottom of his loop and killing them both.

John Davies from Chew Magna has a clear recollection of the tragedy. He says:

It was on the 7 June 1975 that Chew Magna held their annual Summer Fayre, organised by the committee of The Chew Magna Society. I was on that committee, as was Jim Hamilton.

The afternoon's entertainments – cake stalls, children's races, Punch & Judy and all that sort of thing – was to take place in a field alongside Tunbridge Farm on the southern edge of the village.

Jim Hamilton, who lived in Tunbridge Close with his wife Muriel, had a half-share of a light aircraft, shared with a man from nearby Dundry. I recall Jim, who was an engineer working with the tobacco company Wills, in Bristol, used to say that on his Saturday afternoon flights he would circle the area and keep an eye-out on his back garden. Murial would put a sheet on the washing line when it was time for him to come home for tea. I understand the aircraft was garaged at Lulsgate.

During our planning of the Summer Fayre Jim offered to do a low-level pass above the fayre's proceedings. This stunt was not generally advertised, but certainly committee members knew about it. And so it was that whilst I was organising some youngsters ready to do their egg-and-spoon race, I heard the plane coming, and we all stopped to watch.

What happened next I'm not exactly sure? Certainly it was more than a low-level flypast. The plane did some aerobatics, which was a surprise, even to me. There was a loop the loop, and a roll. But then on the next pass, the plane took a dive and crashed into a field no more than 300 yards from the village gathering. Some folks made a move towards the incident which was in an adjacent field, though I recall I was rooted to the spot. The aircraft had descended, nose first, and was going more-or-less vertically downwards when it hit the ground. It seemed obvious to me that there was no hope of survival.

Another of the organising committee who was on site was Mike Rowe, local funeral director and part-time fireman. He no doubt responded as a fireman and with the local fire station only some 100 yards from the summer fayre proceedings it was only a few minutes before there was an appliance at the site of the crash. But there was nothing they could do. I recall Mike telling me 'they (the plane occupants) were obviously dead'.

It was news to me when I learned there were two on board; I had imagined it was only Jim. It was hearsay that Jim was the passenger and the pilot was the other co-owner.

Sources: Air Safety Network Occurrence Number 19510; Flight Global/Archive 0143.pdf, 24 January 1976; Catherine Soper, Chew Magna, January 2011; Catherine Soper's son, January 2011; David Young, Bishop's Sutton, January 2011; Simon Ford, Chew Magna, February 2011; John Davis, Chew Magna, February 2011.

6 September 1975   • RAF Harrier • Serial Number Not Known • Number 233 Operational Conversion Unit • Home Base – RAF Wittering • Peterborough, Cambridgeshire

As the pilot was getting out of this Harrier on the runway, the ejector seat accidentally fired. He was thrown 30ft into the air and tragically died shortly after arriving at Yeovil Hospital.

The accident occurred during an RNAS Yeovilton Air Show day but out of sight of the main crowd. Minutes before the incident, the pilot had been putting his aircraft through its paces in a spectacular performance before a crowd of 35,000 spectators. A large section of the crowd was unaware of the tragedy because at that precise moment a loud thunder explosion announced the arrival of the Red Arrows.

4232484 Flight Lieutenant Stephen Beckley, aged twenty-nine, is buried in the All Saints churchyard, Wittering, near Peterborough, in Row 4, Grave 78. He was born on 6 March 1946.

Source: *Western Gazette.*

1976

16 January 1976   • Westland WS-58 Wessex H.U.5 • Serial Number XT758 • Number 848 Naval Air Squadron • Home Base – RNAS Yeovilton • Ilchester, Somerset • Detached to HMS *Bulwark*

This helicopter suffered a control system failure 5ft above the deck of the ship.[22] It crashed into the Atlantic Ocean some 50 yards off the starboard bow of HMS *Bulwark* and some 750 nautical miles or so south-west of the Azores. The crew of Sub Lieutenant M.J. Crabtree, Sub Lieutenant A.K. Naughton and LACMN (Leading Aircrewman) G.S. Watson were all safely rescued by the ship's SAR.

The aircraft was still floating and an attempt by divers to secure a strop from the crashed aircraft to the ship's crane failed. The aircraft sank into the 3,000m depth of the ocean.

16 June 1976   • Morane-Saunier MS.880B Rallye Cub • Serial Number G-BAOE •
Westward Aviation Co. Ltd

At 7.42 p.m, this aircraft encountered poor visibility and low cloud over the
Blackdown Hills on a flight out from Dunkerswell airfield, near Honiton, Devon. It
was both seen and heard circling, before it finally went into a descending turn to the
left from which it did not recover. It crashed just beyond the hedge alongside the lane
and 100 yards from Moorseek Farm, Buckland St Mary, near Taunton.

The pilot, Mr Ken Cooper of Bishops Rise, Torquay, was badly injured and died
later from his injuries at Musgrove Park Hospital in Taunton. Mr Bob Foster and his
wife Margaret of High Street, Budleigh Salterton, Devon, both died at the scene.

Eyewitness Mr Clifford Smith of Folly Farm, Buckland St Mary, was driving a
tractor in the farmyard of Moorseek Farm when he heard a revving noise overhead.

'I looked up and saw the plane about 20–30ft above the farmhouse,' he said. 'It
revved up again and seemed to gain height and then it stopped altogether and dived
into the hedge. The engine just cut out and it went straight down.'

Sources: AAIB Report EW/C565; and *Western Gazette*, 18 June 1976.

21 September 1976 • Hawker Hunter F.4 • Serial Number WT772 • Fleet Requirements
and Air Direction Unit (FRADU) • Home Base – RNAS Yeovilton • Ilchester, Somerset

This aircraft suffered an engine failure shortly after taking off.[23] The pilot, Mr Peter
Millard of Lower Street, Merriot, ejected safely. In a strange sequence of events the
aircraft continued to fly and somehow landed safely on its belly in fields between the
nearby villages of Queen Camel and Charlton Adam.

Mrs Margaret Reeve was in a field near her home, Vale Farm Cottage, when she
saw the jet crash. 'It came over very low,' she said. 'Then a yellow parachute appeared.
The plane went on very low and burst into flames as it hit a tree. It went on leaving a
trail of flames behind it.

'It broke down a tree as it went through a hedge, on through another hedge and
into a third field.

'The pilot landed in another field. I came back and called the fire brigade, then
went to look for him. He fired a flare when a helicopter came over.'

The aircraft was returned to RNAS Yeovilton and ended up on the fire dump of
that unit in April 1977. It was burnt out shortly afterwards.

Source: *Western Gazette*, 24 September 1976.

24 October 1976   • Piper PA-28-140C Cherokee • Registration Number G-AYDT •
Operator – West London Air Service

The aircraft was being piloted by a Frenchman who was returning from Lydd airport, near Deal in Kent, and supposedly heading for the airfield at White Waltham,

Buckinghamshire. The research vessel *Edward Forbes* received an emergency message at 7.05 p.m. reporting that a light aircraft had run out of fuel over the Bristol Channel just north of Weston-super-Mare. Making full speed towards St Thomas Point in Sand Bay, and about half a mile north-east of St Thomas Point, the pilot was spotted in the water. This was at about 7.30 p.m. The ship launched its small boat to pick him up, but unfortunately the pilot had by this time succumbed to the cold water and drowned. His body was not recovered.

The aircraft wreckage lies on the floor of the Bristol Channel and at a depth of about 2m. Scuba divers often visit the wreck because of its shallow depth. The site of the wreckage is marked on the coastal chart for the area.

Source: *Bristol Evening Post*, 25 October 1976.

1978

12 May 1978 • McDonnell-Douglas Phantom F.G.1 • Serial Number XT868 • Number 892 Naval Air Squadron • Home Base – RN Detachment • RAF Leuchars, Scotland

The aircraft was practising for a flying display at RAF Leuchars when its starboard wing tip hit the ground.[24] The aircraft then cart-wheeled along the runway and both crew ejected, but along the ground. The observer was killed.

Commander Carl Cedric Nelson Davis, the senior naval officer at RAF Leuchars, was seriously injured when, during the ejection process, he hit a fence.

CO14999L Lieutenant (O) John Gavin, aged thirty-one, was born on 21 January 1947. He is buried in the Royal Naval Cemetery at St Bartholomew's in Yeovilton village. His final resting place is shown in Appendix 2.

24 May 1978 • Hawker Hunter F.4 converted to T.8 • Serial Number XF991 • Fleet Requirements and Air Direction Unit (FRADU) • Home Base – RNAS Yeovilton • Ilchester, Somerset

This aircraft took off from Yeovilton and crashed after an engine explosion.[25] Mr Richard Statham, the pilot, and his passenger, Sub Lieutenant Alan Brooks, who was twenty-two years of age, both successfully ejected from the stricken aircraft. Mr Statham worked for the Air Works Services at RNAS Yeovilton and was an ex-RAF pilot.

The aircraft had taken off at approximately 10.30 a.m. and soon after the take-off things started to go seriously wrong with the engine. The pilot attempted to steer the stricken aircraft back to RNAS Yeovilton but did not have enough height to do so, and so he gave the order to abandon the aircraft. The Hunter hit the ground and skidded into Brearley Brook near Martock. When fire tenders from Yeovil and RNAS Yeovilton arrived the aircraft was almost completely burnt out.

Both of the crew were taken to Yeovil Hospital, where Sub Lieutenant Brooks needed stitches to a nose injury. Mr Statham was kept in overnight with a back injury.

Source: *Western Gazette.*

10 September 1978 • Rockwell Commander 114 • Registration Number HB-NCM • Air Espace SA • Switzerland

The accident occurred in poor weather during an attempted Visual Flight Rules (VFR) flight from Exeter to Leicester. The aircraft ran into low cloud as it entered a valley which passes through the hills to the South East of Bristol. Whilst in a cloud and during a turn to the left, the aircraft descended and hit the edge of a clay pit; it then crashed inverted into a pile of timber, killing all four of the occupants instantly. The accident occurred near Waterloo Farm, Dundry, Bristol at approximately 0830 hours in the morning.

It is concluded that the accident was caused by the pilot continuing the flight over hilly terrain at low altitude after encountering adverse weather conditions.

The aircraft burned fiercely and was only a short way from an empty Bristol airport runway when the accident occurred. The three men and one female did not survive the incident. Three of the occupants were Swiss and one was British. The pilot, aged thirty-three, was a Swiss national. The occupant of the front right-hand passenger seat was a British national, aged thirty-seven, and living in Switzerland.

Source: AAIB Report No 4/79 Ref. EW/C637.

21 September 1978 • Scottish Aviation Bulldog T.1 • Serial Number XX530 • Number 3 Flying Training School • Home Base – RAF Leeming • Yorkshire

The pilot made an emergency landing on Cochcayne Ridge, Bilsdale Moor in Yorkshire.[26] Unfortunately, he had chosen an area of very soft peat moor and the wheels sank into the ground on touching down. Both the crew were killed when the aircraft stopped dead in the soft peat.

2616559 Flight Lieutenant John D. (Jack) Piercy BSc RAF was born on 2 October 1947 at Worcester Park, north-east Surrey. He was aged thirty when he lost his life and is buried in Our Lady and St Benedict's churchyard, Ampleforth, Yorkshire, Grave 252.

The student pilot, CO25993D Midshipman Mark Simon RN was born on 13 March 1959 and was aged nineteen when he was killed. He came from Dartford, Kent. His place of burial is not known. He belonged to HMS *Heron*, RNAS Yeovilton, and was attached to 3FTS for pilot training.

22 September 1978 • D.H.82 Tiger Moth II • Serial Number T8191 • Historic Flight •
Home Base – RNAS Yeovilton • Ilchester, Somerset

This aircraft underwent a forced landing at Brue Farm, Alford, near Castle Cary, where it overturned and crashed in a field belonging to farmer John Farthing.[27] The pilot, Lieutenant Commander David Bridger was practising for the Lulsgate airport open day, due to be held that Sunday on 24 September.

He was flying at 1,400ft in an inverted position when the engine suddenly stopped and would not restart. Righting the aircraft, he glided down to the first suitable field that he could see. On landing he clipped the hedge and the aircraft ended up in an inverted position, with the pilot hanging from his safety straps. He released himself and thankfully sustained no injuries from the accident.

The aircraft was sent to Lee-on-Solent before finally being sold at auction at Sotheby's, registering as G-BWKM on 26 November 1994. It then went to Welshpool airport where it transferred into the private ownership of APB Leasing.

Source: *Western Gazette.*

26 October 1978   • Percival P.57 Sea Prince T.1 • Serial Number WP309 • Number 750 Naval Air Squadron • Home Base – RNAS Culdrose

The undercarriage of this aircraft collapsed while taxiing along the runway at RNAS Yeovilton, Somerset, whilst being piloted by Flight Lieutenant A. Dorey RAF.[28] It was written off and went to the fire dump at Yeovilton and was last seen there in 1989.

1979

6 March 1979   • Westland WS-58 Wessex H.U.5 • Serial Number XT465 •
Number 846 Naval Air Squadron • Home Base – RNAS Yeovilton • Ilchester, Somerset

On a routine arctic training flight in Norway, the helicopter was coming in to land on the island of Andoeya, in a prepared landing area. It hit a single power cable and its tail broke off.[29] The aircraft crashed into the ground, killing its crew.

CO212861l Lieutenant (P) Bernard Clifford Brunsden, aged thirty, was born on 12 July 1948 at Bushley, in Hertfordshire. He was cremated at the Yeovil Crematorium. He lived with his wife in married quarters at Houndstone Camp, Yeovil.

CO24449C Sub Lieutenant (P) Herbert James Clarke, aged twenty-four, was born on 20 March 1955 in Lisburn, Northern Ireland. He is buried in Lisburn Cemetery.

D075147K Leading Aircrewman Lyall Douglas Bradbury, aged thirty, was born on 10 June 1948. Although he survived the initial impact, he unfortunately died in the ambulance and on the way to the hospital. He is buried in the cemetery at Peebles. He lived with his wife in married quarters at Houndstone Camp, Yeovil.

Source: *Western Gazette*.

3 August 1979   • Lockheed F104-G Starfighter • Serial Number 22+25 • Marinefliegergeshader 1 • Home Base – Federal Republic of West Germany

This aeroplane had successfully taken part in the RNAS Yeovilton Air Day. The pilot, Kapitanleutnant Manfred Sturmer, approached the airfield making a very low and tight final turn, ready for a fast fly by.

The aircraft slipped sideways into the ground about half a mile from the airfield and a quarter of a mile from the village of West Camel, killing the pilot. The pilot was also the squadron leader and this was to be his final air display flight before retiring. This was the first fatal air day crash at RNAS Yeovilton in thirty-two years.

A local policeman from Yeovil received an unexpected fright during this tragic accident. His job had been to patrol the lanes around the airfield and was tasked with keeping the traffic moving. He had stopped his police motorcycle to watch the aircraft landing, when suddenly this aeroplane, clearly in trouble, headed straight towards him in an inverted position. Hastily he had to kick-start his motorcycle, something that he always achieved on the first attempt. This time he took several times to get his motorcycle started and he managed to get out of the area just before the aircraft screamed overhead and crashed.

This aircraft was nicknamed 'The Widowmaker' by the West Germans. There were 916 Starfighters supplied to Germany; 292 of them crashed, killing 115 of its pilots.

1980s

1980

April 1980 • Jet Provost • Serial Number Not Known • Number 3 Flying Training School • Home Base – RAF Leeming • Yorkshire

Flight Lieutenant McDonald RAF was flying one of a pair of Jet Provosts to the Royal Navy airfield at Yeovilton, Somerset, from his home base at RAF Leeming, Yorkshire.

As he was approaching RNAS Yeovilton, his aircraft suddenly had a flame out. Quickly breaking formation, he attempted to relight his engine, which briefly occurred. By this time, he was out of sight of Yeovilton and the other aircraft, so he immediately transmitted a Mayday call and descended to 2,000ft and attempted another relight. This attempt failed. As he had visually acquired RNAS Yeovilton again, McDonald decided to make a dead-stick landing.

He was starting to make his final approach at a height of 600ft when another aircraft turned finals in front of him. The control tower at Yeovilton was unable to prevent this from happening. By now he was faced with the situation of being down to 200ft and the runway ahead of him blocked.

He needed to make an instantaneous decision. McDonald chose to land on a taxiway that was parallel to the runway, even though the end of the taxiway was much further upwind than the end of the runway. Making a text-book landing, he succeeded in bringing the aircraft safely to a halt. Even though he would have been justified in ejecting, at great personal risk he stayed with his aircraft and saved it.

208581 Flight Lieutenant Paul Thomas McDonald, a Royal Air Force flying instructor, was awarded the Queen's Commendation for Valuable Service in the Air.

Source: Supplement to the *London Times*, 24 March 1981.

1 December 1980 • Sea Harrier F.R.S.1 • Serial Number XZ454 • Number 800 Naval Air Squadron • Home Base – RNAS Yeovilton • Ilchester, Somerset • Detached to HMS *Invincible*

Sea Harrier F.R.S.1 of 800 Squadron, Serial No XZ454, was the squadron's first aircraft loss.[1] This aircraft hit the top of the ramp of HMS *Invincible* on a planned overshoot and was written off. Lieutenant Commander Michael (Mike) Stephen Blissett DFC successfully ejected from the aircraft but suffered some injuries. The Ministry of Defence DASA site gives the location of the crash as being 25 nautical miles south of Land's End, Cornwall.

1981

17 March 1981   • Hawker Hunter F.4 converted to T.8 • Serial Number XF977
• Fleet Requirements and Air Direction Unit (FRADU) • Home Base – RNAS Yeovilton •
Ilchester, Somerset

This aircraft crashed into the English Channel after engine failure, some 12 nautical miles south-west of Start Point in Devon.[2] The pilot, Mr J. Stewart-Smith safely ejected and was picked up by an SAR Whirlwind helicopter and taken to the nearby HMS *London*.

6 October 1981   • Westland WS-58 Wessex H.U.5 • Serial Number XT448 •
Number 845 Naval Air Squadron • Home Base – RNAS Yeovilton • Ilchester, Somerset •
Detached to HMS *Hermes*

Flying from the NAS at Jacksonville, USA, to USMAS at New River and whilst over the sea,[3] this aircraft's skin section of the tail rotor detached itself and yaw control was lost. The helicopter successfully auto-rotated down to the sea but rolled over to its port side and sank into 15ft of water. Due to the exceptionally heavy seas, the aircraft was destroyed and not recovered.

Lieutenant P.S. Doyne-Ditmas, Corporal I.C. Tyrell, AEA (Air Engineering Artificer) D. Sampson, Pilot Officer J. Anderson, AEA N. Howard and Sub Lieutenant P. Lynch were all saved and rescued by an SAR helicopter.

1982

22 April 1982   • Westland WS-58 Wessex H.U.5 • Serial Numbers XT464 and
XT473 • Number 845 Naval Air Squadron • Home Base – RNAS Yeovilton • Ilchester,
Somerset • South Atlantic Conflict

On 21 April, two Wessex H.U.5 helicopters from the Royal Fleet Auxillary, Tidepool (XT464 and XT473, No 845 Naval Air Squadron), led by HMS *Antrim's* Wessex H.A.S.3 (XP142 of 100 Flight, No 737 Naval Air Squadron), successfully inserted SAS men on to the Fortuna Glacier, South Georgia. The troop's task had been to observe Argentine troops that had invaded the island. The following day, the SAS put in a call to be extracted due to the terrible weather conditions they were experiencing.

All three helicopters returned to pick up the troopers. Both of the H.U.5 helicopters suffered white-outs in the blizzard they were experiencing and crashed while attempting to lift the SAS troops off the glacier. Fortunately, despite the fact that the helicopters were fully laden, no serious injuries were sustained among the troopers or the helicopters' crews.

The Wessex H.A.S.3, XP142 (pilot Lieutenant Commander Ian Stanley, navigator Lieutenant Chris Parry) successfully returned to HMS *Antrim* with its passengers. Quickly, the crew removed much of its dipping sonar gear in order to save weight, and about three hours later, successfully returned to the glacier to rescue the remaining seventeen SAS troopers and naval personnel.

This aircraft is now part of the collection of the Fleet Air Arm Museum at RNAS Yeovilton, near Ilchester, Somerset. Both the pilot and navigator of XP142 were awarded the DSO for their exploits on that day.

23 April 1982 • Sea King H.C.4 • Serial Number ZA311 • Number 846 Naval Air Squadron • Home Base – RNAS Yeovilton • Ilchester, Somerset • South Atlantic Conflict

This squadron detached to HMS *Hermes* during the Falklands War. The Sea King was employed in a logistics moving mode at the time, but crashed into the sea in the darkness. Although Flight Lieutenant R.W. Grundy RAF was almost immediately picked up by Sea King XZ574, the petty officer aircrewman could not be found. He was in the main cabin of the aircraft when it went down and became the first fatality of the Falklands War.

A memorial service was held for him at his local parish church, All Saints in Easton, Portland. He left behind a wife, Ellie.

He was a very keen sportsman and his shipmates from HMS *Osprey* and RNAS Yeovilton remember him to this day because of the perpetual trophy awarded in his name. It is called the 'Ben Casey trophy'.

D136093W Petty Officer Aircrewman Kevin Stuart (Ben) Casey, aged twenty-six, was born on 23 January 1956 in Rugby, Warwickshire. He was listed as 'Missing Presumed Drowned'.

4 May 1982 • Sea Harrier F.R.S.1 • Serial Number XZ450 • Number 800 Naval Air Squadron • Home Base – RNAS Yeovilton • Ilchester, Somerset • Detached to HMS *Hermes* • South Atlantic Conflict

As the pilot attacked Goose Green for a cluster bomb attack, his Sea Harrier was hit by radar-controlled anti-aircraft fire.[4] The pilot's body was recovered, still in his ejector seat, by the residents of Goose Green. He was buried very close to the spot where the aircraft crashed by the Argentinians and was given a full military funeral.

His grave lies near to Goose Green, surrounded by a white fence, and is today tended by residents from that settlement. On his gravestone are engraved the words 'In proud memory of a dearly loved husband, son and brother, shot down while flying for the country he loved'.

This F.R.S.1 was the first aircraft of this type to fly. It had a limited instrumentation fit at this juncture in 1978 and flew before the first three development aircraft, XZ438, XZ439 and XZ440.

CO20574N Lieutenant (P) Nicholas Taylor, aged thirty-two, was born on 28 May 1949. He lived in Ryme Intrinseca, near Yeovil, with his wife Clare (who was a serving WRNS second officer at the time) and their son Harry. Although technically living in Ryme Intrinseca, he actually lived much nearer to the village of Closworth, where the villagers knew him well. He was also the first British battle casualty of the Falklands War.

Source: *The Times*, 6 May 1982.

6 May 1982   • Sea Harrier F.R.S.1 • Serial Numbers XZ452 and XZ453 • Number 801 Naval Air Squadron • Home Base – RNAS Yeovilton • Ilchester, Somerset • Detached to HMS *Invincible* • South Atlantic Conflict

In the early hours of the morning, two aircraft were sent to investigate a suspicious contact near the still burning HMS *Sheffield*. The weather was absolutely atrocious, with low cloud, fog and rain. Contact with the flight was lost and the aircraft never returned. It was assumed that the planes had collided in mid air, killing both their pilots.[5] XZ452 was flown by Lieutenant Commander (P) John Edward Eyton-Jones and XZ453 was flown by Lieutenant William Alan Curtis.

CO16085B Lieutenant Commander John Edward Eyton-Jones, aged thirty-nine, was born on 24 April 1943 in Northampton. He lived close to RNAS Yeovilton at Troubridge Park, Ilchester, along with his wife Sally and two daughters. He was listed as 'Missing Presumed Killed'.

CO27154R Lieutenant (P) William Alan Curtis, aged thirty-five, was born on 11 July 1946 at Preston in Lancashire. His wife Pamela was expecting their first child in July that year. He was a well-known and liked man within the village of West Chinnock and he lived in Higher Street. A memorial service for him took place at the nearby church in Merriot, Somerset. He was listed as 'Missing Presumed Killed'.

In the church of St Mary's in West Chinnock, Somerset, there is a memorial to him which reads: 'In memory of Lieutenant William Alan Curtis, RN killed in action in the Falkland Islands on 6 May 1982, aged thirty-five years. Given by the villagers of West Chinnock.'

The brass memorial is located just inside the church entrance on the right and is next to the Roll of Honour from the two world wars.

On 1 May 1982, Lieutenant Curtis was credited with the shooting down by Sidewinder missile of a Canberra aircraft belonging to Grupo 2 of the Argentine air force. He was subsequently awarded a Mention in Dispatches.

17 May 1982   • Sea Harrier F.R.S.1 • Serial Number XZ438 • Number 809 Naval Air Squadron • Home Base – RNAS Yeovilton • Ilchester, Somerset

This aircraft was being tested by British Aerospace and Aeroplane and Armament Experimental Establishment (A&AEE). It was on the Yeovilton ski ramp trailing 330-gallon under-wing tanks.[6] The aircraft encountered an asymmetric fuel load condition in the empty tanks and the pilot, Lieutenant Commander David Poole RN successfully ejected but sustained minor injuries. The aircraft was written off. This aircraft was one of the first three production aircraft and had first flown before June 1979.

19 May 1982   • Sea King H.C.4 • Serial Number ZA294 • Number 846 Naval Air
Squadron • Home Base – RNAS Yeovilton • Ilchester, Somerset • South Atlantic Conflict

While cross-decking troops between HMS *Hermes* and HMS *Intrepid* a loud 'thump'
closely followed by a 'bang' was heard from those up on the deck of HMS *Intrepid*. It
came from the approaching helicopter. It was at about 300ft and coming in to land
on that ship.

The aircraft dipped once before diving into the sea. Incredibly, nine members of
the SAS managed to escape from the open door of the aircraft before it quickly
slipped beneath the waves of the South Atlantic. Bird feathers were found floating
on the water by the rescuers and it was suspected at the time that the Sea King had
sustained a bird strike, possibly by a black-browed albatross which has a massive wing-
span of some 8ft. Some doubt has since been cast on this theory.

Lieutenant R.I. Horton, Sub Lieutenant P.J. Humphreys and seven SAS troops were
rescued by a boat from HMS *Brilliant* and a Sea King of No 826 Naval Air Squadron.[7]

The casualties in this tragic accident were high. The aircrewman from the Sea King
was lost. In addition, eighteen members of the Special Air Service from D and G
Squadrons, one Royal Signals JNCO and one RAF officer were also killed. Their
bodies were not recovered.

PO35079S Corporal Aircrewman Michael David Love DSM, Royal Marines, aged
  twenty-two. He was born on 22 August 1959 in Preston, Lancashire.
23860354 WO2 Lawrence Gallagher BEM, 22nd SAS (formerly Royal Engineers).
  He was aged thirty seven.
24057552 Sergeant Sidney Albert Ivor Davidson, 22nd SAS (formerly the Parachute
  Regiment). He was aged thirty-four.
24154552 Acting Sergeant William Clark Hatton QGM, 22nd SAS (formerly the
  Parachute Regiment). He was aged thirty-one.
24325221 Acting Corporal Raymond Ernest Armstrong, 22nd SAS (formerly Royal
  Green Jackets). He was aged twenty-nine.
24221177 Acting Sergeant John Leslie Arthy, 22nd SAS (formerly the Welsh Guards).
  He was aged twenty-seven.
23969493 WO1 Malcolm Atkinson, 22nd SAS (formerly the Coldstream Guards). He
  was aged thirty-six.
24122095 Acting Corporal William John Begley, 22nd SAS (formerly Royal Corps of
  Transport). He was aged thirty-two.
24145047 Acting Sergeant Paul Alan Bunker, 22nd SAS (formerly Royal Army
  Ordnance Corps). He was aged twenty-eight.
23948859 Sergeant Philip Preston Currass QGM, 22nd SAS (formerly Royal Army
  Medical Corps). He was aged thirty-four.
24076141 Acting Sergeant William John Hughes, 22nd SAS (formerly the Welsh
  Guards). He was aged thirty-four.
24184150 Acting Sergeant Phillip Jones, 22nd SAS (formerly the Welsh Guards). He
  was aged twenty-seven.
24380988 Acting Corporal John Newton, 22nd SAS (formerly Royal Electrical and
  Mechanical Engineers). He was aged twenty-two.

24048957 Acting Warrant Officer 2 Sergeant Patrick O'Connor, 22nd SAS (formerly the Irish Guards). He was aged thirty-three.

24110456 Corporal Edward Thomas Walpole, 22nd SAS (formerly Royal Green Jackets). He was aged thirty-six.

24442111 Lance Corporal Paul Neville Lightfoot, 22nd SAS (formerly Royal Signals). He was aged twenty-one.

24369281 Acting Corporal Robert Allan Burns, 264 SAS Signal Squadron. He was aged twenty-two.

24398283 Acting Corporal Michael Vincent McHugh, 264 SAS Signal Squadron. He was aged twenty-two.

24256419 Corporal Stephen John Godfrey Sykes, 264 SAS Signal Squadron. He was aged twenty-five.

241956847 Corporal Douglas Frank McCormack, Royal Signals. He was aged twenty-six.

4232387 Flight Lieutenant Garth Walter Hawkins, Royal Air Force. He was aged thirty-nine.

20 May 1982   • Sea King H.C.4 • Serial Number ZA290 • Number 846 Naval Air Squadron • Home Base – RNAS Yeovilton • Ilchester, Somerset • Detached to HMS *Invincible* • South Atlantic Conflict

---

This helicopter was the one that 'mysteriously' landed in the bay of Agua Fresca (located on the Straits of Magellan) and was destroyed by its crew. It landed approximately halfway between the town of Punta Arenas and Puerto del Hambre in southern Chile when ZA290 became 'separated' from its carrier, HMS *Invincible*.

It has been rumoured that the aircraft was connected with Operation Mikado, a bold but cancelled attempt to attack the Argentine air base that housed the Exocet missiles on the Argentine mainland. The nearest Argentine military base at Rio Gallegos was approximately 100 miles away from the final position of the helicopter. It has been suggested that the aircraft dropped off eight SAS men before the crew destroyed the aircraft by burning it. The helicopter crew then surrendered to the Chilean authorities.

Lieutenant Alan Reginald Courtenay Bennett RN and Lieutenant Richard Hutchings RM were both awarded the Distinguished Service Cross. The DSC is awarded for 'gallantry during active operations against the enemy at sea'.

Leading Aircrewman Peter Blair Imrie was awarded the Distinguished Service Medal. For naval ranks up to the rank of chief petty officer the medal is awarded for 'for bravery and resourcefulness on active service at sea'.

The true reason for being at that place and at that time has never been revealed; suffice to say that medals are not usually awarded to anyone who gets lost!

23 May 1982   • Sea Harrier F.R.S.1 • Serial Number ZA192 • Number 800 Naval Air Squadron • Home Base – RNAS Yeovilton • Ilchester, Somerset • Detached to HMS *Hermes* • South Atlantic Conflict

---

About an hour before midnight Lieutenant Commander (P) Gordon Walter James Batt DSC was the last of three aircraft to launch from HMS *Hermes* to fly on a sortie to attack Stanley airfield during the Falklands War. His aircraft was seen to explode ahead of HMS *Hermes* before crashing.[8] The pilot was killed and lost at sea during the early evening of 23 May. The cause of the explosion was never established but is thought to have been a premature bomb explosion. In the Roll of Honour, his date of death is recorded as 24 May.

Lieutenant Commander Batt had flown twenty-nine operational missions in his Sea Harrier before he was lost on active service.

CO15622P Lieutenant Commander Gordon Walter James Batt DSC, aged thirty-seven, was born on 10 February 1945 at Worksop, Nottinghamshire.

A memorial to him can be found in the form of a large stone with his details engraved upon it. These also refer to an oak tree next to the stone, which is dedicated to him in the churchyard at All Saints church, Martock in Somerset. This church is also the second largest in Somerset.

25 May 1982   • Number 845 Naval Air Squadron Personnel • Home Base – RNAS Yeovilton • Ilchester, Somerset • Detached to *Atlantic Conveyor* • South Atlantic Conflict

On 23 May, the flight was transferred to the *Atlantic Conveyor*. An Argentine air attack by two Super Étendard fighters took place on 25 May. The ship was hit by two Exocet missiles and she was sunk three days later. This ship became the first British merchant vessel to be lost to enemy action since the end of the Second World War.

Six Wessex H.U.5s of No 848 Naval Air Squadron, a Lynx of No 815 Naval Air Squadron and three Chinooks from No 18 Squadron RAF were lost in this attack. Amongst the dozen men killed were two members of No 845 Naval Air Squadron based at RNAS Yeovilton.

D137112E LAEM (Leading Air Engineering Mechanic) Don Pryce, aged twenty-six, was born on 13 January 1956 in Odstock Hospital, Salisbury in Wiltshire. LAEM Pryce was killed and his body recovered from the sea by the crew of HMS *Alacrity*. Despite their attempts to revive him, they failed. He was buried at sea on the same day off the Falklands Islands at 51° 07'S 055° 27'W.

D176381K Air Engineering Mechanic (Radio) 1 Adrian John Anslow, aged twenty, was born on 9 September 1961 at Wordsley, Stafford, West Midlands. The sea is his grave.

25 May 1982   • Westland WS-58 Wessex H.U.5 • Serial Numbers XS480; XS495; XS499; XS512; XT476 and XT483 • Number 848 Naval Air Squadron • Home Base – RNAS Yeovilton • Ilchester, Somerset • Detached to *Atlantic Conveyor* • South Atlantic Conflict

These helicopters were lost with the MV *Atlantic Conveyor*. All were destroyed by fire on the ship. The remains of the aircraft went down with the ship.

29 May 1982   • Sea Harrier F.R.S.1 • Serial Number ZA174 • Number 801 Naval Air Squadron • Home Base – RNAS Yeovilton • Ilchester, Somerset • Detached to HMS *Invincible* • South Atlantic Conflict

During the Falklands War, HMS *Invincible* rolled in heavy seas to the east of the islands as she was making a turn and this aircraft slipped over her side and was lost.[9] The pilot, Lieutenant Commander (P) Guy James Michael Wheatley Broadwater, ejected safely and was rescued by helicopter.

1 June 1982   • Sea Harrier F.R.S.1 • Serial Number XZ456 • Number 801 Naval Air Squadron • Home Base – RNAS Yeovilton • Ilchester, Somerset • Detached to HMS *Invincible* • South Atlantic Conflict

This was 801 Squadron's final aircraft loss of the Falklands conflict. It was brought down by an Argentine 'Roland' surface-to-air missile position just south of Port Stanley.[10] The pilot, Flight Lieutenant Ian (Morts) Mortimer successfully ejected and after spending eight hours in his dinghy was finally rescued, cold but safe, at 2.30 a.m. by Lieutenant Commander Keith Dudley of No 820 Naval Air Squadron in Sea King H.A.S.5., Serial No XZ574. His crew were Sub Lieutenant J.A. Carr, Sub Lieutenant M. Finucane and LACMN Trotman.

19 August 1982   • Hawker Hunter F.4 converted to G.A.11 • Serial Number XE682 • Fleet Requirements and Air Direction Unit (FRADU) • Home Base – RNAS Yeovilton • Ilchester, Somerset

The aircraft concerned suffered a major bird strike near RNAS Yeovilton and had to make a nose wheels-up landing upon a bed of foam.[11] It sustained serious damage in doing so. The aircraft was assessed as having received Category 5 damage and was beyond economical repair. The aircraft's last known location was at RNAS Culdrose, where it was heavily used for 'spares' before finally ending up on the station's fire dump.

   This plane formed part of the Blue Herons Flying Display Team that was in operation from 1975 to 1980. On 6 September 1975, the unit made history as the first civilian aerobatics team to fly military aircraft. They were briefly resurrected for the RNAS Yeovilton Air Day in 1984 and also for the RNAS Culdrose Air Day in 1986.

16 December 1982   • Hawker Hunter F.4 converted to T.8 • Serial Number WT702 • Fleet Requirements and Air Direction Unit (FRADU) • Home Base – RNAS Yeovilton • Ilchester, Somerset

This aircraft was exercising from HMS *Exeter* with another aircraft. After a pairs low-level pass, WT702 climbed 10° and its right wing dropped at 400ft.[12] The aircraft turned sharply to the right and it dived into the sea and sank off the Isle of Wight,

3 miles north-west of the Nab Tower. The pilot, Mr John F. Mullins, was killed. His body was recovered from the sea.

Source: www.fradu-hunters.co.uk.

1983

21 January 1983   • Sea Harrier F.R.S.1 • Serial Number ZA177 • Number 899 Naval Air Squadron • Home Base – RNAS Yeovilton • Ilchester, Somerset

The aircraft developed an inverted spin in a mock dog fight with a Hunter aircraft at 11,000ft. The student pilot, Lieutenant (P) K. Fox, sustained injuries when he ejected. The aircraft came down near Cattistock, Dorset, and narrowly avoided a large housing estate, crashing within 150 yards of a house. Mr Tony Herring, the kennels huntsman of the Cattistock Hunt, was tending the pack at the time and he was reported as saying that he saw the jet fly low over the village, turn over and then crash into the ground.

This aircraft had two kills during the Falklands War. At the time this aircraft was flown by Flight Lieutenant Dave Morgan RAF of No 800 Naval Air Squadron over Choiseul Sound, Falkland Islands. Its Sidewinder missiles brought down two Skyhawks of Grupo 5 of the Argentine air force.

Source: *Western Gazette.*

16 May 1983   • Hawker Hunter F.4 converted to G.A.11 • Serial Number XE716 • Fleet Requirements and Air Direction Unit (FRADU) • Home Base – RNAS Yeovilton • Ilchester, Somerset

This aircraft suffered an engine failure at low level and crashed into the English Channel at West Bay, Dorset, some 2 nautical miles from the runway at Portland. The pilot, Mr R.M. 'Dan' Carter, safely ejected 2 miles from the end of Portland runway and was rescued by helicopter. This aircraft was originally an RAF Hawker Hunter F.4 and was one of forty converted to G.A.11 and fitted with the Rolls-Royce Avon 113 engine. It was transferred to the Royal Navy in 1962.[13]

15 June 1983   • Sea Harrier F.R.S.1 • Serial Number XZ500 • Number 800 Naval Air Squadron • Home Base – RNAS Yeovilton • Ilchester, Somerset • Detached to HMS *Hermes*

This plane failed to recover from an inverted spin during a test flight over the Bay of Biscay.[14] The pilot, Lieutenant (P) Simon Hargreaves, successfully ejected from an inverted position from a height of 1,000ft. He was rescued by helicopter.

During the Falklands War, this aircraft was being flown by Flight Lieutenant John Leeming of No 800 Naval Air Squadron when he shot down a Skyhawk of the 3rd Nav Ftr & Attack Escuadrilla by means of his 30mm cannon. This successful attack occurred over the Falklands Sound. The attack was confirmed.

10 October 1983 • Westland Wessex H.U.5 • Serial Number XT450 • Number 845 Naval Air Squadron • Home Base – RNAS Yeovilton • Ilchester, Somerset • Detached to HMS *Hermes*

This aircraft made a heavy landing in Saros Bay, Turkey, during a NATO exercise.[15] The starboard oleo collapsed and the main rotor blades hit the ground while still turning. It was declared a Category 4 loss. Sub Lieutenant A.J. Marshall and his crewman, Leading Airman M.J. McLoughlin were unhurt. The passengers, who also escaped unhurt, were the Rev. Hillard, Captain A.J. Berry RM, Corporal Bentley RM, Marine Galloway, Flight Lieutenant Partridge RAF, Mr J. Hands and Mr R. Hammond, both of the Independent Television News network.

20 October 1983 • Sea Harrier F.R.S.1 • Serial Number ZA194 • Number 899 Naval Air Squadron • Home Base – RNAS Yeovilton • Ilchester, Somerset

This aircraft, flown by Major W. O'Hara USMC, an exchange officer from the US Marine Corps, came down near West Knighton, Dorset, after control restriction during a combat manoeuvre. The pilot successfully ejected. The aircraft was written off.[16]

During the Falklands War this aircraft was flown by Lt Martin Hale of No 800 Naval Air Squadron. He used a Sidewinder missile to shoot down a Dagger from Grupo 6.

7 December 1983 • Westland WS-58 Wessex H.U.5 • Serial Number XT459 • Number 845 Naval Air Squadron • Home Base – RNAS Yeovilton • Ilchester, Somerset

Whilst turning on the auto-stabilisation system and in level flight, this aircraft flew into the ground near the airfield at Bardufoss, Norway.[17] The helicopter broke up and Sub Lieutenant D.A. Edwards, Leading Aircrewman P. Imrie and seven other Norwegian troops they were transporting were injured. The wreckage of the aircraft finally ended its days at Park Aviation Supply at Faygate.

1984

16 March 1984 • Sea Harrier F.R.S.1 • Serial Number XZ496 • Number 801 Naval Air Squadron • Home Base – RNAS Yeovilton • Ilchester, Somerset • Detached to HMS *Illustrious*

This aircraft came down in the North Sea off Norway when its engine failed on its approach to HMS *Illustrious*.[18] The pilot, Lieutenant Commander Michael William Watson, successfully ejected and was slightly injured. He was picked up by an 814 Squadron Sea King after spending ten minutes in the sea.

During the Falklands War this aircraft had a confirmed kill by Lieutenant Commander Mike Blisset of No 800 Naval Air Squadron. By use of its Sidewinder missiles it brought down a Sky Hawk of Grupo 4 of the Argentine air force.

9 June 1984   • Socata Rallye 110ST Galopin • G-BGKB • Dunkeswell Airfield • Honiton, Devon • Privately Owned

The aircraft took off from Dunkeswell airfield at 9.55 a.m with the pilot and two passengers. The trip was meant to be a sixteenth birthday treat for one of them. The aircraft was next seen over the town of Wellington, near Taunton. It was flying straight and level with no hint of any problems. Several people then saw the aircraft near Wiviliscombe and Langley Marsh, where it flew in a figure-of-eight pattern at about 1,200ft.

Eyewitnesses then reported that the aircraft flew straight and level for about fifteen seconds when suddenly they saw the wings of the aircraft fold up and sweep back. The aircraft then dived vertically into the ground near the water filter station at Maundown, Somerset (Grid Reference 067291). It did not catch fire on impact.

The pilot of the aircraft, twenty-eight-year-old Andrew Meads, sixteen-year-old Rob Davey (whose birthday it was) and sixteen-year-old Steven Pearson were killed. It was reported that the cause of the accident was a wing spar that suffered an upward overload failure.

Sources: AAIB Report 12/84 reference EW/C875/01; ex-policeman Tom Lovegrove of Williton, who was the policeman on duty at the crash site.

31 October 1984   • Hawker Hunter T.8C • Serial Number XL584 • Fleet Requirements and Air Direction Unit (FRADU) • Home Base – RNAS Yeovilton • Ilchester, Somerset

This aircraft crashed into the sea just off the coast at Portland.[19] It was carrying out a high-speed, low-level run for the Fraser Gunnery Range in poor visibility when the accident occurred. Tragically, the pilot, the well-liked and respected Mr L.E. (Ted) Clowes was killed.

1 December 1984   • Sea Harrier F.R.S.1 • Serial Number XZ458 • Number 800 Naval Air Squadron • Home Base – RNAS Yeovilton • Ilchester, Somerset

This aircraft was operating from HMS *Illustrious*. During Exercise High Tide, it sustained a low-level bird strike at 500ft. This caused engine failure near Fort William, Scotland.[20] The pilot, Lieutenant (P) Collier, successfully ejected, although he sustained minor injuries. The aircraft came down near Kilmonivaig Farm, Gairlochy, north of Fort William.

1985

7 February 1985   • Sea Harrier T.4.N • Serial Number ZB606 • Number 899 Naval Air Squadron • Home Base – RNAS Yeovilton • Ilchester, Somerset

During mid-afternoon, this aircraft took off on a routine training flight. It suddenly plunged into the ground and exploded in a field yards from the main A37 road at Sticklebridge, between Ilchester and Lydford, approximately 3 miles north of RNAS Yeovilton.[21] The normally very busy trunk road was fortunately not carrying much traffic at that time, which was extremely lucky because pieces of the wreckage were scattered across the road.

CO25679L Lieutenant (P) Andrew James George, aged twenty-five, who was born on 10 May 1959, was killed. His last resting place is in the Royal Navy Cemetery at St Bartholomew's, Yeovilton village. His final resting place is shown in Appendix 2.

CO31640E Midshipman (O) Paul Duncan Norman, aged twenty-five, was born on 30 June 1959 and he was also killed. He is buried in the Royal Navy Cemetery at St Bartholomew's, Yeovilton village. His final resting place is shown in Appendix 2.

29 November 1985 • Hawker Hunter F.4 converted to G.A.11 • Serial Number WV267 • Fleet Requirements and Air Direction Unit (FRADU) • Home Base – RNAS Yeovilton • Ilchester, Somerset

The pilot made a safe emergency landing at RNAS Yeovilton, Somerset, after the aircraft suffered a bird strike.[22] This was the second bird strike that had happened to this particular aircraft. In August 1982, it suffered its first, which resulted in the aircraft being sent to RAF Abingdon where it was repaired and modernised further. It was then returned to RNAS Yeovilton in October 1984 before suffering its second and final bird strike.

The second incident resulted in the aircraft being classified as Category 3 damage (repairable). The category of damage was then upgraded to Category 5. As a result the aircraft was not repaired and in due course was allocated to the RNAS Culdrose School of Aircraft Handlers, Culdrose in Cornwall.

It was kept in a ground-running condition so that trainee aircraft handlers could learn how to control and move an aircraft around safely. The military career of this aircraft ended in 1993 when it was finally put up for disposal.

The last known location of this aircraft was at the European Warbird Organisation based in California, USA.

1986

25 March 1986   • Westland Wasp H.A.S.1 • Serial Number XT439 • Number 829 Naval Air Squadron • Home Base – RNAS Portland

---

This helicopter crash-landed after loss of control at the RNAS Yeovilton outstation at Merryfield, near Ilton in Somerset.[23] After a heavy landing it ended up lying on its side, with its main rotor blade twisted and broken. The tail rotor drive shaft was also severed. Lieutenant A.J. Symons of Royal Naval Standards Flight (Rotary Wing) and Lieutenant A.L. Davison of Hydra Flight both received minor injuries.

The aircraft was later sold as a civilian helicopter. Its last known location, as of June 2010, was at Hemel Hempstead in Hertfordshire, where it was privately owned by the Alan Allen Aviation Collection and placed in a state of preservation.

16 April 1986   • Sea Harrier F.R.S.1 • Serial Number XZ491 • Number 801 Naval Air Squadron • Home Base – RNAS Yeovilton • Ilchester, Somerset • Detached to HMS *Ark Royal*

Uncertain of the position because of an instrument malfunction, short of fuel and some 60 miles away from the HMS *Ark Royal*, the engine of this aircraft flamed out.[24] The pilot, Lieutenant Commander Andrew Bruce Sinclair of No 801 Naval Air Squadron, safely ejected. The aircraft crashed about 10km south-west of the island of Benbecula. The Ministry of Defence DASA site gives the location of the crash as being 120 nautical miles west of the island of Tiree, the most westerly island of the Inner Hebrides. The aircraft was recovered and its remains were sent to the Park Aviation Supply Yard, Faygate, Surrey. This aircraft yard is now closed and the remains of this aircraft were last sighted in 2007.

This aircraft had seen active service during the Falklands War.

17 June 1986   • Harrier G.R.3 • Serial Number XW916 • Number 233 Operational Conversion Unit • Home Base – RAF Gutersloh • West Germany

---

A flight of four Harriers was detached from its home base of RAF Gutersloh to RAF Wittering for the day.[25] The aircraft took off from RAF Wittering for a low-level sortie but on approaching RNAS Yeovilton found the weather made the sortie unsuitable.

The leader authorised practice diversions to RNAS Yeovilton. On a ground-controlled approach to the airfield, the leader's electrics failed and power was lost, causing the nose to drop. The pilot, Flight Lieutenant Gerry A. Humphries, immediately called for full power but the engine did not respond. The aircraft was successfully abandoned and crashed just off the runway. The pilot was slightly injured in the incident.

1987

23 July 1987　　• Sea King Mk 42B • Serial Number ZF527 • Westlands
Helicopter Limited • Home Base – Westland's Airfield • Yeovil, Somerset

Whilst carrying out EH101 sonar dipping trials, this helicopter suffered a loss of power on the No 2 engine and ditched into the Mediterranean Sea off St Raphael, southern France. As it hit the water it bent the tail fuselage but still remained afloat. It sank after the flotation bag ruptured while the aircraft was under tow.

This aircraft had been recently sold to the Indian navy and was due to be delivered to them with the Indian Serial No IN514.

Source: www.ukserials.com.

15 October 1987　　• Sea Harrier F.R.S.1 • Serial Number ZA190 • Number 801
Naval Air Squadron • Home Base – RNAS Yeovilton • Ilchester, Somerset • Detached to
HMS *Ark Royal*

Whilst flying towards a mock raid by Buccaneers, this aircraft ingested a large bird at 250ft over the Atlantic. The engine caught fire and failed.[26] The Ministry of Defence DASA site gives the location of the crash as being 85 nautical miles south-west of the island of Tiree, the most westerly island of the Inner Hebrides. The pilot, Lieutenant D. O'Meara, successfully ejected.

This particular aircraft had performed well in the Falklands War and was credited with two kills: Lieutenant S. Thomas RN, 801 NAS, HMS *Hermes* (2 Daggers) and one shared kill, Lieutenant Commander David Braithwaite RN, 801 NAS, HMS *Hermes* (1 Puma).

24 October 1987　　• Socato MS.892A Commodore 150 • Registration Number
G-ATWZ • Privately Owned

The aircraft was taking off from the grass/gravel runway at Westbury-sub-Mendip unlicensed airfield. The runway is 540m long and is narrow, with a width of 20m. This aircraft crashed on this date, but little is known about the actual incident.

As a result of the crash the aircraft was deregistered. By this time it had flown a total of 1,307 hours. The AAIB have recorded it as Bulletin 1/88 which is not available. The AAIB does confirm, however, that the accident did indeed occur. This is recorded in AAIB Bulletin No 9/94, Ref. EW/G94/07/08, which refers back to this incident.

1988

14 June 1988 • Hawker Hunter F.4 converted to G.A.11 • Serial Number WT809 • Fleet Requirements and Air Direction Unit (FRADU) • Home Base – RNAS Yeovilton • Ilchester, Somerset

The aircraft was on its final approach to land at RNAS Yeovilton when it suffered an engine flame out.[27] The pilot, Lieutenant Commander (P) David Dawson Braithwaite RN, instantly reacted by using his remaining height and speed to change his flight path and avoid any populated areas. He ejected at the last possible moment through the canopy, and the aircraft finally crashed safely into some woodland that was close to the B3151 road. The fuselage of the aircraft remained largely intact. Before finally coming to rest the aircraft had also ploughed through a pig slurry pit, picking up a lot of its undesirable contents on the way.

The aircraft came to rest just a few hundred yards away from the Ilchester Primary School and the main A303 road. A grateful local council sent an official letter of thanks to RNAS Yeovilton regarding the actions of the pilot.

Source: *Western Gazette.*

1989

10 June 1989 • Hawker Sea Fury F.B.11 • Serial Number TF956 • Royal Navy Historical Flight • Home Base – RNAS Yeovilton • Ilchester, Somerset

This aircraft suffered a hydraulic failure shortly after take-off from RNAS Prestwick.[28] The pilot retracted the undercarriage but only one wheel locked. In an effort to free the wheel the pilot selected 'Undercarriage down' and this occurred. However, unbeknownst to the pilot, a hydraulic pipe had burst and the wheel that didn't lock went down again and locked into position. Despite the best efforts of the pilot to free the undercarriage, including bouncing the aircraft off the runway and going up and down for about three hours, nothing would work. The pilot, Lieutenant Commander John Beattie, was ordered to bale out. He took the plane up to 6,000ft and abandoned it over the Irish Sea, off Prestwick, Scotland. He was picked up by a Sea King helicopter.

27 July 1989 • McDonnell-Douglas Phantom F.G.1 • Serial Number XV576 • Number 111 Squadron RAF • Home Base – RAF Leuchars • Fife, Scotland

The aircraft undershot on approach to landing at RNAS Yeovilton and crash-landed.[29] It was returned to RAF Leuchars by road and withdrawn from use in January 1990. The aircraft was finally scrapped in Adams Scrapyard, Glasgow, in April 1992.

4 October 1989   • Sea Harrier F.R.S.1 • Serial Number ZA191 • Number 801 Naval Air Squadron • Home Base – RNAS Yeovilton • Ilchester, Somerset • Detached to HMS *Ark Royal*

This aircraft hit the mast of HMS *Ark Royal* during a fly-past and ditched into the sea.[30] The pilot, Lieutenant Paul Rowland Simmonds-Short, safely ejected 13 nautical miles west of Portland Bill, Dorset.

This Sea Harrier had a record of one shared kill during the Falklands War (Flight Lieutenant Leeming RAF, 800 NAS, HMS *Hermes* (A109 helicopter)). On another occasion the aircraft attacked the Argentine supply vessel *Bahia Buen Suceso*, and it was damaged by anti-aircraft fire, sustaining a hit in the tail. This was swiftly repaired and the aircraft became battle ready after a few hours.

By the middle of June 1982 this aircraft had flown seventy-one operational sorties, dropped a total of two LG bombs and expended 600 30mm cannon shells.

1 December 1989   • Sea Harrier F.R.S.1 • Serial Number XZ451 • Number 801 Naval Air Squadron • Home Base – RNAS Yeovilton • Ilchester, Somerset • Detached to HMS *Ark Royal*

The forward reaction control valve seat diaphragm of this aircraft failed and the seat detached, jamming the controls. The Sea Harrier then crashed into the Mediterranean Sea near the Acmi Range, which lies off Decimomannu, Sardinia.[31] The pilot, Lieutenant (P) Michael Frederick Auckland, ejected from his crashing aircraft but sustained serious injuries in the process. He was picked up by a local fishing vessel.

He was later fated to die in another aircraft crash in February 1996 at the rank of lieutenant commander. This is documented later on in the book.

This particular aircraft had a good record during the Falklands War. It was credited with a total of three kills (Lieutenant Commander 'Sharkey' Ward RN, 801 NAS, HMS *Invincible* (Pucara, C130), and Lieutenant A. Curtis RN, 801 NAS, HMS *Invincible* (Canberra)).

1990s

1990

10 April 1990 • Hawker Hunter F.4 converted to T.8.C • Serial Number XF985 • Fleet Requirements and Air Direction Unit (FRADU) • Home Base – RNAS Yeovilton • Ilchester, Somerset

Returning from an exercise over the English Channel near Portland, the aircraft suffered a severe control restriction of a jammed aileron.[1] The cause was later reported as being the failure of a pin in the port aileron hydraulic jack. Despite trying to regain control of the aircraft, the civilian pilot, Mr Richard (Rick) Lea, aged forty-six, from Glastonbury, had to abandon her.

He was acclaimed as a local hero after he had skilfully steered the stricken aircraft away from the Herrison Hospital, which almost stood alone in the countryside. 'As it screamed over the roof of the psychiatric hospital eyewitnesses heard a popping sound and a bang.'

The aircraft crashed into a hillside near Roman Farm, Charminster, Dorset. At that time the hillside was covered in sheep and the aircraft killed dozens of them and their newborn lambs, as it created a 15ft crater in the ground at its point of impact. Rescuers were almost immediately on the scene to discover the crater and the smouldering wreckage, with the pilot parachuting down to them.

'He was dazed and had bitten his lip, but he was so calm you would have thought it was an everyday experience,' said first-aider Rebecca Buchan, nineteen, first on the scene.

A naval SAR helicopter was soon on the scene and airlifted the pilot away to the military hospital at RAF Wroughton, near Swindon, for a check up.

Source: *Western Gazette*, 12 April 1990.

8 May 1990 • Sea Harrier F.R.S.1 • Serial Number XZ460 • Number 800 Naval Air Squadron • Home Base – RNAS Yeovilton • Ilchester, Somerset • Detached to HMS *Invincible*

The aircraft flew into the Mediterranean Sea near Cabocogiari, Sardinia, just after take-off from HMS *Invincible* while taking part in Exercise Dragon Hammer.[2] The crash killed the aircraft's pilot and he was lost.

This aircraft saw active service during the Falklands War. The aircraft was being piloted by Lieutenant Commander Batt when he scored a direct hit with a bomb on the Argentine intelligence-gathering ship, *Narwhal*. The bomb had been released too low, and as expected by the pilot it did not function because the safety device that prevented it from exploding did not have time to unwind.

CO30357L Lieutenant (P) Stephen James Holmes, aged thirty, was born on 11 April 1960 at Birkenhead, near Liverpool.

14 July 1990 • Hawker Sea Fury T.20 • Serial Number WG655 • Royal Navy Historical Flight • Home Base – RNAS Yeovilton • Ilchester, Somerset

---

The aircraft was outbound from RNAS Yeovilton to a display at Silverstone. When passing over Bruton, Somerset, the engine suddenly cut out. The power plant became a dead piece of metal and the aircraft began to lose height rapidly.[3] The pilot spotted a large field and he prepared for a forced wheels-up emergency landing. Initially the aircraft ran along the ground successfully but the field had a hidden slope and the aircraft began to turn. In the middle of this open countryside the crew found themselves heading toward a small stand of three oak trees.

The port wing of the aircraft struck the first tree and resulted in the fuselage swinging between the two other trees. Consequently the starboard wing and cockpit side struck the second tree, severed the port wing and split the fuselage in two. The pilot, Lieutenant Commander John Beattie, was hardly hurt, but the chief engineer, Chief Petty Officer Eric Young, wasn't so lucky. He suffered broken ribs and a dislocated shoulder. Later investigation showed that a corroded con rod had been the cause of the engine failure.

After the accident, the remains were inspected and deemed unrepairable then put up for disposal. The remains went initially to New Zealand where the wing folding mechanism wound up in Fury ZK-SFR. Chuck Greenhill, who houses his fine collection of aircraft at Kenosha, Wisconsin, has always had an interest in aircraft with Naval connections. He purchased the remains and had them shipped to Kenosha where Tim McCarter and his crew went to work. After thousands of man-hours, the project began to look like a Sea Fury, but with the other aircraft projects in the hangar it was decided to ship the plane to Sanders Aeronautics, the 'Sea Fury Kings', for completion.

On May 24, 2005 Brian Sanders took N20MD up for a successful first post-restoration flight – the first time the aircraft had flown in 15 years.

Sources: www.sandersaircraft.com; www.stringbag.flyer.co.uk.

1991

10 May 1991 • Sea Harrier F.R.S.1 • Serial Number ZD609 • Number 801 Naval Air Squadron • Home Base – RNAS Yeovilton • Ilchester, Somerset

---

This aircraft suffered a pitch control restriction, probably caused by the ingress of a foreign object while acting as No 2 during a three-aircraft low-level loose tactical formation flight.[4] The pilot, Lieutenant Henry George Murray Mitchell, ejected successfully at 100ft, although he was injured in the process.

A curious sequence of events then occurred. By ejecting, the aircraft's centre of gravity was changed and it climbed clear of the ground. The No 3 aircraft, whose radio had failed, joined up with the pilotless aircraft thinking it was leader. He followed it through a series of manoeuvres for two minutes until the aircraft finally crashed into Wentwood Forest, near Penhow, Chepstow, Gwent. The Ministry of Defence DASA site gives the location of the crash as being 1 nautical mile north-east of Parc Seymour, Gwent.

12 September 1991 • Tornado G.R.1 • Serial Number ZA540 • Number 27 Squadron RAF • Home Base – RAF Marham

---

The crew of two were flying a low-level training mission over the Bristol Channel when they noticed warning captions connected with the fly-by-wire system.[5] The crew heard a bang and a solid jolt came from the rear of the aircraft. Flying controls instantly became hard to control. As the aircraft climbed to 1,000ft a left-hand engine fire was indicated. At this point the captain made a Mayday call.

Another hard jolt was felt and at 5,000ft the nose pitched down and the aircraft commenced a gentle roll to the left without pilot guidance. At this point, and with complete loss of control of the aircraft, the crew successfully ejected south of Steep Holme Island. Unfortunately, neither the accident flight recorder nor any significant wreckage was recovered from the Bristol Channel.

The crew of the aircraft were Flight Lieutenants A. Edwards and W.C.J. Ball.

Source: Defence Analytical Services and Advice for National Statistics – Aircraft Accidents and Associated Deaths and Major Injuries 1990–2007.

1992

15 February 1992   • Hawker Hunter F.4 converted to T.8 • Serial Number WV363 • Fleet Requirements and Air Direction Unit (FRADU) • Home Base – RNAS Yeovilton • Ilchester, Somerset

---

This aircraft was detached to Lossiemouth and to carry out mock air raids against HMS *Battleaxe*. The pilot was informed that his aircraft was on fire and ditched 70 miles north of the Isle of Lewis.[6] Flight Lieutenant Spon Clayton ejected successfully and was quickly located by a Royal Dutch Navy P-3C. He was then picked up by RN Lynx ZD251 and flown to Stornoway and safety. This same officer was later to eject from a Harrier crash successfully in 2001 and this is documented later on in the book.

28 May 1992   • Sea Harrier F.R.S.1 • Serial Number ZA193 • Number 800 Naval Air Squadron • Home Base – RNAS Yeovilton • Ilchester, Somerset • Detached to HMS *Invincible*

The control column of this aircraft disconnected from the reaction controls whilst hovering alongside HMS *Invincible* in the eastern Mediterranean, off Cyprus.[7] The aircraft ditched into the sea alongside the ship. The pilot, Lieutenant Peter Wilson, ejected safely.

This aircraft was credited with the downing of a Dagger aircraft during the Falklands War. It was piloted at the time by Lieutenant Commander David A. Smith RN, 800 NAS, HMS *Hermes*.

1993

8 January 1993   • Cessna 172 RG Cutlass • Registration Number G-BOUH •
Privately Owned

The aircraft was on a flight from Leicester to Westbury-Sub-Mendip, a grass airstrip orientated 11/29 with a length of 540me and width of 20m. The airstrip is situated on the site of a disused railway line and is positioned on a raised embankment. The weather at the time of the accident was fine with good visibility and a surface wind of 2600/06 kt.

On arrival at the airstrip the pilot examined the runway by completing two low level fly pasts. He elected to land on Runway 11 and after completing the normal landing checks positioned the aircraft on long finals in order to give him plenty of time to establish a stabilised approach. After a normal landing the aircraft began to slew to the left. This was corrected but was followed by a further sudden yaw to the left. The left landing gear departed the runway causing the aircraft to descend the bank and collide with a hedge. The pilot and passengers vacated the aircraft using the normal exits without injury.

The pilot reported that he should have examined the airstrip more closely before visiting by air as the dimensions of the strip left little margin for error. The aircraft's departure off the side of the runway was compounded by the fact that it touched down initially two to three feet left of the centre line.

There was substantial damage to both of the wings, propeller and landing gear of this aircraft. The pilot and his two passengers were unhurt. The time of the accident was 2.15 p.m.

Source: AAIB Bulletin No 3/93, Ref. EW/G93/01/03.

23 June 1993   • Cameron A-180 Hot Air Balloon • Registration Number G-BTYE •
Privately Owned

The commander stated that, at the conclusion of a one hour's flight, he made a firm but otherwise normal landing in a field of grass. The wind at the time was 6 kt from the north-west which dragged the basket for about 10m before the envelope deflated and the basket tipped on to its side.

One passenger immediately complained of pain in her left leg but asked the commander not to call for assistance. Later that evening she went to hospital where a suspected cracked tibia was diagnosed and a plaster cast was fitted. The plaster cast was removed five days later.

The commander was unaware that the passenger, a senior citizen, had a medical history of weak bones in her left leg. The passenger stated that the commander was not to blame for the accident.

The incident occurred at 8.25 p.m. at Rice Farm, Meare near Glastonbury. With the pilot were eight passengers. The accident was classified as a Category 4.

Source: AAIB Bulletin No 9/93, Ref. EW/G93/06/23.

23 October 1993 • Cameron A-210 Hot Air Balloon • Registration Number G-BTCK • Privately Owned

The balloon departed from Dinnington, Somerset at 1600hours on a pleasure cruise. The wind was calm at the departure time. However, some 30 minutes later, the pilot noted that the wind strength over the hills was stronger, and that landing was made difficult by the adjacent hills. On touchdown, the balloon tipped over and dragged for a short distance.

The pilot reported that one passenger, a 76 year old lady, did not hear the command to get into the landing position and knocked into another passenger. She was shaken at the time, but the extent of her injury was only revealed to the pilot one week later.

Source: AAIB Bulletin No 1/94, Ref. EW/G93/10/26.

4 November 1993 • Piper PA-31-350 Navajo Chieftain • Registration Number G-VIPP • Privately Owned

This aircraft had previously completed a trip with passengers that day. It later left Harwarden for Filton airport but on take-off a strong smell that reminded the pilot of paraffin permeated the aircraft. On approaching Filton the pilot selected the gear-down lever, and although this felt normal, he noticed that the gear transit light and the gears down light had not illuminated. The pilot tried the procedure again but was unsuccessful and so he initiated a go-round procedure. He made several attempts over the next hour to get the landing gear down.

In the meantime, the pilot had established a radio link with engineers on the ground to discuss the problem with the gear. He then flew slowly past the air-traffic control tower to enable a visual inspection from the ground. The pilot was informed that the gear appeared to be fully retracted and that there was no outward sign of a hydraulic leak.

He then re-established the aircraft on the racetrack pattern and briefed his assistant and his passengers on the gear-up landing and evacuation procedures. For the gear-up landing the pilot had decided to land on the main runway, rather than the grass, because he did not wish to manoeuvre the aircraft close to the ground, and because there were numerous obstructions in the grass areas; the weather had not changed significantly since his first approach. He agreed with ATC that he would carry out an ILS to a visual approach on Runway 27 and commenced his approach. At 500ft on QFE 1005 mb he became visual with the runway, selected the master switch off, and the ground clearance switch on to retain radio contact with ATC. Subsequently, at approximately 50ft to 100ft agl, the pilot retarded the throttles, feathered the propellers, leaned the mixtures and pulled the fire wall shut-off valves. He held the aircraft off the runway while reducing speed and touched down gently just below 80 kt. Retardation was gradual and the aircraft remained on the centre line until it came to a stop. The crew and the passengers, who were uninjured, evacuated using all available exits. The AFS were already in attendance and quickly confirmed that the aircraft was secure.

On later examination it was found that a faulty hydraulic pipe had disconnected, causing the problem.

Source: AAIB Bulletin No 1/94, Ref. EW/C93/11/1.

1994

5 January 1994   • Sea Harrier F.R.S.1 converted to F.A.2 • Serial Number XZ495 • Number 899 Naval Air Squadron • Home Base – RNAS Yeovilton • Ilchester, Somerset

This aircraft suffered engine failure over the Bristol Channel, 5 nautical miles east-south-east of Lundy Island.[8] The pilot, Lieutenant (P) Peter Neil Wilson, ejected safely and was picked up seven minutes later by a 22 Squadron RAF helicopter from Chivenor.

This aircraft saw service during the Falklands War, finally returning to the UK on board HMS *Invincible* on 17 September 1982.

16 April 1994   • Sea Harrier F.R.S.1 • Serial Number XZ498 • Number 801 Naval Air Squadron • Home Base – RNAS Yeovilton • Ilchester, Somerset • Detached to HMS *Ark Royal*

This aircraft was shot down by a Bosnian Serb surface-to-air Missile 9 (SA16 – Man Portable) near Goradze, Bosnia.

Two Sea Harriers were guided onto Bosnian-Serb armour on the outskirts of Gorazde by SAS forward air controllers. These were stationed on top of the Hotel

Gardina which has a commanding view of the town. The Sea Harriers, under the rules of engagement, were to make a low pass over the area to try and stop the armour advancing on the city. It was on this pass that XZ498 was hit and the pilot ejected. The pilot ejected and landed in the Muslim held lines of the city. The pilot was later handed over to the SAS team in the city. They and the pilot subsequently escaped and evaded and were picked up by a French forces Puma.

The pilot, Lieutenant (P) Lieutenant Nick Richardson, subsequently wrote a book about this incident titled *No Escape Zone*.

This aircraft saw service during the Falklands War, finally returning to the UK on board HMS *Invincible* on 17 September 1982. The dramatic voice recording of the events surrounding this can be downloaded from the following website: http://airserbia.com

Source: www.aeronautics.ru.

2 May 1994   • Cameron A-250 • Hot Air Balloon • Registration Number G-BUZY • Construction Number 2936 • Privately Owned

The balloon had taken off from Taunton at 6.45 a.m. and the crash occurred at 7.45 a.m. The total number of persons on board consisted of the pilot and seventeen passengers. The pilot and eight passengers suffered minor injuries. The balloon came down near Williton, Somerset, and the accident was classified as a Category 3. It was a relatively new balloon, having been manufactured in 1993.

On landing in a field of long grass, the balloon bounced at least once with what the passengers described variously as a 'crash' and 'a real thud'. The commander stated that after landing from a normal approach, he was pulling 'enthusiastically' on the parachute line which spills air rapidly from the top of the balloon on landing, when the basket tipped over and he was pulled out by the pressure being exerted by the parachute line. A passenger who was sharing the pilot's compartment also fell out at the same time.

Following the loss of two occupants, the residual lift of the balloon exceeded its weight and it began to climb. The commander, who was slightly injured from his exit from the basket, ran after the balloon calling on the passengers to pull on the parachute line to reduce the lift of the envelope. Before the dazed and confused passengers were able to comply with the commander's instructions, the balloon had climbed to a 100ft. Once the parachute line had been pulled the balloon began a rapid descent. At some stage, one of the passengers had pulled a rotation line which allows the balloon to rotate about its vertical axis and the passengers were now facing in the direction of the travel of the balloon instead of the preferred orientation for landing of having their backs to the direction of travel. The basket's initial ground contact was with the A358 road. It then bounced into a 7ft-high hedge before toppling on its side and back on to the pavement bordering the road. The balloon's recovery team and friends of the passengers who had been following the flight in cars were quickly on the scene and dealt with the injured passengers. The emergency services were quickly on the scene and attended to the injured passengers and several passengers were taken to hospital. None were detained.

The commander considered that a faster than average horizontal speed, a higher than usual vertical speed and the hard nature of the ground combined to produce a firm but not exceptionally heavy landing and, in the absence of any other factors, he would not have anticipated any other problems on touchdown. However, he considered that the additional factors of the unexpectedly high back pressure on the parachute line together with the possibility that the passenger who was occupying the pilot's compartment with him may not have been holding on as briefed, exacerbated the situation to the point where the accident occurred.

Source: AAIB Bulletin No 9/94, Ref. EW/G94/05/06.

27 June 1994   • Sea Harrier T.4.N • Serial Number XW268 • Number 899 Naval Air Squadron • Home Base – RNAS Yeovilton • Ilchester, Somerset

This aircraft had a heavy landing at RNAS Yeovilton during an instrument approach, bursting its tyres and sustaining a collapsed starboard outrigger.[9] The aircraft was consequently written off, probably due to its age (twenty-four years).

It was formally a RAF Harrier T.2., being first flown on 5 November 1970. It was then modified by the RAF into a T.4.A. Later, in 1990, the aircraft was transferred to the Royal Navy and was one of three converted to a T.4.N. The aircraft went into private ownership in December 2008, and the owner was planning to restore it for exhibition purposes. In April 2011, the restored aircraft was on display in the City of Norwich Aviation Museum, Old Norwich Road, Horsham St Faith, Norwich.

1 July 1994   • Jodel DR 1050-M1 Sicile Record • Registration Number G-BTIW
• Privately Owned

The aircraft was taking off from the grass/gravel Runway 11 at Westbury-Sub-Mendip unlicensed airfield, for a flight to Bristol Airport. The runway is 540m long, and is narrow with a width of 20m. The runway runs along a raised embankment, which is the track of a disused railway line, and is partly bounded by a hedge. The pilot reported that the aircraft lifted off normally, but at around 60 kt the left wing dropped and it yawed left, causing the left wing to strike the hedge. The aircraft continued left and struck the ground in the field to the left and below the level of the runway. The stall warning horn did not sound during the short flight. The aircraft turned over after impact, breaking off the outboard section of each wing, and throwing clear the engine, fuel tank and instrument panel. The pilot, who was wearing a lap and diagonal harness, evacuated the aircraft through the broken canopy.

The weather at the time was good, with the reported surface wind calm to 0900/10 kt.

AAIB records indicate two other similar occurrences at this airfield. The first was an MS.892A Rallye, registration G-ATWZ, on take-off from Runway 29 on 4 October 1987 (AAIB Bulletin No 1/88). The other was a Cessna 172 RG, registration G-BOUH, while landing on Runway 11 on 8 January 1993 (AAIB Bulletin No 3/93).

The pilot suffered minor injuries but the aircraft was written off. It was beyond economical repair. This aircraft was built in 1965 as Construction No 618.

Source: AAIB Bulletin No 9/94, Ref. EW/G94/07/08.

23 July 1994   • Cameron A-120 Hot Air Balloon • Registration Number G-SKYP •
Privately Owned

This accident occurred at Castle Cary, Somerset, at 7 a.m. The balloon was carrying the pilot and five passengers, one of whom was classified as having a serious injury, whilst two other passengers sustained minor injuries in the incident. The accident was classified as a Category 3. The balloon was built in 1991.

The balloon took off at 0545 hours with five passengers. The surface wind was light and forecast to remain so for the duration of the flight. However, after 45 minutes, the pilot observed that the surface wind had increased to 12 to 15 kt and decided to land as soon as a suitable landing site became available. At first, no suitable sight could be seen, but after a few minutes, the pilot located two possible sites and descended to low level to make his landing approach. The first field proved to be unsuitable and the pilot continued to the second at about 50ft agl. The landing area was constrained by power cables to the right and a barn at the far end of the field. The pilot rebriefed his passengers on the correct procedures for a fast landing. Just before touchdown, the pilot noted that despite the fact that the parachute and turning vents were all sealed, the balloon was rapidly deflating. He applied maximum heat and warned the passengers to 'hold tight' as the landing would be 'positive'. On touchdown the basket turned over and two elderly passengers in the rear of the basket were thrown out sustaining minor injuries in the process. The reduction in weight caused the balloon to become airborne again. On the second landing, the son of one of the elderly passengers was no longer in the correct landing position and suffered a fractured ankle.

The pilot attributed the injuries to a heavier than expected landing caused by the rapid deflation of the balloon envelope in unexpected low level windshear and when the balloon was already in a fast cooling mode.

Source: AAIB Bulletin No 10/94, Ref. EW/G94/07/31.

15 December 1994 • Sea Harrier F.R.S.1 • Serial Number XZ493 • Number 800 Naval Air Squadron • Home Base – RNAS Yeovilton • Ilchester, Somerset • Detached to HMS *Invincible*

This aircraft ditched alongside HMS *Invincible* in the Adriatic Sea off Bosnia when yaw control in the hover was lost.[10] The pilot, Lieutenant (P) David John Kistruck, ejected successfully and was picked up by a Spanish helicopter. The remains of the aircraft were salvaged over a four-day period from 720m of water. The nose section of this aircraft was recovered and fitted to a Harrier G.R.3 airframe and is now on display at the Fleet Air Arm Museum with the prefix 001. At the time of the crash the aircraft had flown for just over 2,684 hours.

This aircraft saw action in the Falklands War, returning to the UK on HMS *Invincible* on 17 September 1982. Plate 14, taken at the 1995 air day at RNAS Yeovilton by Brian Pittard, shows the tail section of the aircraft. Its number can be clearly seen right at the very end of the fuselage.

1995

7 April 1995 • EH Industries E.H.101 • Serial Number ZF644 • Home Base – Westland's Airfield • Yeovil, Somerset

During a high-altitude test flight from Yeovil, the helicopter suffered loss of control due to an uncommanded movement of the tail rotor to full pitch while at 12,000ft. The second pilot and two test engineers parachuted to safety from 10,000ft. The chief pilot of Westland's, Captain John S. Dickens, an ex-Royal Navy pilot, stayed with the helicopter and steered it away from the village of Yarcombe, Somerset. He baled out of the cockpit window at 1,200ft and sustained back injuries as his parachute did not have time to deploy fully.

The other crew members were: Second Pilot Don MacLaine, Flight Test Engineers Alistair Wood and Geoff Douthwaite.

The aircraft crashed into a field close to the A303 Exeter–London road. The accident was found to have been caused by a sub-standard component in the tail rotor pitch control system. This aircraft first flew at Yeovil on 15 June 1989.

11 June 1995 • Avid Speed Wing • Registration Number G-BVFO • Home Base – Branscombe • South Devon

The accident occurred about 2km north of Shepton Mallet at 4.10 p.m. The aircraft sustained damage to the main landing gear and adjacent fuselage area; left the flaperon damaged; the wooden propeller had one blade broken off. The pilot had no passengers with him.

At 1520 hrs, the aircraft took off from Branscombe, South Devon for a flight to Enstone, Oxford. The aircraft was flying at 1,800 feet amsl when, at about 1610 hrs, the engine stopped. The pilot realised that, despite a reminder on his kneepad to 'CHANGE TANKS AT 1700' (local time), he had not done so and the right tank was now empty. He changed to the left tank which contained 40 litres of fuel, but had insufficient time to start the engine; he set up his aircraft for an immediate forced landing. He did not make a MAYDAY call because of a lack of time; he also considered that the open terrain made survival appear certain.

The chosen field had a slight uphill gradient towards the north where wooded hills rose to about 200ft above the selected landing area. The surface wind was estimated to have been 3300/15 kt. A high sink rate developed during the final part of the approach which the pilot was unable to arrest and a heavy landing ensued. The main landing gear collapsed and, when the aircraft had stopped, the pilot, who was wearing lap and upper torso diagonal restraint, escaped uninjured through the main door.

Source: AAIB Bulletin No 8/95, Ref. EW/G95/06/07.

20 October 1995
• Sea Harrier F.R.S.1 converted to F.A.2 in 1993 • Serial Number XZ457 • Number 899 Naval Air Squadron • Home Base – RNAS Yeovilton • Ilchester, Somerset

On taking off from RNAS Yeovilton, this aircraft suffered from a catastrophic engine failure when it shed a fan blade as it increased power to ready for take-off and caught fire.[11] The pilot, Lieutenant Commander (P) Clive William Baylis, made a heavy landing but safely ejected through the fire. The aircraft then rolled down the runway and into the barrier. It ended up with its nose on the runway and the after part just on the grass. The badly burned aircraft was transferred to the Boscombe Down Aviation Collection, which is a nonprofit organisation and not open to the general public. The aircraft was rebuilt using parts from other Harriers.

This aircraft had a very good record in the Falklands War and was credited with a total of four confirmed kills (Lieutenant Commander Andy Auld DSC RN, 800 NAS, HMS *Hermes* (2 Daggers), and Lieutenant Clive Morrel RN, 800 NAS, HMS *Hermes* (2 Skyhawks)).

This aircraft was the highest-scoring aircraft for kills during the Falklands War. By mid-June 1982, this aircraft had flown sixty-six sorties and dropped a total of three 1,000lb bombs at targets. In addition, it had fired three Sidewinder missiles and expended 680 30mm cannon shells.

The aircraft, now painted out in its Falklands colours, is used as a static display in many air shows. It was due to be shown at the RNAS Yeovilton Air Day on 9 July 2011.

1996

14 February 1996   • Sea Harrier F.R.S.1 converted to F.A.2 in 1993 • Serial Number XZ455 • Number 801 Naval Air Squadron • Home Base – RNAS Yeovilton • Ilchester, Somerset • Detached to HMS *Illustrious*

After returning from a NATO operational mission over Bosnia, this aircraft made a night approach to HMS *Illustrious*, but the pilot found that he had to use large amounts of right rudder to maintain a balanced flight. Neither accelerating nor climbing, he then chose to overshoot and flew straight and level above the deck. The aircraft then descended towards the Adriatic Sea and crashed approximately 28 nautical miles north-east of Bari.[12] The pilot, Lieutenant (P) Gavin Peter Phillips, successfully ejected and was rescued by a Sea King helicopter from HMS *Illustrious*. The aircraft was recovered from 215m of water and the wreck was held in storage at Everett Aero, Sproughton, near Ipswich, Suffolk. In March 2010, the aircraft was reported to be in private hands in Queensbury, Bradford.

This aircraft had a record of two confirmed kills during the Falklands War (Flight Lieutenant Tony Penfold RAF, 800 NAS, HMS *Hermes* (1 Dagger), and Lieutenant Commander R. (Fred) Frederickson, 800 NAS, HMS *Hermes* (1 Dagger)).

23 February 1996   • Sea Harrier T.4A (N) • Serial Number XZ445 • Number 899 Naval Air Squadron • Home Base – RNAS Yeovilton • Ilchester, Somerset

This aircraft came down at 2.40 p.m. on the Blackdown Hills, near Wellington, Somerset.[13] A trail of damage was left from Burnworthy towards the Wellington Monument along the top of the hill. The aircraft exploded and caught fire on Leigh Hill. A lot of debris was left by a large pond, including the tail section that bore the words 'Royal Navy'. It was reported that visibility in the area at the time was down to 200 yards.

By a strange quirk of fate, the Harrier flew very low over the author near Wellington as he was heading northwards on the M5 and, unbeknown to him, it crashed moments later.

By an awful coincidence the aircraft came down close to a local public house. It is called the Merry Harriers and can be found at Forches Corner, Clayhidon, Devon.

At the subsequent inquest, the coroner, Mr Michael Rose, was told that the aircraft was meant to team up with another Sea Harrier. Their mission was to try to intercept three low-flying tornadoes. The inquest was also told that the Sea Harrier did not have any way of warning the pilot of his close proximity to the ground. In 2002, the Ministry of Defence finally admitted responsibility for the accident and Stephen Brooke's wife and daughter were awarded £530,000 damages. The MoD barrister, Phillipa Whittle, said in court, 'The MoD acknowledges responsibility. I apologise to Mrs Brookes for the death of her husband. It was an avoidable accident.'

There is a memorial close to the spot where the aircraft crashed. This takes the form of a bench with a small plaque inscribed with the names of the two men. The bench is located in the copse that the aircraft crashed through on its way to its final resting place. My thanks to Kevin Giddings for this piece of information.

CO31991N Lieutenant Commander (P) Michael Frederick Auckland, aged thirty-two, was born on 15 June 1963. He was cremated at the Yeovil Crematorium. His final resting place is shown in Appendix 2.

D183471X Chief Petty Officer Air Engineering Artificer Stephen Robert Brookes, aged thirty-one, was born on 8 June 1964. Stephen was the husband of Helen and he had a teenage daughter called Kayleigh. He is buried in the Royal Navy Cemetery in St Bartholomew's at Yeovilton village. His final resting place is shown in Appendix 2.

Source: *Western Gazette*, 2 May 2002.

4 August 1996   • MW5 (K) Sorcerer • Registration Number G-MYGS • Privately Owned

---

The accident site for this incident was about 238° (M) or 105 nautical miles from Sandy, Bedfordshire, and the flight time was about two hours. The pilot was killed when his microlight aircraft crashed near the village of Wyke Champflower, near Bruton in Somerset. The aircraft caught fire and virtually burnt out at the impact site.

The area in which aircraft crashed comprised a large field of open pasture, bounded on its northern and eastern sides by public roads and transected by a pair of 11 kV high tension electricity supply cables on 6.5 metres high wooden poles running parallel with the eastern edge of the field, approximately 100m from the boundary. A set of telephone cables on wooden poles ran down the eastern edge of the field, at the boundary with the road. The north-eastern corner of the field was fenced off into what was effectively a small paddock area, in which several horses grazed.

The right wing of the aircraft had become entangled with the western-most of the pair of high tension cables, at a location approximately 200m to the south of the paddock area at the north-eastern corner of the field. When the emergency services first arrived at the scene the remains of the aircraft were still hanging by its right wing, partially suspended from the electricity cable which had become trapped in an aileron pulley bracket at the junction of the main spar and lift strut. The electricity cable was heavily stretched but still intact, and it was evident that during the period immediately following impact, prior to the electrical supply fault detectors finally disconnecting the supply, current had passed through the aircraft structure to earth at those points where the nose and tail of the aircraft contacted the ground. The resulting discharge of current to earth had ignited the tailplane and fuselage pod, and a fierce post impact fire destroyed most of these areas; not only the fabric and plastic parts of the aircraft, but also parts of the aluminium frame. There was no evidence of arcing or fire at the point where the left outer wing contacted the ground, almost certainly because the metal structure was insulated from the ground at this point by the surrounding non-metallic wing skins and tip fairing.

Source: AAIB Bulletin No 12/1996, Ref. EW/C96/8/1.

10 December 1996 • Sea Harrier F.R.S.1 converted to F.A.2 in 1994 • Serial Number XZ492 • Number 899 Naval Air Squadron • Home Base – RNAS Yeovilton • Ilchester, Somerset

This engine crashed into the Mediterranean Sea off of Tunisa after an engine failure.[14] The pilot, Lieutenant (P) Paul Reza Blackburn, successfully ejected. The wreckage was recovered, but written off as a Category 5 loss. It then went to the Fleet Air Arm Investigation Centre for examination before finally being sent to the Park Aviation Supply at Faygate.

This aircraft achieved one confirmed kill during the Falklands War. That was by Lieutenant Commander Neil Thomas RN, 800 NAS, HMS *Hermes* (Skyhawk).

1997

24 June 1997 • Sea Harrier T.8 • Serial Number ZD991 • Number 899 Naval Air Squadron • Home Base – RNAS Yeovilton • Ilchester, Somerset

Two minutes after taking off from RNAS Yeovilton, a muffled explosion was heard by the pilot and this was immediately followed by a fire warning.[15] After a short circuit of the airfield, an emergency landing was made at Yeovilton and the aircraft was taxied on to the grass, where the crew quickly vacated it. Hot gases from a crack in the exhaust had caused the failure of the engine heat blanket and had damaged the aircraft's structure. The aircraft was declared a Category 4 repair and it was sent initially to RAF St Athan, near Barry in Glamorgan, the home of the Defence Aircraft Repair Agency (DARA). From there it went to British Aerospace at Chadderton for repair. After that it was delivered to Everett Aero/GD Metals at Sproughton in Suffolk for disposal.

The aircraft has since been refurbished and is used as a static display. It was last displayed in the UK at the Bentwaters Park Air Show in Suffolk in June 2010. In September 2010, the aircraft belonged to the PALIS (Cultural Promotion of Glorious Historical Collections) Foundation, Patriarhou Grigoriou 1–3 and Voliagmenis Avenue 1674, Glyfada, Greece. This is located quite close to Athens.

10 September 1997 • AS355FI Twin Squirrel • Registration Number G-PASE • Shorts Tucano T.1 • Serial Number ZF164

This incident was not an accident, but could quite easily have been. I have included this near miss as it illustrates how dangerous the skies above Somerset can still be:

> The helicopter pilot reported that the aircraft had departed from Filton Aerodrome when tasked with a search for a missing person in the vicinity of Wookey, Somerset. It carried a crew of one pilot and two police observers. At 1431 hrs, the aircraft was about to begin the search and was heading about

260° at an airspeed of 60 kt at 500ft agl. The aircraft was in receipt of a Flight Information Service from Yeovilton Radar. The helicopter was not fitted with a High Intensity Strobe Lights system.

Simultaneously, the pilot heard 'a whoosh' and felt a jolt. He saw a Tucano aircraft flying away below the helicopter in the 'half past eleven' relative position and saw an object flying off the helicopter in his right peripheral vision.

There were no handling difficulties with the helicopter. The pilot informed Yeovilton of the situation, carried out a precautionary landing in the nearest available field and shut down. A mobile telephone was used to confirm with Yeovilton that the helicopter had landed safely and also to request engineering support from the operator's base at Filton. Yeovilton Radar was unaware of the presence of the Tucano.

The Tucano was on the low level portion of a training navigation sortie from its base at Linton-on-Ouse to St. Mawgan. The front seat was occupied by a 'fast-jet refresher' student pilot, who had a total of 206 hours flying experience, of which 140 hours were on the Tucano type. An instructor was occupying the rear seat. The aircraft had just completed a turn by the Wells television transmitter mast from heading 190° on to heading 243° using 60° bank and was in a gentle descent to return to its minimum operating height of 250ft having just flown over a ridge. The instructor was 'head down' at the time folding his chart and did not see the helicopter at all. The student indicated that the helicopter 'appeared out of nowhere' about 40 seconds after the completion of the turn. He initiated a hard push in order to pass underneath the helicopter before losing sight of it. No impact was felt in the Tucano, which continued its flight to St. Mawgan. When in contact with St. Mawgan Approach Control, the crew were informed of the collision in the Wells area. With the aid of the rear view mirror, the damage to the top of the fin and rudder was noted. An external inspection was carried out by another Tucano aircraft on a similar sortie, a low speed handling check was carried out, followed by a successful landing.

Source: AAIB Bulletin No 2/98, Ref. EW/G97/09/06.

28 November 1997 • Robinson R.22 Beta Helicopter • Registration Number G-FLYU • Privately Owned

The helicopter was flown to the hover in a field over sloping ground that was assessed by the pilot to be unsuitable for a landing near Hestercombe House, Taunton. The weather was fine with good visibility, occasional showers and a surface wind of 240°/14 kt. Having decided to land elsewhere he hover taxied, at approximately 5ft above the surface, to find a more suitable landing area.

Whilst taxiing he turned to the right from his initial into wind heading of 240° onto a heading of approximately 100°. As he did so the right skid lifted and the aircraft started to sink rapidly to the left. Corrective cyclic control was applied but this failed to prevent the helicopter rolling rapidly to the left and the left skid striking the ground. The main rotor blades then struck the ground and the helicopter came to rest on its left side. The pilot and passenger, who were wearing lap diagonal seat belts, vacated the aircraft without injury. The pilot assessed the cause of the accident as being due to a sudden and strong gust of wind.

Source: AAIB Bulletin No 2/98, Ref. EW/G97/11/10.

2000s

2000

26 July 2000 • Sea Harrier F.R.S.1 converted to F.A.2 in 1990 • Serial Number ZE695 • Number 899 Naval Air Squadron • Home Base – RNAS Yeovilton • Ilchester, Somerset

This aircraft was on a delivery flight to RNAS Yeovilton from British Aerospace, Dunsfold. It was due to become part of the No 899 Naval Air Squadron. As the aircraft landed in the undershoot area at Yeovilton, the nose-wheel tyre suddenly burst.

The aircraft went off the runway and on to the grass, causing the nose wheel to collapse. As it slid over the grass the aircraft then caught fire. It was at this point that the pilot ejected. The Harrier came to rest at the edge of No 847 Naval Air Squadron dispersal and was classified as having suffered Category 4 damage. The pilot suffered a broken ankle.

With the announcement that the Sea Harrier fleet was to be withdrawn, it was taken out of use earlier than expected and it was declared a Category 5 loss. The aircraft departed St Athan by road on 24 September 2002 for scrapping. Later it was bought by a private collector from Everett Aero, Sproughton, Suffolk.

Although this aircraft was originally built as an F.R.S.1 it never flew as such. In 1993 she was the first converted F.A.2 to be handed over to the Royal Navy. On 27 September 2010, this aircraft was displayed hanging from the roof of the Tate Gallery, London, in a vertical position. She had feathers tattooed on to her flying surfaces. Her nose was just above the floor and was displayed as part of the Fiona Banner Exhibition along with Sepecat Jaguar XZ118, which was lying on the floor in an inverted position. For photographs of this remarkable display visit: www.richardbaker.photoshelter.com.

16 November 2000 • Sea Harrier T.8 (originally RAF Harrier T.4 but converted to T.8) • Serial Number ZD992 • Number 899 Naval Air Squadron • Home Base – RNAS Yeovilton • Ilchester, Somerset

The aircraft launched at 3.40 p.m. from RNAS Yeovilton, simulating a take-off from an aircraft carrier ramp. One of the aircraft's engines suddenly caught fire in the air. It crashed heavily to the ground but within the boundaries of the naval air station.[1] The fire was soon extinguished.

Lieutenants Walsh and Paul Reza Blackmore both successfully ejected but sustained injuries. They were taken to the nearby Yeovil District Hospital for a check up.

The aircraft was classified a Category 5 write-off. The last known location of the fuselage in 2009 was at Sproughton, Suffolk, which is about 3km from Ipswich. For a photograph of the aircraft's battered condition at this time go to: www.demobbed. org.uk.

2001

1 June 2001   • Cricket MKIV Gyroplane • Registration Number G-BXEM •
Privately Owned

The pilot had gone to Henstridge airfield in Somerset with the intention of obtaining some aviation fuel, arriving there about mid-morning. He met the owner of G-BXEM during the course of the afternoon who agreed that the pilot, who had not received any training on this specific type of aircraft, could fly it.

The pilot gave the owner a 'thumbs up' as he passed him on the taxiway and continued to taxy to Runway 25. During the second take-off the pilot again had difficulty establishing a controlled 'balanced' position; the nose was seen to rise violently and the stabiliser wheel at the rear of the airframe struck the ground. Thereafter the nose descended again and the nose-wheel was seen to strike the ground hard before the craft almost jumped airborne in a right-wheel-low attitude. Some eyewitnesses thought the craft was carrying out another 'short hop', but as the craft approached the end of the runway, power was applied abruptly and the gyroplane carried out a steep left-banked turn to downwind.

As the gyroplane rolled out on the downwind leg it was seen to descend slightly and then establish level flight. Almost immediately the aircraft started an oscillation in pitch which continued the length of the downwind leg. One witness thought it was still pitching when it entered a steep turn to final. Some witnesses thought that the gyroplane's speed downwind was higher than normal, and others judged that the downwind leg had been angled towards the runway and that the final turn was therefore commenced from a position closer than normal to the runway centreline. An instructor who watched the gyroplane fly downwind was concerned to see the pitch oscillations, but as the aircraft began the final turn he considered that the pilot had recovered control and he therefore looked elsewhere. The bank was then seen by others to reduce slightly before being reapplied to the point where eyewitnesses estimate the rotor was at 90° to the ground. From this attitude the gyroplane was seen to fall sideways into the ground from an estimated height of around 100 feet with no change in bank angle. At no time during this sequence were witnesses aware of any apparent problem with the engine.

The aircraft hit the ground on its left side and came to rest a short distance away with the pilot trapped beneath the wreckage. Rescuers freed the pilot and attempted resuscitation but without success.

The pilot died at the scene. The accident was classified as a Category 3.

Source: AAIB Bulletin No 5/2002, Ref. EW/C2001/6/01.

8 October 2001   • Sea Harrier F.R.S.1 converted to F.A.2 in 1995 • Serial Number ZD614 • Number 800 Naval Air Squadron • Home Base – RNAS Yeovilton • Ilchester, Somerset

Just after 10.30 a.m., the pilot radioed that he was experiencing engine problems and was unable to land.[2] The pilot, Squadron Leader Spon Clayton RAF, sustained injuries as he ejected and landed on the concrete of the runway. He was first taken to the sick bay at RNAS Yeovilton for treatment, before being transferred to the nearby Yeovil District Hospital. This was the pilot's second successful ejection (he had previously ejected from a Hunter in 1992).

The aircraft failed to stop and overran the No 22 runway. It smashed through a wooden fence with great force and ran across a field before finally ending up in the River Yeo. There it was almost fully submerged up to its tailplane. On the way to the river it had lost its nose cone and a wheel. To view photographs of this aircraft submerged, visit: www.davebellamy.co.uk.

Due to the risk of heavy river pollution, the Environment Agency was called out. The aircraft had an almost full fuel tank and had sustained substantial hydraulic fluid loss. The agency quickly put into place oil-catching booms that floated on the surface of the river and the pollutant effect was reduced to its bare minimum.

The aircraft was recovered from the river on 10 October 2001 by a mobile crane, but it was classified as a Category 5 write-off. It first went to RAF St Athan and then to Everett Aero, Sproughton, on 16 September 2002. Its last known location was recorded as Sproughton in 2009; the aircraft was in private hands.

Source: *Western Gazette*, 11 October 2001.

2002

1 May 2002   • Sea Harrier F.A.2 • Serial Number ZH807 • Number 800 Naval Air Squadron • Home Base – RNAS Yeovilton • Ilchester, Somerset

This aircraft suddenly jumped its nose wheel chock on the ramp, causing the nose wheel and main undercarriage to retract.[3] The pilot sustained an injury to the spine at the south dispersal side of the runway. The aircraft was classified as having suffered Category 5 damage. Its last known location was with a private owner in Newport, the Isle of Wight. A photograph of the cockpit section can be seen at: http://forums. airshows.co.uk by inputting ZH807 into the search engine.

12 June 2002   • Westland Lynx H.A.S.2 • Serial Number XZ256 • Number 815 Naval Air Squadron • Home Base – RNAS Yeovilton • Ilchester, Somerset • Detached to HMS *Richmond*

The pilot and his observer were both killed when their helicopter plunged into the sea as it headed back towards HMS *Richmond*, approximately 200 miles off the coast of the USA. Petty Officer (Photographer) P. Hanson sustained minor injuries and was rescued by an American Sea Hawk helicopter sent to the scene of the disaster.

CO34632D Lieutenant (P) Rodney Peter Skidmore, aged thirty-nine, was born on 5 March 1963 in Reading, Berkshire. He is buried in the Royal Navy Cemetery at St Bartholomew's church, Yeovilton village. His final resting place is shown in Appendix 2.

VO30755L Lieutenant Jennifer Lucy Lewis, aged twenty-five, was born on 13 March 1977 in Guildford, Surrey. The details of her final resting place are not known.

5 December 2002 • Sea Harrier T.4.N converted to T.8 in 1992 • Serial Number ZB605 • Number 899 Naval Air Squadron • Home Base – RNAS Yeovilton • Ilchester, Somerset • Detached to RAF Wittering, Cambridgeshire

This aircraft crashed on take-off from RAF Wittering at the commencement of a training mission.[4] Lieutenant Commander London, the instructor and the Royal Navy's top pilot at the time, received fatal injuries after he ejected from the plane shortly before it hit the ground and burst into flames. The other pilot, Lieutenant Nathan Gray, received minor injuries.

Convention dictates that when a dual-seat aircraft is about to crash the instructor does not eject until the student is safely out. By the time Lieutenant Commander London ejected from the plane it had rolled upside down and he was fired down into the ground from approximately 40ft. A rotor blade in the engine had broken off during the Harrier's short take-off run. This caused the engine to explode and the accident to happen.

Lieutenant Commander London's bravery had been recorded on BBC1's *999* programme just a week before his death. It involved a reconstruction of a dramatic incident that had happened while he was flying a Harrier. He was showered with shards of Perspex and thrown into temperatures of -60°C when his cockpit shattered at 40,000ft. In these circumstances many pilots would have ejected, but Lieutenant Commander London managed to land the Harrier safely on its aircraft carrier, despite it initially spinning out of control. He had also built up a remarkable reputation as a trainer of young pilots, becoming known for his desire to keep flying rather than seeking promotion by pursuing desk jobs.

CO26086N Lieutenant Commander Martin (Jak) London MBE, aged forty-three, is buried in the Royal Navy Cemetery at St Bartholomew's in Yeovilton village. His final resting place is shown in Appendix 2.

2003

26 May 2003   • Cesna 120 • Call Sign G-AJJT • Home Base – East Pennard
Farm • Shepton Mallet, Somerset • Privately Owned

The pilot was practising circuits at a farm strip where he kept the aircraft. He
had gone around from the first two approaches as he was unhappy with his
speed and position. On the third approach he found he was about 5mph faster,
but considered this acceptable and so he continued. On rounding out the aircraft floated a little and touched down further into the strip than normal.

During the rollout the pilot became concerned because he was unsure about
the length of strip remaining. Since the aircraft was a tail wheel type, he had to
strain forwards in order to look over the engine cowling to try and see the fence
that delineated the end of the strip. In so doing the pilot thought he relaxed
the backpressure that he had been maintaining on the control column. He then
applied the brakes but with more force than he had intended, locking the wheels
and causing the aircraft to skid forward about three metres. At this time the aircraft was travelling at approximately 20mph and it tipped forwards, striking the
propeller on the ground. The strike broke the wooden propeller and stalled the
engine. The aircraft then continued to tip forwards until it came to rest on its roof.

As the aircraft rolled over, the pilot had the presence of mind to switch 'OFF'
the magnetos and electrical master switch. He then found himself upside down
in his seat, held in by his seat belt. He supported himself against the roof with
one hand and released the seat belt with the other, lowering himself onto the
roof before opening his door and vacating uninjured from the aircraft …

The accident occurred at 11 a.m., with damage to the fin, windscreen, propeller,
starboard wing and wing strut of the aircraft.

Source: AAIB Bulletin No 8/2003, Ref. EW/G2003/05/20, Category 1.3.

11 June 2003   • Sea Harrier F.A.2 • Serial Number ZH805 • Defence Aviation
Repair Agency • Home Base – St Athan • Cornwall

This aircraft was being piloted by Lieutenant Commander Robert Anthony Schwab
RN and had recently undergone a major service known as a scheduled base maintenance. As part of the flight test, the pilot, an experienced Sea Harrier maintenance
test pilot, was required to test the aircraft's stall characteristics.

The aircraft successfully completed its engine checks at 40,000ft and descended to
24,000ft to begin its stalling checks. The aircraft showed a slight tendency to yaw, so the
pilot abandoned the first stall attempt. When he tried again, the right wing suddenly
dropped and the aircraft yawed rapidly to the right. The pilot attempted stall recovery.

It became immediately apparent that the aircraft had departed from normal flight
and was in the incipient stage of a spin. At this point he carried out the incipient spin

recovery procedure and then full spins recovery actions. Despite attempting a number of spin recovery techniques it became obvious that the aircraft was showing no signs of righting itself. At 10,000ft, and with no sign of a recovery happening, he made a Mayday call to Cardiff Approach.

He successfully ejected after the aircraft went into an unrecoverable spin. He was picked up by an SAR helicopter within twenty minutes. The pilot became the 7,000th airman to be saved by a Martin Baker ejection seat. The aircraft crashed into the Bristol Channel near Lee Bay in North Devon and was destroyed upon impact.

Source: Military Aircraft Accident Summary, 1 December 2005.

28 June 2003   • Vans RV-6 • Serial Number G-BZUY • Privately Owned

The pilot had planned a local flight in CAVOK conditions with a light and variable surface wind. Runway 23, approximately 15m wide and edged with cereal crop approximately 60cm tall, was the runway in use and its grass surface was dry and bumpy.

The pilot reported that during the take-off run from Franklyn's Field, near Wells in Somerset, the aircraft hit a series of bumps, became airborne at a low speed and drifted to the left. The left wing tip ran into the cereal crop, the aircraft yawed to the left and came to rest inverted. The pilot believes that the windscreen rollover bar prevented further injuries to him and his passenger. The accident was graded a 1.3 accident.

* CAVOK – Ceiling and Visibility O.K.
Source: AAIB Bulletin No 9/2003, Ref. EWG2003/06/34.

12 July 2003   • Fairey Firefly A.S.5 • Serial Number WB271 • Royal Navy Historical Flight • Number 727 Naval Air Squadron • Home Base – RNAS Yeovilton • Ilchester, Somerset

The Fairey Firefly was taking part in the Flying Legends Air Show at Duxford airfield, Cambridgeshire.[5] It was seen to be flying quite normally in sunny and clear conditions, when suddenly the aircraft rolled upside down and then nose dived into a field alongside the busy M11, 1 nautical mile south-east of the town and well away from the spectators. Unfortunately, both the pilot and his civilian aircraft fitter/navigator, Mr Neil Rix, aged twenty-nine, were killed.

CO29287A Lieutenant Commander William (Bill) Morris Murton, aged forty-five, was born on 3 April 1958. He is buried in the churchyard of St John the Baptist at Pitney, near Langport.

At the time of his death he was the commanding officer of No 727 Naval Air Squadron and based at Roborough, near Plymouth, Devon. On 6 December 2001, the Royal Naval Flying Training Flight was commissioned as 727 Naval Air Squadron, at Plymouth City airport with Chipmunks, and in January 2007 the squadron relocated to RNAS Yeovilton.

24 August 2003   • Fournier RF4D • Serial Number G-AVWY • Privately Owned

After a normal takeoff the pilot accelerated the aircraft to 50 kt whilst remaining approximately 5ft above the ground. He then selected the landing gear up but, distracted by his map interfering with the landing gear control lever, he allowed the aircraft to descend and the propeller struck the ground, breaking off 4 inches from each tip. He climbed the aircraft to about 10ft but due to engine vibration, closed the throttle. With insufficient runway remaining to land straight ahead, he opened the throttle to an acceptable level of vibration in order to clear a stone wall and decided to land in a field in the overshoot. He believed he had enough momentum at that power setting to clear a fence in the field but shortly before reaching it, the aircraft stalled, hitting the fence and ground simultaneously. One of the fence posts failed the right hand wing close to its root and the aircraft came to rest on its right hand side.

The pilot commented that he retracted the landing gear too early and had not appreciated the higher stalling speed resulting from flying at a higher all up weight than usual.

The aircraft had taken off from Halesland airfield, Somerset, at 2.50 p.m. The aircraft was damaged beyond economical repair and classified as a Category 5. Halesland airfield is a grass-strip airfield and can be located upon the Mendip Hills, about 6 miles west of Wells, just north of the village of Draycott.

Source: AAIB Bulletin No 11/2003, Ref. EW/G2003/08/41.

2004

28 February 2004   • Cameron Z-105 Hot Air Balloon • Serial Number G-BZVU • Privately Owned

Prior to the flight, the commander had obtained official weather information that gave a predicted wind from 340° at 5 kt. The flight had begun at Ashton Court near Bristol and had headed to the South toward Glastonbury. There had been no problems with the balloon and after about 1 hour 15 minutes in the air, a landing area was selected in farm land to the North of Glastonbury, close to the village of Polsham. The original landing area was intended to be beyond some farm buildings, between fencing and a field boundary hedge but, whilst approaching this area, the commander noticed that there were cows in the field. He aborted the approach and levelled the balloon; he then also assessed that the approach into this field would have to be very steep. It was at this point that he noticed power cables (33Kv type), in the path of the balloon which traversed the field beyond the boundary hedge. He assessed the distance to the power cables and, having decided that they were far enough away for the balloon not to encounter them, he then decided to land in the field and so recommenced the approach. On landing the commander became aware that the wind speed on the ground was higher than he had anticipated and, as the balloon was deflating, it was dragged toward the power cables by the wind, due to 'Spinnaker Effect'. As it slowed to halt, the deflating envelope settled onto the 33 Kv power lines with a resulting 'flash' and 'pop' as the lines were shorted together. The balloon's basket then came to rest; the commander evacuated the four passengers from the balloon and ordered them to move up wind. None of the passengers or the commander was injured during the accident.

A short time later the balloon envelope was blown from the power cables by the wind and settled in the field. After contacting the Power Company, the balloon was packed away. When the balloon was subsequently inspected, it was discovered that the contact with the power lines had burnt several holes in the envelope.

Source: AAIB Bulletin No 5/2004, Ref. EW/G2004/02/12.

8 December 2004 • Westland Lynx H.A.S.3 • Serial Number XZ724 • Number 815 Naval Air Squadron • Number 229 Flight • Home Base – RNAS Yeovilton • Ilchester, Somerset

---

The aircraft was carrying out a search over the English Channel, 19 miles south-east of the Lizard, for a possible man overboard from HMS *Montrose*, when contact with it was lost at 7 p.m. It plummeted vertically into the sea from 100ft at a high rate of descent and about 2 miles from the ship, 12 miles east of Lizard Point. There was no 'black box' fitted to this aircraft and therefore the cause could not be established. The wreckage was located on the seabed in an upright position with both engines shut down. The bodies of all four crew were recovered from the Lynx. From August 2007, all Lynx were fitted with cockpit voice recorders.

D228327L Leading Aircraft Engineering Mechanic Richard James (Nookie) Darnell, aged thirty-one, was born on 8 January 1973. He is buried in the Royal Navy Cemetery at St Bartholomew's church, Yeovilton village. His final resting place is shown in Appendix 2.

CO38226F Lieutenant David John Cole, aged thirty-four, was born on 8 April 1970. He is buried in the Royal Navy Cemetery at St Bartholomew's church, Yeovilton village. His final resting place is shown in Appendix 2.

CO39689C Lieutenant (O) James Murray Mitchell, aged twenty-nine, was born on 28 May 1978. He is buried in the Royal Navy Cemetery at St Bartholomew's church, Yeovilton village. His final resting place is shown in Appendix 2.

CO38948C Lieutenant (P) Robert Alexander P. Dunn, aged twenty-nine, was born on 22 September 1975. He is buried at the Barnhill Cemetery, Broughty Ferry, Dundee in Scotland. His grave can be located in Section KK, Grave LAIR 411.

2005

22 January 2005   • Jet Ranger 206B • Registration Number G-BXLI • Heli-Flight •
Home Base – Staverton • Gloucestershire

The pilot had planned to fly with some friends from Staverton Airport, near
Gloucester, to a private landing site in the Torbay area but, due to deteriorating
weather, landed at Topsham to the south of Exeter Airport. After a period of
several hours, the weather had not improved so the pilot decided to return to
Staverton. Although on the outbound trip he had routed south via the Bristol
Channel and the M5 corridor, an area of low lying terrain, he elected to return
to Staverton via Sidmouth, and communicated this to Exeter ATC, advising
them that he would be flying at an altitude of 900ft. As he approached Sidmouth,
he then informed Exeter that he was going to go north towards Wellington and
Taunton. This route would take the helicopter over the Blackdown Hills, which
rise to a height of some 1,000ft amsl. Witnesses in an area approximately 5 nm
south of Taunton generally heard, but did not clearly see, a low flying helicopter
and one heard a 'bang'. A subsequent S.A.R effort failed to locate the helicopter, due to very poor weather conditions, and it was found by a dog walker the
following morning. All four occupants had received fatal injuries in the accident. No pre-accident defects were found during the wreckage examination.

Roy Stevens, aged fifty-four, died along with forty-four-year-old Allan Tartagila and
his fifteen-year-old son, James, as well as fifty-nine-year-old Peter John Bloxhome. All
of the bodies were recovered from the wreckage.

Source: AAIB Bulletin No 1/2006, Ref. EW/C2005/01/03.

30 April 2005   • ARV Super 2 (ARV1) • Registration Number G-TAVR • Home Base
– Not Known

The accident occurred during a takeoff from a private airstrip under light
wind conditions. The aircraft struck the edge of a wood and then some power
cables. There was no evidence of any mechanical malfunction. Examination of
a Pilot Operating Handbook for the aircraft type showed that the airstrip was
unsuitable for the operation of the aircraft and, with the existing meteorological
conditions, the take-off distance available was less than was required for take-off.

The accident occurred at Naish Farm, Clapton in Gordano, Bristol. The crash killed
the pilot. It was the first crash involving this type of aircraft for over twenty-five years.

Source: AAIB Bulletin No 12/2005.

12 June 2005   • Sea King H.C.4 • Serial Number ZA311 • Number 846 Naval Air
Squadron • Home Base – RNAS Yeovilton • Ilchester, Somerset

This aircraft was taking off at night from Camp Abu Naji, Al Amarah, Iraq.[6] Whilst attempting a transition to the hover it was caught in a downwash from an RAF Merlin helicopter and rapidly lost height. The tail cone hit a wall and was severed by the main rotor blade. The aircraft hit the ground and the undercarriage was torn off. It was declared a Category 4 loss. ZA311 was returned to the UK and struck off charge. Parts of it were then used to rebuild ZF115.

10 July 2005   • Colt 105A Hot Air Balloon • Registration Number G-BPZS •
Privately Owned

The balloon took off from a site on the western outskirts of Bath at 1820 hrs. Whilst flying to the north-east of Farmborough, the pilot decided to land in a field adjacent to, and to the west of, the A39 road. The pilot reported that he instructed the other people on board (two passengers and a qualified pilot) to check for hazards, but it was not until the balloon had descended to approximately 15ft agl that the pilot became aware of a line of power cables in his path. He attempted to initiate lift by using the burners but, when it became apparent that the balloon would make contact with the cables, the pilot instructed the passengers to get down in the basket and he turned off the propane fuel supply.

The uprights of the basket struck the cables, causing the wires to meet, short out and break. The cables then fell across the A39 road and struck a passing car, causing minor damage to the car, but no injury to the car's occupants. The pilot subsequently landed the balloon approximately 200m from the point of impact with the cables where the envelope was deflated and the occupants alighted and were able to walk away. Local police, a police helicopter and ambulance services all attended the scene. One of the wires had caught passenger on their back and another passenger was affected by sparks. Both were subsequently treated in hospital for minor burns.

The pilot provided both his weather forecast and details of the actual conditions at the time of the accident. Both of these were in good agreement with 'aftercast' information supplied by the Met Office. There were light north-easterly winds of around 7 kt, no cloud below 5,000ft and the surface visibility was in excess of 15 km. Sunset was at 2024 hrs.

Aerial photographs of the accident site, taken by the police revealed that the pole supporting the cables near to their point of contact with the basket was located about approximately 10m to the east of the A39 road and was obscured by trees, making both the pole and wires difficult to see from the air. The pilot noted that he had elected to land in the field close to the road in order to facilitate easy access for the recovery vehicle, and to minimise damage to the field. Had he chosen to land close to the centre of the field this incident would most likely not have occurred since the field was relatively large and its central area was free from obstructions.

Source: AAIB Bulletin No 1/2006, Ref. EW/G2005/07/11.

2006

6 May 2006   • Lynx AH Mk 7 Helicopter • Serial Number XZ614 • Number 847 Naval Air Squadron • Home Base – RNAS Yeovilton • Ilchester, Somerset

On Saturday 6 May 2006, a Lynx A.H. Mk 7 XZ614 of 847 Naval Air Squadron Detachment, assigned to the Joint Helicopter Force (Iraq) based at Basra Air Station, was conducting a local area reconnaissance over the city of Basra. It was its second mission of the day. The aircraft exploded in mid-air and crashed on to the rooftop of a residential building in the centre of Basra. The five occupants of the aircraft were fatally injured. There were no immediate fatalities on the ground; however, the incident sparked local unrest and there were reports that several civilians died during the resultant rioting. The conclusion was that the aircraft had been shot down by a hostile surface-to-air missile.

CO32739W Lieutenant Commander (P) Darren Andrew Chapman RN, aged forty. He was born on 16 September 1965 in Mansfield. His last resting place can be found at St Mary's church, Charlton Mackerell, near Somerton in Somerset.

555123 Captain David Ian Dobson, Army Air Corps, was serving as an army pilot with 847 Naval Air Squadron. He was born on 28 May 1978 in Devizes, Wiltshire, and was aged twenty-seven when he died. It is not known where he is buried.

5205010G Wing Commander John Coxen RAF, aged forty-seven, was born on 21 September 1959 at Liverpool. He was detached from RAF Benson and his grave can be found in the Benson churchyard at Benson in Oxfordshire.

8245481J Flight Lieutenant Sarah-Jayne Mulvihill RAF, aged thirty-two, was born on 10 June 1973. She was also detached from RAF Benson. She was the first British servicewoman to have been lost to enemy action in twenty-two years. There is a memorial plaque dedicated to her memory at Kent International Airport, Manston, Kent. She was cremated at Barham Crematorium, where the RAF provided a fly-past.

PO61751Q Marine Paul Michael Collins, aged twenty-one, was born on 20 July 1984 in Manchester. He was cremated at the Exeter and Devon Crematorium, Topsham Road, Exeter, after a service for him was held at the Commando Training Centre Royal Marines, midway between Exeter and Exmouth.

1 June 2006   • Paramotor Aircraft • Sky School Flight Centre Limited • Cyprus • Privately Owned

Paul 'Scruff' McGeogh MID, aged forty-one, previously of the 40 Commando Royal Marines, Norton Manor Camp, Taunton, lost control of his Paramotor aircraft after a twenty-minute 'fun' flight in Cyprus. The Paramotor somehow went into a spin and crashed into the ground from about 1,000ft. He had only recently retired from the Royal Marines.

In 2001 he was part of an operation at the Qala-I-Jangi jail near the town of Mazar-I-Sharif, Afghanistan. He was a sergeant in the Special Boat Service at the time (SBS). He was famously pictured on several occasions with his face covered by a shemagh.

McGeogh was also filmed standing firing a general-purpose machine gun over the walls of the jail in full view of the Taliban. He was one of an eight-man team and was in the first wave of SBS men sent to Afghanistan when the British deployment began.

He was an experienced parachutist and had completed a four-day training course on the holiday island with British-based Sky School Flight Centre Ltd.

Mr Michael Rose, the West Somerset coroner, heard how Mr McGeogh had completed two 360° turns at the end of his flight and was attempting a third when the tragedy occurred. The coroner was informed that: 'He may have pulled too aggressively on hand toggles used to steer and was unable to recover stability during a crucial five seconds in which he began to spiral and lose altitude.'

Instructions to release the toggles and cut the engine power, relayed to him from the ground on a one-way radio, went unheeded and the pilot went into a face-down spiral dive. He hit the ground at about 60mph and died from multiple injuries.

The Cypriot authorities stated that the flying school had breached the country's regulations by not registering itself or the aircraft, although the coroner stated this was not a key factor in the accident. Mr Ledger, the owner of Sky School Flight Centre Ltd, claimed he had approached the police in Cyprus to check he was not in breach of the law.

The coroner recorded a narrative verdict, saying:

> The deceased, having completed a Paramotor training course in Cyprus was undertaking a 360-degree turn when the Paramotor he was turning started to bank steeply and went into a spiral dive resulting in his death. In all probability the fatality would not have occurred if the risks of such turns had been more fully understood at the time of the incident and appropriate training given.

According to the British Hang Gliding and Paragliding Association, 'a Paramotor is the simplest of all powered aircraft and consists of small 2-stroke petrol engine driving a propeller, worn like a backpack, under a paraglider wing. It provides thrust to take off, climb and maintain level flight.'

Source: *Somerset Western Gazette*, 16 December 2008.

16 July 2006   • Europa • Registration Number G-BWCV • Privately Owned

The aircraft was cruising at 3,500ft near the Severn Estuary with the engine at about 4,000 rpm, when, without warning, smoke entered the cockpit accompanied by a burning smell. The aircraft yawed and the nose dropped. The pilot then realised that the engine had stopped, although the propeller was still rotating.

The pilot, who also had approximately 1,000 hours gliding experience, reported that the aircraft attained an unusually high rate of descent as he manoeuvred it towards two adjacent fields which he had selected for the landing. He also reported a severe reduction in elevator effectiveness. He briefed the passenger and switched off the master switch, pulled the circuit breakers and turned off the fuel. He became aware of power lines running across the larger of the two fields so he made his approach to the smaller field, which was later measured to be 290m diagonally. His workload was high as he had to avoid several trees and pylons in the vicinity, and the electric trim was unavailable as the master electric switch had been turned off. The smoke in the cockpit however, had cleared. The gear and flaps were lowered and the aircraft touched down. Once on the ground the pilot, drawing upon his gliding experience, elected to retract the single wheeled landing gear in an attempt to decelerate more rapidly. Whilst this probably reduced the risk of tipping the aircraft over, it caused the propeller to break off and the flaps to retract. The loss of drag from the freewheeling propeller, the lack of flaps and the fact that the wheel still rotated all combined to reduce the deceleration rather than to increase it. The aircraft then struck a dense hedge at the far end of the field causing major damage to the composite fuselage structure fore and aft of the cockpit.

Both occupants suffered minor injuries and exited through the doors. The police, fire and ambulance services attended the scene.

Source: AAIB Bulletin No 3/2007, Ref. EW/C2006/07/20.

2007

8 July 2007 • Cessna 150 • Registration Number G-HFCI • Privately Owned

The aircraft took off from the Clutton Hill Farm Strip in Somerset and was seen to climb away at an unusually steep attitude to a height of approximately 200ft. Witnesses reported that the engine appeared to stop and the aircraft rolled rapidly to the left and entered a vertical descent. The aircraft struck the ground and there was an extensive post-impact fire. Both occupants were fatally injured.

The crash site was near to Kings Lane, Clutton in Somerset, and occurred shortly after 4 p.m. The pilot of the Cessna 150 aircraft, Robert Gunter and thirteen-year-old Jamie Clapp, from Mangotsfield in South Gloucestershire, were killed. This report indicated that the pilot, aged thirty-three, was found to have traces of ecstasy in his blood that appeared to have been taken a few hours before his flight.

Source: AAIB Bulletin No 7/2008, Ref. EW/C2007/07/01.

31 July 2007 • Pegasus Quantum 15-912 • Registration Number G-TUSA • Private Microlight • Westonzoyland Airfield

The pilot intended to undertake a local flight with a passenger who had flown in a microlight on two previous occasions. The surface wind was approximately 270°/5 kt and the pilot chose tarmac Runway 16 for departure. As the pilot began to rotate the aircraft during the takeoff, it veered to the right and collided with a fence near the edge of the runway, which brought it to a stop. The pilot and passenger, who were both wearing full harnesses and helmets, received minor injuries in the accident which left the trike severely damaged.

The pilot was unable to offer a cause of the accident, other than possible windshear. Given the light wind reported, it would be surprising for this to be the cause of such a loss of control.

The foot rests for both the pilot and passenger were connected to allow either person to use them to steer the nose wheel. An inadvertent passenger input on the right foot rest might have been sufficient to cause it to veer to the right as described.

Source: AAIB Bulletin No 12/2007, Ref. EW/G2007/07/13.

2008

9 May 2008   • Streak Shadow • Serial Number G-CBGI • Privately Owned

The aircraft departed a farm strip at Wadswick, close to Corsham in Wiltshire, at approximately 1905 hrs for a flight to Glastonbury and back, the pilot having reviewed the weather at the Met Office website at around 1630 hrs. The flight was uneventful until the aircraft passed Radstock on the return leg, whilst following a north-easterly course. With approximately 12 miles to run, the pilot saw a flash of lightning ahead, together with a very dark sky and heavy rain. He decided to turn the aircraft to the south and make a precautionary landing. After a few minutes he selected a suitable field to the south of the village of Hinton Charterhouse and planned the circuit. Downwind, base leg and final approach were conducted without any problems; however, the light had suddenly deteriorated due to the nearby storm clouds, and this resulted in the pilot flaring the aircraft too high. The pilot became aware of a hedge 'looming up' as the aircraft had by now flown a little too deeply in to the field. It struck the ground heavily and cart wheeled before coming to rest in an inverted attitude. The aircraft was severely damaged. The passenger sustained only minor injuries and exited the wreckage of the aircraft without difficulty. He then assisted the pilot, who received serious chest injuries, to vacate the aircraft via the broken canopy. The emergency services arrived promptly after being summoned using the pilot's mobile telephone.

Source: AAIB Bulletin No 8/2008, Ref. EW/G2008/05/16.

14 June 2008   • Pioneer 200 Alpi • Serial Number G-CEVJ • Privately Owned

During the final stages of the approach to land, the pilot found that movement of the control stick became impeded by a kneeboard strapped to his thigh. In an attempt to free the controls he pulled back hard on the control stick. The stick then freed suddenly, resulting in a full-aft control input being applied and the aircraft stalling into the ground.

The pilot and passenger departed Franklyns Field, a small grass airstrip, at 1100 hrs local time and conducted a short flight consisting of two circuits to test engine cooling performance. During final approach to land back at the airfield, aft movement of the control stick became impeded. In an attempt to free the controls the pilot pulled back hard on the stick, which then freed suddenly and resulted in a full-aft control input being applied to the aircraft. The aircraft pitched nose high and stalled into the ground from a height of approximately 10ft, causing extensive damage to the aircraft but no injuries to the pilot or passenger. The pilot realised that the kneeboard strapped to his left thigh had slipped round and caused the restriction in control stick movement.

Source: AAIB Bulletin No 9/2008, Ref. EW/G2008/06/16.

9 August 2008   • Red Arrows Display Team • BMI Baby Boeing 737 • Near Miss

After the terrible fire that destroyed the pier at Weston-super-Mare in Somerset, the Red Arrows were performing above it in poor weather. Bristol airport officials instructed the air-display team to climb to 2,500ft, being unaware of an approaching Boeing which was under the control of Cardiff airport. Luckily, the leader of the Red Arrows spotted the airliner through the cloud and, with his group, performed a dramatic evasion manoeuvre.

A report by the air-safety board blamed the near-miss on air-traffic controllers at Cardiff. They failed to tell their Bristol counterparts that the BMI Baby holiday flight was due to cross the Red Arrows' path.

The Boeing, which carries 158 people, was cruising at 2,500ft when the Red Arrows were told to climb to the same altitude. The lead pilot spotted the Boeing as the Red Arrows made height and quickly told his colleagues to 'level off' at 1,500ft. They watched as the jet came terrifyingly close – 900ft (270m) vertically and 0.7 miles horizontally – of a crash.

Source: *Independent*, 14 March 2009.

22 August 2008   • Maule M5-235C Lunar Rocket • Serial Number G-RAIN •
Privately Owned

Whilst approaching to land at Perrow Farm, the aircraft struck the bank of the airstrip boundary ditch and pitched nose-down. It came to rest inverted, approximately 50 m further on. There was no fire. The pilot, who was uninjured, vacated the aircraft through the cabin door but the passenger, who suffered serious injuries, had to be assisted from the aircraft.

The pilot advised that he was deliberately low and slow on approach which, together with a gust of tailwind, resulted in an uncontrollable sink into the obstacle. Pilot Nigel Humphries was at the controls of the Maule light aircraft when it crashed on farmland between Crickham and Clewer, near Cheddar, on Friday evening.

But amazingly, 57-year-old Mr Humphries was able to pull himself from the wreckage, having suffered only a cut hand.

He then managed to call the emergency services himself, and fire crews cut a female passenger - the aunt of Mr Humphries' wife Cressida – from the upside-down craft.

The passenger, Isobel Paterson, aged 87, was then transported to hospital by air ambulance. She received treatment for a broken elbow, but also escaped serious injury.

Fire crews doused the wrecked plane with foam to prevent any fire risk, before calling in crash investigators from the Civil Aviation Authority.

The Mercury understands Mr Humphries had taken Ms Paterson on a sight-seeing flight, and had been returning to his private airstrip at Perrow Farm when the accident occurred at around 6.30pm.

The plane hit difficulties as it came into land, and somersaulted twice before coming to rest.

Father-of-one Mr Humphries, who has been flying for 37 years and uses the plane to commute to work in Exeter, told the Mercury on Saturday at his relief that no one had been seriously hurt.

He said: 'I am fine, and Isobel has a broken elbow but will be fine. It happened when we were coming in to land on my airstrip.'

'I am pretty hacked off, but physically I am alright. We were both very lucky.' Crash experts are still investigating the cause of the accident, but witnesses say they are amazed that no one was killed.

Peter Churches, who runs Perrow Farm, was one of the first on the scene.

He said: 'I was milking when I heard all the sirens, and it looked like all the fire crews in Somerset were here.

'The plane is a mess - it's very lucky it didn't catch fire. I'm amazed they were able to walk away.'

Perrow Farm is in Crickham, near Wedmore, Somerset. Customers at the nearby Trotter Inn watched in amazement as the aircraft came to grief a mere two fields away from the pub.

Sources: AAIB Bulletin No 11/2008, Ref. EW/G2008/08/17; *Weston, Worle and Somerset Mercury*, 1 September 2008.

9 October 2008 • RAF 2000 GTX-SE Micro-Light • Serial Number G-CBCJ •
Privately Owned

The AAIB report showed that this aircraft had flown from Henstridge to Little Rissington airfield in Gloucestershire. Its purpose was to have its 'Permit to Fly' annual inspection. G-CBCJ, in the company of another microlight, left Henstridge later than planned, which meant that they did not leave Little Rissington until 4.07 p.m. The flight had a planned time of eighty-four minutes and Henstridge was due to close at 6 p.m. The other pilot noted that from 5 p.m. onwards it became very cold and damp.

All went well with the return journey and at 5.50 p.m. it started to become dark. By this time, unlit ground features were becoming hard to make out. At about 5 nautical miles away from Henstridge, things started to go wrong:

Pilot B attempted to call G-CBCJ on the Henstridge Radio frequency but received no reply. Approximately one nm further on he looked towards the airfield and checked his flight instruments before looking again towards where he expected to see G-CBCJ. He could not see the other gyroplane and, concerned that he may have caught up with it, he turned to the right and reduced speed. As he did so, he looked to his left and saw what he believed to be a white blade spiralling down in an eccentric circle at 60–120 rpm. He also recognised the colour of G-CBCJ's airframe and watched the aircraft descend until it reached the surface of the field below. He considered that it was too dark to conduct a safe field landing and continued on to Henstridge Airfield where he landed safely and contacted the emergency services.

Numerous witnesses around the village of Kingston Magna reported hearing noises like misfiring or pinking, followed by what sounded like a very large backfire. The witnesses who were immediately below the flight path described seeing a gyroplane much lower and louder than normal, hearing a loud bang and seeing a cloud of debris fall from the sky. Several witnesses went immediately to the large field into which the aircraft had descended, arriving within minutes of the accident. The pilot had suffered fatal injuries.

A witness in the village of Buckhorn Weston, about 1 nm north of the accident site, reported seeing a pair of gyroplanes fly overhead. The witness was concerned that one was 'swaying' from side to side. However, based on the witness's description, it appears this was not the accident gyroplane but the one flown by Pilot B. This witness described the accident gyroplane as flying straight and not giving cause for any concern.

Despite immediate help, the pilot, former army officer Brain Errington-Weddle, aged fifty-seven, was pronounced dead at the scene at 7.15 p.m. The crash occurred close to Back Lane and Pill Meadows in Kingston Magna.

He lived in Folly Lane, Blandford St Mary. Brian had been a member of the RAOC and from the tributes that were given to him on the RAOC website it appears that he was a well-liked and respected officer. He was also a member of the Hash House Harriers and was their webmaster. Brian and his wife regularly took part in the Monday-evening runs that took place.

Sources: AAIB Bulletin No 3/2010, Ref. EW/C2008/10/2; *Western Gazette*.

2009

24 May 2009 • CASA 1-131E Jungmann • Serial Number G-JUNG • Privately Owned

This aircraft was a Spanish plane that was built in 1952 and overhauled in 1984. It had been examined five days before it took off from Henstridge airfield and had been given the all clear. Later investigations showed that the fuel pump had shown signs of wear and was not supplying enough fuel to the engine.

The pilot was trying to raise funds for his local church at Hindon, near Salisbury. He had agreed to take five people on a flight in his aircraft in order to raise £250 for the church funds of St John the Baptist.

On the flight it was reported that the engine was misfiring badly and the pilot decided to make an emergency landing when the engine cut out. Unfortunately, the aircraft hit a telephone wire at Stourton Candle as it came in to land. The pilot, Mr Kenneth Hugh Wilson, aged sixty-three, of Hindon, suffered severe head injuries and, despite wearing a helmet, was killed in the crash. His passenger, Emma Kenrick-Piercy, aged twenty-five, received serious neck injuries; she was airlifted to hospital by the Dorset Police Air Support Unit helicopter.

During the accident flight the passenger recalled looking forward at the 'float-type' fuel gauge, which she described as 'bouncing up and down'. Then, without warning, the engine ran down smoothly and stopped. The aircraft turned right, towards what the passenger described as a 'big green lush field.' The pilot transmitted a Mayday on the Henstridge frequency, reported the engine failure and gave his position as somewhere west of Stalbridge. He placed the aircraft in a glide and made an approach to a field near the village of Staunton Caundle. The passenger commented that the pilot appeared very calm and in control of the situation. As they neared the ground the passenger saw a set of telegraph cables and realised that they would not clear them. The aircraft struck the cables, causing it to decelerate rapidly and pitch nose-down. It impacted the ground nose first and then pitched over inverted.

Sources: *Western Gazette*, 17 June 2010; AAIB Bulletin No 4/2010, Ref. EW/ C2009/05/01.

2010

21 May 2010   • Westland Sea King H.C.4 • Serial Number ZA298 • Number 846 Naval Air Squadron • Home Base – RNAS Yeovilton • Ilchester, Somerset

During an operational tour to Afghanistan, and approaching a forward operating base near Nad Ali, Helmand province, this aircraft was fired upon by the Taliban. It was hit by a rocket-propelled grenade which penetrated the starboard side. Luckily, it passed out through the port side without exploding.[7] Five British troops, who were on board, sustained very light injuries. The aircraft was declared a Category 4 and airlifted by Chinook to Camp Bastion before being returned to the UK and VAHS Fleetlands for repair.

24 October 2010   • 'Corpulent Stump' Rocket • Length 12ft • Weight 110lb

A miniature rocket was launched in an attempt to send it up to around about 20,000ft. At this point, the fuel would have been expended and a parachute would have deployed to bring the rocket safely back to earth. It was one of two that had been fired from a portable scaffold on Cheddar Moor by a group of ten rocket enthusiasts. The rockets had been cleared to fire by the Civil Aviation Authority and Bristol airport.

After its launch something went wrong and, after a few thousand feet, the rocket split in two, falling back to earth at approximately 100mph.

Mr Martin Corkish, a father of two, was working on a building extension to his home in Clewer, near Wedmore, Somerset. He heard a loud whistling noise and a 7ft section of the rocket's tailend slammed into his garden just 12ft away from his house. The front half of the rocket came down half a mile away in a field of cows, near Glendale Cottage; it was witnessed by Mrs Wendy Major and her son Chris. Luckily, this part of the rocket had a much gentler landing as its descent was controlled by parachute.

Source: *Daily Mail*, 26 October 2010.

2011

1 January 2011   • Cameron A120 Hot Air Balloon • Blenheim Balloon Team

An early morning high-altitude flight, led to tragedy on New Year's Day 2011. A hot air balloon caught fire and plunged to the ground as it was attempting to reach 20,000ft (6,096m). It plummeted to earth and fell on to Pratten's Bowls Club Green at Charlton Lane, Midsomer Norton, narrowly missing a row of houses. As the canopy collapsed the basket was also seen to be on fire.

The whole event was made worse by the fact that the ground crew following the balloon were members of the victims' families. The passenger, the scoutmaster of the Blenheim Scouts, had been given the ride as a gift by his teenage son, who normally flew as the co-pilot of this particular aircraft.

The very experienced pilot, Lee Pibworth, aged forty-two, and his passenger, Allan Burnett, aged fifty-five, were both killed. Mr Pibworth was cremated at the Bristol Crematorium, Bedminster Down, while Mr Burnett was buried at St Oswald's church in Bedminster Down.

5 March 2011   • Westland Wasp H.A.S.1. Helicopter • Serial Number G-BZPP (ex-XT793) • Starduster Too SA300 • Serial Number G-STOO • Yeovilton Flying Club • RNAS Yeovilton, near Ilchester, Somerset

This helicopter was in a low hover near St Bartholomew's church, Yeovilton village. The fixed-wing Starduster Too aircraft, of the same aero club, was undertaking 'touch and goes' on Runway 4 when it appears it was hit from behind, quite close to the crash gate that enters Yeovilton village. The Starduster Too pilot was taken to hospital with serious head injuries. The wreckage of the helicopter is now at Thruxton.

Source: AAIB Bulletin No 7/2011, Ref. EW/G2011/03/0.

19 June 2011   • Hughes 369E (500E) • Serial Number G-KSWI

This small helicopter, built in 1986 by McDonnell Douglas, crashed near Cinnamon Lane, Glastonbury, at approximately 2.20 p.m. The aircraft came down near the Berewall Junior Girls' Boarding House, not far from Glastonbury Tor. The port side of the helicopter's skids were torn off in the crash, although the aircraft did remain upright. The pilot, who was the only person on board, was taken to Frenchay Hospital, Bristol, with a serious head injury. The registered owner of the aircraft at the time was Mr Kevin Stuart Williams.

24 July 2011   • Robinson R.44 Raven • Serial Number G-ROTG • Redhill Aerodrome

An experienced pilot, forty-five-year-old Chris Watts, who was the managing director of Aldwick Court Hospitality in North Somerset and flying alone at the time, crashed into fields about 5 miles from Bude, Cornwall, at about 3.30 p.m. The incident occurred in a field between Marhamchurch and Week St Mary. The aircraft crashed into fields and caught fire, exploding on impact. Unfortunately, the pilot lost his life in the accident.

Source: BBC, *This is Somerset*.

FLEET AIR ARM ROYAL NAVY CEMETERY PLAN

						Garden of Remembrance				
K	I	2	3	4	5					
J	I	2	3	4	5	7	8	9	10	
I	I	2	3	4	5	7	8	9	10	11

To church ⟶
Path from church gate

H	I	2	3	4	5	7	8	9	10	11
G	I	2	3	4	5	7	8	9	10	11
F	I	2	3	4	5	7	8	9	10	11
E	I	2	3	4	5	7	8	9	10	11
D	I	2	3	4	5	7	8	9	10	11
C	I	2	3	4	5	7	8	9	10	11
B	I	2	3	4	5	7	8	9	10	11
A	I	2	3	4	5	7	8	9	10	11

Notes:
1. Grave 6 has not yet been allocated in any row.
2. My numbers match the CWGC records and, where they have them, the Roll of Honour.
3. All these last resting places have been physically checked by the author.

Churchyard Part

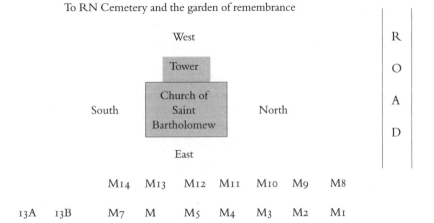

To RN Cemetery and the garden of remembrance

West   R

Tower   O

South   Church of   North   A
         Saint
         Bartholomew   D

East

M14   M13   M12   M11   M10   M9   M8

13A   13B   M7   M   M5   M4   M3   M2   M1

APPENDIX 2

NAMES OF THOSE BURIED IN THE ROYAL NAVAL CEMETERY AT YEOVILTON VILLAGE

Grave	Name	Rank	Died	Age
E1	ACHESON, Michael Ernest Brabazon	Sub Lieutenant (A) RN	5/10/44	20
B10	ADAMS, Harry Frederick	Aircraft Artificer 3	20/9/52	27
B8	AGNEW, Alan Munro	T/A Sub Lieutenant (A) RN	2/4/54	22
E3	AYLWARD, Cecil John Winston	Leading Airman	22/4/45	19
H2	BADGER, Noel Gordon	Radio Electrical Mechanician (A)	21/8/70	17
B9	BLAKE, George Peter	Commander (E) RN	5/2/53	35
H10	BLEACKLEY, Colin	Aircraft Artificer 1	29/1/69	26
H1	BOOTH, Frederick Robert Duncan	Lieutenant RN	24/7/68	26
D5	BRINE, Timothy Paul	Junior Cook	5/12/72	17
A8	BROOKES, Stephen Robert	Chief Petty Officer (Air Engineering Artificer) (M)	23/2/96	31
D10	BROOKS, Keith	Radio Electrical Mechanician (A) 1	20/7/59	19
H7	BUCKINGHAM, John	Aircraft Mechanician (A/E)	17/10/86	38
B5	CARTER, Richard	Electrical Mechanic (A) 1	17/8/74	22
G9	CATON, David Henry	Naval Airman Mechanic 1 (O)	17/3/66	26
C11	CAWOOD, Frank AFC	Lieutenant Commander RN	31/1/55	31
I8	CLARKE, Kevin John	Warrant Officer Master at Arms	23/4/07	50
M4	CLEARY, Joseph	Air Mechanic (E) 2	22/4/41	22
K2	COLE, David John	Lieutenant RN	8/12/04	34
G3	CONIBEAR, Graham Victor	Sub Lieutenant (A) RNVR	11/7/46	22
D3	CONSTABLE, Peter DSC	Lieutenant (A) RN	12/7/44	23
M10	COOK, George	Midshipman New Zealand RNVR	8/4/42	19
C1	COSSILL, Royce Ivan	Sub Lieutenant (A) RNZNVR	10/2/43	21
I11	CUTHBERT, Robert Richard	Lieutenant RN	25/6/94	33

Grave	Name	Rank	Died	Age
K1	DARNELL, Richard James (Nookie)	Leading Air Engineering Mechanic (M)	8/12/04	31
I7	DAW, James Barnaby Pearce (Barney) BSc	Lieutenant RN	17/10/92	25
A10	DOBINSON, John Terence	POCK (Petty Officer Cook)	14/2/90	34
J3	DODD, Paul Richard	Leading Air Engineering Mechanic (L)	1/2/98	27
A3	DONEGAN, Patrick	Commander RN	14/1/77	44
F5	DUNBAR–DEMPSEY, David John	Commander RN	2/3/71	37
M6	DUNCAN, T.	Sub Lieutenant (A) RN	6/7/41	N/K
M8	DUNN, Harold S. MBE	Lieutenant Commander (Retired) RN	1/10/41	N/K
J1	ELLIS, John Timothy	Lieutenant Commander RN	8/5/89	35
M5	EUSTACE, John P.	Lieutenant RN	21/5/41	24
I4	EVES, Patricia Aileen	Petty Officer Wren Writer	27/10/96	33
F11	EYTON-JONES, Richard Hugh	Lieutenant (P) RN	23/8/62	24
F1	FEENEY, John Joseph BSc	Lieutenant Canadian RNVR	27/6/45	24
C7	FERGUSON, William Alistair Maitland DSC	Lieutenant Commander RN	1/5/58	34
C4	FERRERS-GUY, John Humphrey	Midshipman (Air) RNVR	16/9/43	19
E7	FIELDHOUSE, Derek Frederick (Mick)	Lieutenant Commander (P) RN	28/1/63	36
G2	FORBES, Leslie Keith	Sub Lieutenant (A) RNVR	11/7/46	20
A5	GAVIN, John	Lieutenant RN	12/5/78	31
I1	GEORGE, Andrew James	Lieutenant RN	7/2/85	25
C5	GLASS, Francis BSc(Eng)	Commander RN	1/12/71	42
E11	GOLBY, Clifford Bentley	Naval Air Mechanic (E) 1	29/2/60	22
B11	GOLDSACK, Peter Russell	Lieutenant RN	30/11/49	23
G8	GOLLOP, Leslie George	Sub Lieutenant RN	17/1/68	19
E8	GRIFFITHS, Clifford Harry	Radio Electrical Mechanician (Air) 1	25/6/60	20
E4	GROGAN, Jack Armstrong	Lieutenant RCNVR	19/5/46	26
J10	GUTHRIE, Ashley James	Air Engineering Technician 1	13/10/06	22
A1	HALEY, William John	Aircraft Mechanician 1	19/11/74	35
F4	HARES, John Anthony	Sub Lieutenant (A) RNVR	23/7/45	20
B1	HARRISON, William	Sub Lieutenant (A) RNZNVR	19/9/42	21
G4	HILL, Arthur Patrick Francis	Acting Leading Naval Airman	26/12/48	21
E9	HILLION, Anthony	Electrical Mechanic (Air) 1	12/6/60	25
B3	HOBBS-WEBBER, Dudley Niccolls	Lieutenant RN	4/11/54	23

Grave	Name	Rank	Died	Age
B7	HOLSEY, John Joseph	Leading Air Mechanic (A)	10/8/56	23
K5	HORNER, Mark (Jack)	Lieutenant RN	9/12/08	42
M3	HOWES, Joseph William James	Leading Airman	19/3/41	N/K
G1	HUGHES, Gordon Booth	Petty Officer Airman	9/11/45	21
M13	JOHNSON, Alan R.	Sub Lieutenant RCNVR	22/5/42	N/K
D7	JONES, Alec Daniel	Radio Electrical Mechanician (Air) 2	14/2/60	17
C10	JONES, Colin Edward George	Lieutenant RN	31/1/55	31
D8	KEMSLEY, Anthony William George	Lieutenant (E) (P) RN	20/1/60	24
H5	KENDALL, John Alan (Jak)	Lieutenant RN	22/9/70	27
I3	KITCHEN, Roy	Chief Petty Officer Air Engineering Artificer	2/2/88	40
J8	LANGTHORP, Steve	Petty Officer Air Engineering Mechanic	7/7/07	44
A11	LEWIS, Philip	Lieutenant RN	26/11/80	32
A4	LIDDELL, Gilbert Elliot	Chief Petty Officer Weapons Engineering Artificer (WL)	28/8/89	32
I5	LLOYD, Paul Victor	Squadron Leader RAF	13/4/89	40
J7	LONDON, Martin R. (Jak) MBE, QCBA	Lieutenant Commander RN	5/12/02	43
M14	LUKE, James Carlyone	Lieutenant RN	5/6/42	21
D1	MAISEY, Richard Geoffrey Dennis (Geoff)	Sub Lieutenant (A) RNVR	20/3/44	19
D2	MALLEE, G.	Off.M.S.D. 1E.KL MLD (Marine-Luchtvaartdienst) is the naval aviation branch of the Royal Netherlands Navy	26/4/44	22
C9	MARGOLIOUTH, Joseph Maurice	Sub Lieutenant RN	17/8/55	22
A7	MASSINGHAM, Janet Beryl	Wren WA (AB)	6/2/79	23
E10	McCARTHY, Alan	Petty Officer Air Fitter (A/E)	6/4/60	30
H3	McKENZIE, Donald Robert	Lieutenant RN	24/7/68	30
M11	McMILLAN, Rex	Sub Lieutenant (A) RNZNVR	22/4/42	20
D9	MILLER, Robin William Hart	Lieutenant (O) RN	19/9/59	26
K4	MITCHELL, James Murray	Lieutenant RN	8/12/04	29
C8	MOORE, Michael Anthony	Lieutenant RN	1/5/58	27
H11	NEWBERRY, Ernest Edward Astell	Petty Officer Electrician (Air)	19/4/66	36
13A	NEWITT, Dennis	Private	5/5/42	19

Grave	Name	Rank	Died	Age
J2	NICHOLSON, Graham Bruce	Lieutenant Commander RN	30/11/93	35
F2	NORCOTT, Harry	Lieutenant (A) RNVR	17/7/45	24
I2	NORMAN, Paul Duncan	Midshipman RN	7/2/85	25
B2	O'BRYEN, William Stanislaus	Sub Lieutenant (A) RNVR	26/11/42	26
D4	OLDS, David Leonard	Sub Lieutenant (A) RNZNVR	21/8/44	23
H8	PARKER, Geoffrey	Chief Petty Officer	2/4/67	34
G5	PHILLIPSON, Gordon Thomas	EM(Air)	15/10/72	22
G10	PREUS, Hugh Ian Robert (Bob)	Sub Lieutenant RN	8/3/65	22
A9	RIGLEY, Dennis Brian	Air Engineering Mechanician (L) 2	23/9/80	33
A2	ROPER, Derek	Petty Officer Air Engineering Mechanician (L)	24/1/81	34
F10	SCOTT, David Graeme	Acting Sub Lieutenant RN	23/8/62	24
M9	SCOTT, Arnold Charles	Sub Lieutenant (A) RNVR	16/10/41	20
M7	SIMMONDS, Douglas	Sub Lieutenant (A) RNZVR	25/9/41	N/K
G11	SIMMS, Brian Malcolm	Naval Air Mechanic 1	22/3/64	19
I10	SKIDMORE, Rodney (Rod)	Lieutenant RN	12/6/02	39
J5	SMITH, Russell (Smudge)	Petty Officer Air Engineering Artificer (L)	21/5/99	30
J9	SMITH, Stuart Frederick	Lieutenant Commander RN	15/11/02	55
F9	SNEDDON, Eric	Lieutenant RN	20/2/64	22
M2	STAFFORD-CLARK, John	Sub Lieutenant (A) RNVR	26/2/41	20
H9	STARLING, David John (Pete)	Lieutenant RN	29/9/66	25
F7	STEENSON, George Alexander	Sub Lieutenant RN	20/2/64	20
F8	STEVENS, Anthony Daniel	Lieutenant (O) RN	9/2/66	27
C2	STEVENS, John Paul	Sub Lieutenant RNR	13/5/43	20
H4	SUTTON, Ian Scott	Acting Sub Lieutenant RN	1/5/69	21
G7	THOMAS, Simon Scott	Lieutenant RN	17/3/66	31
M12	THOMSON, Alexander Neilson	Sub Lieutenant (A) RNZNVR	22/4/42	21
C3	TUTEIN, H.	Res JE LT MLD	27/6/43	26
E2	WADDINGTON, Peter	Sub Lieutenant (A) RNVR	3/2/45	23
B4	WEEKS, Roy Keeble	Sub Lieutenant RNR	2/8/43	21
M1	WELLS, Derrick Stanley Thomas	Midshipman (A) RNVR	26/9/40	19
F3	WENYON, Louis Morley DSC	Lieutenant (A) RNVR	17/7/45	25

Grave	Name	Rank	Died	Age
I9	WEST, Christopher Peter	Lieutenant Commander RN	17/1/94	51
J4	WIDGERY, David Greenaway OBE	Commander RN	7/5/92	47
13B	WILLIAMSON, Gerald Vyvian	Sub Lieutenant (A) RNVR	25/1/40	36
K3	WILSON, Andrew Stott	Lieutenant RN	22/3/03	36
D11	WOOD, Brian Christopher	Lieutenant RN	25/7/58	25
E5	WORBEY, Leslie George	Ordinary Seaman	12/9/71	17

The Garden of Remembrance

This can be found in the top right-hand corner of the RN Cemetery, next to the wooden hut. It contains the cremated remains of those who lost their lives in service, plus those who had retired from the Royal Navy.

Name	Rank	Died	Age
AUCKLAND, Michael Frederick	Lieutenant	23/2/96	32
BOWEY, William Albert (Jim). Actually buried in Portland Cemetery near Weymouth, Dorset.	Leading Aircraftman	24/4/02	31
BEALE, Toby Damian. Stone memorial. He was part of the crew of HMS *Grafton*, Type 23 frigate, flying Lynx helicopter in night encounter training exercise with three missile corvettes of the Singapore navy. The aircraft crashed about 90 miles NE of Singapore. His co-pilot, Lt Cdr Andy HURRY was rescued.	Lieutenant	23/9/98	27
BRUNSDEN, Bernard Clifford	Lieutenant	6/3/79	30
CHILDS, Tina Janet	Leading Wren	1/11/75	20
COWLING, Christopher Michael	Petty Officer Electrician	22/1/80	29
STEWART, Alexander. Brass plaque on far wall against field. This officer was lost at sea after an aircraft accident.	Lieutenant	3/5/70	29

Photographs of all of the gravestones within the Fleet Air Arm Cemetery can be seen at http://www.flickr.com/photos/harlowirish/sets/72157613313552388/.

NOTES

1940s

1 Cummings, C., *The Price of Peace – A Catalogue of RAF Aircraft Losses Between VE-Day and End of 1945* (Nimbus Publishing, 2004).
2 Ibid.
3 Ibid.
4 Webb, D.C., *UK Flight Testing Accidents 1940–1971* (Air Britain Ltd, 2002).
5 Halley, James J. MBE, *Broken Wings, Post-War Royal Air force Accidents* (Air Britain, 2000).
6 Ibid.
7 Sturtivant, R. with Burrow, M. & Howard, L., *Fleet Air Arm Fixed Wing Aircraft since 1946* (Air Britain, 2004).
8 Halley, J., *Broken Wings.*
9 Local information.
10 Sturtivant, R., Burrow, M. & Howard, L., *Fleet Air Arm Fixed Wing Aircraft.*
11 Webb, D.C., *UK Flight Testing Accidents.*
12 Cummings, C., *Last Take Off – A Record of RAF Aircraft Losses 1950 to 1953* (Nimbus Publishing, 2000).
13 Halley, J., *Broken Wings.*
14 Webb, D.C., *UK Flight Testing Accidents.*
15 Halley, J., *Broken Wings.*
16 Ibid.
17 Sturtivant, R., Burrow, M. & Howard, L., *Fleet Air Arm Fixed Wing Aircraft.*
18 Halley, J., *Broken Wings.*
19 Webb, D.C., *UK Flight Testing Accidents.*
20 Sturtivant, R., Burrow, M. & Howard, L., *Fleet Air Arm Fixed Wing Aircraft.*
21 Ibid.
22 Ibid.
23 Halley, J., *Broken Wings.*
24 Sturtivant, R., Burrow, M. & Howard, L., *Fleet Air Arm Fixed Wing Aircraft.*
25 Ibid.
26 Ibid.

1950s

1 Webb, D.C., *UK Flight Testing Accidents.*
2 Halley, J., *Broken Wings.*
3 Sturtivant, R., Burrow, M. & Howard, L., *Fleet Air Arm Fixed Wing Aircraft.*
4 Halley, J., *Broken Wings.*
5 Webb, D.C., *UK Flight Testing Accidents.*
6 Ibid.
7 Halley, J., *Broken Wings.*
8 Ibid.
9 Ibid.
10 Ibid.
11 Ibid.
12 Webb, D.C., *UK Flight Testing Accidents.*
13 Ibid.
14 Halley, J., *Broken Wings.*
15 Ibid.
16 Ibid.
17 Ibid.
18 Ibid.
19 Sturtivant, R., Burrow, M. & Howard, L., *Fleet Air Arm Fixed Wing Aircraft.*
20 Halley, J., *Broken Wings.*
21 Ibid.
22 Ibid.
23 Ibid.
24 Ibid.
25 Ibid.
26 My thanks to Brian Lewis for supplying me with details of Vampire and Meteor jet crashes which he took the time and trouble to take note of during the 1950s. His initial list gave me the start I needed to find out more information.
27 Halley, J., *Broken Wings.*
28 Ibid.
29 Ibid.
30 Ibid.

31 Flight Global/Archive 1953 0777.pdf.
32 Flight Global/Archive 1953 0808.pdf.
33 Halley, J., *Broken Wings*.
34 Ibid.
35 Sturtivant, R., Burrow, M. & Howard, L., *Fleet Air Arm Fixed Wing Aircraft*.
36 Halley, J., *Broken Wings*.
37 Ibid.
38 Ibid.
39 Ibid.
40 My thanks to Brian Pittard from Stoke-sub-Hamdon for supplying me with help and information. He was a member of the now defunct Aviation Archaeologists Association of Somerset.
41 Halley, J., *Broken Wings*.
42 Ibid.
43 Ibid.
44 Ibid.
45 Sturtivant, R., Burrow, M. & Howard, L., *Fleet Air Arm Fixed Wing Aircraft*.
46 Halley, J., *Broken Wings*.
47 Ibid.
48 Ibid.
49 Ibid.
50 Ibid.
51 Ibid.
52 Brian Lewis.
53 Sturtivant, R., Burrow, M. & Howard, L., *Fleet Air Arm Fixed Wing Aircraft*.
54 Brian Lewis.
55 Ibid.
56 Halley, J., *Broken Wings*.
57 Ibid.
58 Ibid.
59 Sturtivant, R., Burrow, M. & Howard, L., *Fleet Air Arm Fixed Wing Aircraft*.
60 Halley, J., *Broken Wings*.
61 Ibid.
62 My thanks to Brian Lovell of Ilton. He was based at RAF Merryfield in the early 1950s. Some of the photographs shown are his and I am grateful for his permission to use them.
63 Halley, J., *Broken Wings*.
64 Ibid.
65 Ibid.
66 Sturtivant, R., Burrow, M. & Howard, L., *Fleet Air Arm Fixed Wing Aircraft*.
67 Halley, J., *Broken Wings*.
68 Ibid.
69 Ibid.
70 Sturtivant, R., Burrow, M. & Howard, L., *Fleet Air Arm Fixed Wing Aircraft*.
71 Halley, J., *Broken Wings*.
72 Sturtivant, R., Burrow, M. & Howard, L., *Fleet Air Arm Fixed Wing Aircraft*.
73 Ibid.
74 Halley, J., *Broken Wings*.
75 Ibid.
76 Ibid.
77 Sturtivant, R., Burrow, M. & Howard, L., *Fleet Air Arm Fixed Wing Aircraft*.
78 Halley, J., *Broken Wings*.
79 Sturtivant, R., Burrow, M. & Howard, L., *Fleet Air Arm Fixed Wing Aircraft*.
80 Halley, J., *Broken Wings*.
81 Sturtivant, R., Burrow, M. & Howard, L., *Fleet Air Arm Fixed Wing Aircraft*.
82 Halley, J., *Broken Wings*.
83 Sturtivant, R., Burrow, M. & Howard, L., *Fleet Air Arm Fixed Wing Aircraft*.
84 Ibid.
85 Halley, J., *Broken Wings*.
86 Ibid.
87 Sturtivant, R., Burrow, M. & Howard, L., *Fleet Air Arm Fixed Wing Aircraft*.
88 Ibid.
89 Halley, J., *Broken Wings*.
90 Ibid.
91 Sturtivant, R., Burrow, M. & Howard, L., *Fleet Air Arm Fixed Wing Aircraft*.
92 Ibid.
93 Halley, J.J., *Royal Air Force Aircraft WA100–WZ999* (Air Britain Ltd, 1983).
94 Sturtivant, R., Burrow, M. & Howard, L., *Fleet Air Arm Fixed Wing Aircraft*.
95 Ibid.
96 Halley, J., *Broken Wings*.
97 Sturtivant, R., Burrow, M. & Howard, L., *Fleet Air Arm Fixed Wing Aircraft*.
98 Ibid.
99 Webb, D.C., *UK Flight Testing Accidents*.
100 Sturtivant, R., Burrow, M. & Howard, L., *Fleet Air Arm Fixed Wing Aircraft*.
101 Ibid.
102 Ibid.
103 Winton, J., *Air Power at Sea – 1945 to Today* (Sidgwick & Jackson, 1976).
104 Sturtivant, R., Burrow, M. & Howard, L., *Fleet Air Arm Fixed Wing Aircraft*.
105 Halley, J., *Broken Wings*.

106 Howard L., Burrow, M. & Myall, H., *Fleet Air Arm Helicopters since 1943* (Air Britain Ltd, 2011).

107 Halley, J., *Broken Wings.*

108 Sturtivant, R., Burrow, M. & Howard, L., *Fleet Air Arm Fixed Wing Aircraft.*

109 Ibid.

110 Halley, J., *Broken Wings.*

111 Sturtivant, R., Burrow, M. & Howard, L., *Fleet Air Arm Fixed Wing Aircraft.*

112 Ibid.

113 Halley, J., *Broken Wings.*

114 Sturtivant, R., Burrow, M. & Howard, L., *Fleet Air Arm Fixed Wing Aircraft.*

115 Ibid.

116 Ibid.

117 Ibid.

118 Ibid.

119 Ibid.

120 Ibid.

121 Ibid.

122 Ibid.

123 Howard, L., Burrow, M. & Myall, H., *Fleet Air Arm Helicopters.*

124 Sturtivant, R., Burrow, M. & Howard, L., *Fleet Air Arm Fixed Wing Aircraft.*

125 Howard, L., Burrow, M. & Myall, H., *Fleet Air Arm Helicopters.*

126 Ibid.

127 Sturtivant, R., Burrow, M. & Howard, L., *Fleet Air Arm Fixed Wing Aircraft.*

128 Webb, D.C., *UK Flight Testing Accidents.*

129 Howard, L., Burrow, M. & Myall, H., *Fleet Air Arm Helicopters.*

130 Sturtivant, R., Burrow, M. & Howard, L., *Fleet Air Arm Fixed Wing Aircraft.*

131 Halley, J., *Broken Wings.*

132 Sturtivant, R., Burrow, M. & Howard, L., *Fleet Air Arm Fixed Wing Aircraft.*

133 Ibid.

134 Ibid.

135 Ibid.

136 Ibid.

137 Halley, J., *Broken Wings.*

1960s

1 Halley, J., *Broken Wings.*

2 Sturtivant, R., Burrow, M. & Howard, L., *Fleet Air Arm Fixed Wing Aircraft.*

3 Ibid.

4 Ibid.

5 Ibid.

6 Ibid.

7 Webb, D.C., *UK Flight Testing Accidents.*

8 Halley, J., *Broken Wings.*

9 Sturtivant, R., Burrow, M. & Howard, L., *Fleet Air Arm Fixed Wing Aircraft.*

10 Halley, J., *Broken Wings.*

11 Ibid.

12 Ibid.

13 Sturtivant, R., Burrow, M. & Howard, L., *Fleet Air Arm Fixed Wing Aircraft.*

14 Webb, D.C., *UK Flight Testing Accidents.*

15 Sturtivant, R., Burrow, M. & Howard, L., *Fleet Air Arm Fixed Wing Aircraft.*

16 Ibid.

17 Halley, J., *Broken Wings.*

18 Webb, D.C., *UK Flight Testing Accidents.*

19 Sturtivant, R., Burrow, M. & Howard, L., *Fleet Air Arm Fixed Wing Aircraft.*

20 Ibid.

21 Webb, D.C., *UK Flight Testing Accidents.*

22 Howard, L., Burrow, M. & Myall, H., *Fleet Air Arm Helicopters.*

23 Ibid.

24 Sturtivant, R., Burrow, M. & Howard, L., *Fleet Air Arm Fixed Wing Aircraft.*

25 Ibid.

26 Ibid.

27 Ibid.

28 Howard, L., Burrow, M. & Myall, H., *Fleet Air Arm Helicopters.*

29 Sturtivant, R., Burrow, M. & Howard, L., *Fleet Air Arm Fixed Wing Aircraft.*

30 Halley, J., *Broken Wings.*

31 Ibid.

32 Ibid.

33 Webb, D.C., *UK Flight Testing Accidents.*

34 Ibid.

35 Halley, J., *Broken Wings.*

36 Sturtivant, R., Burrow, M. & Howard, L., *Fleet Air Arm Fixed Wing Aircraft.*

37 Ibid.

38 Ibid.

39 Ibid.

40 Ibid.

41 Webb, D.C., *UK Flight Testing Accidents.*

42 Sturtivant, R., Burrow, M. & Howard,

L., *Fleet Air Arm Fixed Wing Aircraft*.
43 Ibid.
44 Webb, D.C., *UK Flight Testing Accidents*.
45 Sturtivant, R., Burrow, M. & Howard,
   L., *Fleet Air Arm Fixed Wing Aircraft*.
46 Ibid.
47 Ibid.
48 Webb, D.C., *UK Flight Testing Accidents*.
49 Sturtivant, R., Burrow, M. & Howard,
   L., *Fleet Air Arm Fixed Wing Aircraft*.
50 Halley, J., *Broken Wings*.
51 Sturtivant, R., Burrow, M. & Howard,
   L., *Fleet Air Arm Fixed Wing Aircraft*.
52 Ibid.
53 Halley, J., *Broken Wings*.
54 Sturtivant, R., Burrow, M. & Howard,
   L., *Fleet Air Arm Fixed Wing Aircraft*.
55 Ibid.
56 Ibid.
57 Ibid.
58 Ibid.
59 Ibid.
60 Ibid.
61 Ibid.
62 Ibid.
63 Ibid.
64 Howard, L., Burrow, M. & Myall, H.,
   Fleet Air Arm Helicopters.
65 Sturtivant, R., Burrow, M. & Howard,
   L., *Fleet Air Arm Fixed Wing Aircraft*.
66 Ibid.
67 Ibid.
68 Ibid.
69 Ibid.

70 Ibid.
71 Ibid.
72 Halley, J., *Broken Wings*.
73 Sturtivant, R., Burrow, M. & Howard,
   L., *Fleet Air Arm Fixed Wing Aircraft*.
74 Ibid.
75 Ibid.
76 Ibid.
77 Ibid.
78 Webb, D.C., *UK Flight Testing Accidents*.
79 Halley, J., *Broken Wings*.
80 Ibid.
81 Brian Lewis.
82 Sturtivant, R., Burrow, M. & Howard,
   L., *Fleet Air Arm Fixed Wing Aircraft*.
83 Ibid.
84 Ibid.
85 Ibid.
86 Halley, J., *Broken Wings*.
87 Sturtivant, R., Burrow, M. & Howard,
   L., *Fleet Air Arm Fixed Wing Aircraft*.
88 Halley, J., *Broken Wings*.
89 Sturtivant, R., Burrow, M. & Howard,
   L., *Fleet Air Arm Fixed Wing Aircraft*.
90 Webb, D.C., *UK Flight Testing Accidents*.
91 Sturtivant, R., Burrow, M. & Howard,
   L., *Fleet Air Arm Fixed Wing Aircraft*.
92 Howard, L., Burrow, M. & Myall, H.,
   Fleet Air Arm Helicopters.
93 Sturtivant, R., Burrow, M. & Howard,
   L., *Fleet Air Arm Fixed Wing Aircraft*.
94 Ibid.
95 Ibid.

1970s

1 Sturtivant, R., Burrow, M. & Howard,
   L., *Fleet Air Arm Fixed Wing Aircraft*.
2 Ibid.
3 Ibid.
4 Ibid.
5 Ibid.
6 Webb, D.C., *UK Flight Testing Accidents*.
7 Sturtivant, R., Burrow, M. & Howard,
   L., *Fleet Air Arm Fixed Wing Aircraft*.
8 Ibid.
9 Halley, J., *Broken Wings*.
10 Sturtivant, R., Burrow, M. & Howard,
   L., *Fleet Air Arm Fixed Wing Aircraft*.
11 Ibid.

12 Ibid.
13 Webb, D.C., *UK Flight Testing Accidents*.
14 Sturtivant, R., Burrow, M. & Howard,
   L., *Fleet Air Arm Fixed Wing Aircraft*.
15 Ibid.
16 Howard, L., Burrow, M. & Myall, H.,
   Fleet Air Arm Helicopters.
17 Ibid.
18 Webb, D.C., *UK Flight Testing Accidents*.
19 Sturtivant, R., Burrow, M. & Howard,
   L., *Fleet Air Arm Fixed Wing Aircraft*.
20 Ibid.
21 Howard, L., Burrow, M. & Myall, H.,
   Fleet Air Arm Helicopters.

22 Ibid.
23 Sturtivant, R., Burrow, M. & Howard, L., *Fleet Air Arm Fixed Wing Aircraft*.
24 Ibid.
25 Ibid.
26 Halley, J., *Broken Wings*.

1980s

1 Sturtivant, R., Burrow, M. & Howard, L., *Fleet Air Arm Fixed Wing Aircraft*.
2 Ibid.
3 Howard, L., Burrow, M. & Myall, H., *Fleet Air Arm Helicopters*.
4 Sturtivant, R., Burrow, M. & Howard, L., *Fleet Air Arm Fixed Wing Aircraft*.
5 Ibid.
6 Ibid.
7 Howard, L., Burrow, M. & Myall, H., *Fleet Air Arm Helicopters*.
8 Sturtivant, R., Burrow, M. & Howard, L., *Fleet Air Arm Fixed Wing Aircraft*.
9 Ibid.
10 Ibid.
11 Ibid.
12 Ibid.
13 Ibid.
14 Ibid.
15 Howard, L., Burrow, M. & Myall, H., *Fleet Air Arm Helicopters*.
16 Sturtivant, R., Burrow, M. & Howard,

27 Sturtivant, R., Burrow, M. & Howard, L., *Fleet Air Arm Fixed Wing Aircraft*.
28 Ibid.
29 Howard, L., Burrow, M. & Myall, H., *Fleet Air Arm Helicopters*.

L., *Fleet Air Arm Fixed Wing Aircraft*.
17 Howard, L., Burrow, M. & Myall, H., *Fleet Air Arm Helicopters*.
18 Sturtivant, R., Burrow, M. & Howard, L., *Fleet Air Arm Fixed Wing Aircraft*.
19 Ibid.
20 Ibid.
21 Ibid.
22 Ibid.
23 Howard, L., Burrow, M. & Myall, H., *Fleet Air Arm Helicopters*.
24 Sturtivant, R., Burrow, M. & Howard, L., *Fleet Air Arm Fixed Wing Aircraft*.
25 Halley, J., *Broken Wings*.
26 Sturtivant, R., Burrow, M. & Howard, L., *Fleet Air Arm Fixed Wing Aircraft*.
27 Ibid.
28 Ibid.
29 Halley, J., *Broken Wings*.
30 Sturtivant, R., Burrow, M. & Howard, L., *Fleet Air Arm Fixed Wing Aircraft*.
31 Ibid.

1990s

1 Sturtivant, R., Burrow, M. & Howard, L., *Fleet Air Arm Fixed Wing Aircraft*.
2 Ibid.
3 Ibid.
4 Ibid.
5 Halley, J., *Broken Wings*.
6 Sturtivant, R., Burrow, M. & Howard, L., *Fleet Air Arm Fixed Wing Aircraft*.

7 Ibid.
8 Ibid.
9 Ibid.
10 Ibid.
11 Ibid.
12 Ibid.
13 Ibid.
14 Ibid.
15 Ibid.

2000s

1 Sturtivant, R., Burrow, M. & Howard, L., *Fleet Air Arm Fixed Wing Aircraft*.
2 Ibid.
3 Ibid.
4 Ibid.

5 Ibid.
6 Howard, L., Burrow, M. & Myall, H., *Fleet Air Arm Helicopters*.
7 Ibid.

BIBLIOGRAPHY

Air Accident Investigations Branch Reports

Civil Aircraft Accident Reports

Cummings, C., *Category Five – A Catalogue of RAF Aircraft Losses 1954 to 2009* (Nimbus Publishing, 2009)

———, *Last Take Off – A Record of RAF Aircraft Losses 1950 to 1953* (Nimbus Publishing, 2000)

———, *Final Landings – A Summary of RAF Aircraft Accidents and Combat Losses 1946 to 1949* (Nimbus Publishing, 2001)

———, *The Price of Peace – A Catalogue of RAF Aircraft Losses Between VE-Day and End of 1945* (Nimbus Publishing, 2004)

Fleet Air Arm Roll of Honour

Halley, James J. MBE, *Broken Wings, Post-War Royal Air force Accidents* (Air Britain, 2000)

———, *Royal Air Force Aircraft WA100–WZ999* (Air Britain Ltd, 1983)

Howard, L., Burrow, M. & Myall, H., *Fleet Air Arm Helicopters since 1943* (Air Britain Ltd, 2011)

Jackson, R., *Avro Vulcan* (Robert Stephens Ltd, 1989)

Robertson, B., *British Military Aircraft Serials 1911–1979* (Patrick Stephens Ltd, 1998)

Sturtivant, R. with Burrow, M. & Howard, L., *Fleet Air Arm Fixed Wing Aircraft since 1946* (Air Britain, 2004)

Webb, D.C., *UK Flight Testing Accidents 1940–71* (Air Britain Ltd, 2002)

———, *UK Flight Testing Accidents 1940–1971* (Air Britain Ltd, 2002)

Winton, J., *Air Power at Sea – 1945 to Today* (Sidgwick & Jackson, 1976)

Bath and Wilts Chronicle

Bristol Evening Post

Chard and Ilminster News

Flight Global magazine

The Times

Western Gazette

Armed Forces Roll of Honour – www.forcesmemorial.org.uk/roll-of-honour.asp

Aviation Safety – http://aviation-safety.net

Britannia Aircraft Preservation Trusts website

Commonwealth War Graves Commission – www.cwgc.org

De Havilland aircraft – www.dehavilland.ukf.net

UK Serials – http://www.ukserials.com

My sincere thanks also go to: Brian Lewis; Brian Lovell; Brian Pittard; Chris Collins; the Fleet Air Arm Museum, Yeovilton.

INDEX